Death Valley
WILDFLOWERS

Panamint daisy

*A Visitor's Guide to the Wildflowers, Shrubs and Trees
of Death Valley National Park*

STEVE CHADDE *and* ROXANA FERRIS
ILLUSTRATIONS *by* JEANNE JANISH

DEATH VALLEY WILDFLOWERS
A Visitor's Guide to the Wildflowers, Shrubs and Trees of Death Valley National Park

Text by Steve Chadde *and* Roxana Ferris
Illustrations by Jeanne Janish

Copyright © 2020 by Steve W. Chadde. All rights reserved.

An Orchard Innovations Field Guide
ISBN 9781951682187

The author can be contacted at: *steve@chadde.net*
Ver. 1.1 April 2020

Contents

Introduction 5
Family list of illustrated species 9
Plant descriptions 11

Blue, purple and lavender flowers 12

Pink, rose and magenta flowers 64

Red and orange flowers 86

White and Cream flowers 98

Yellow flowers 148

Green and brown flowers 230

Non-flowering plants 256

Acknowledgments 269
Resources 270
Index 271

ABOVE Death Valley National Park, California and Nevada, USA.

Introduction

DEATH VALLEY NATIONAL PARK is a vast area with much diversity in climate, in soil, and also in altitudinal range (282 feet below sea level to above 11,000 feet). The physiographical features that one can see in the approximately 2,000,000 acres that are included within the borders of the monument are most varied. As far as plants are concerned, all these diversities offer endless possibilities for different types of growing things. The distance between the "lowest spot in the United States" and Telescope Peak, which is often snow-covered, is only 18 air miles. The distance by land, of course, is greater and it includes many types of plant habitats. If you were to walk instead of fly between the two points mentioned, you might see, in season, two-thirds of the kinds of plants growing in Death Valley National Monument. According to the National Park Service, Death Valley has more than 1,000 described plant species ranging from ancient bristlecone pines at the highest elevations to ephemeral spring wildflowers on the low-elevation desert floor.

"**Will the wildflowers be good this year?**" is one of the first questions that comes to mind when planning a trip to Death Valley. To be sure, a few stray flowering annuals and shrubs can be seen here and there, even in the heat of the summer—ones that have received enough moisture to exist from the trickles of water that come down the alluvial fans after summer showers. In fact, some plants can be found in flower in almost every month of the year. The best time to see a spring floral display on the valley floor and alluvial fans is in those years when the rainfall is two or three times the average 1.65 inches per year. A deluge in late October with no more rain through the cold winter months does not bring out the flowers as do the rains that are nicely spaced through the winter and into the warmer spring weather. With the ideal conditions, one may see great stretches of desertgold, clumps of sand-verbena and phacelia, and other plants that make bright patches of color. In normal, and even in dry years, there are some flowers in the spring season. It is well to remember that we are speaking of annual plants, and they are short-lived. With just a few hot spring days, the flower show is over. No wonder desert plants of this type are known as "**ephemerals**" (short-lived). There may be a second crop of plants from the seeds that ripened in the spring, if there are summer and fall showers to start them growing. In the high canyons of the ranges surrounding the valley, where growing conditions are not so harsh, the annuals may flower for a longer period.

But what about the shrubs and shrubby perennials of the valley floor and alluvial fans that must survive the intense heat of one summer season and keep on living into future seasons? (Soil temperatures as high as 190° F. at ground level have been recorded.) There are two general types of vegetation to consider: plants of the washes and larger drainage areas where the watertable is high enough for the shrubs to derive some benefit from it; and plants of alluvial fans and lower slopes where the water table is so low that the shrubs get no moisture whatsoever from it and must live on what rain they get. The latter type of plants has developed all sorts of means to slow down evaporation:

the leaves may be small, or they may be covered with felty hairs, or they may have a varnished surface, or they may just drop off when the hot weather arrives in Death Valley.

Temperature and moisture—though they are vital—are not the only factors that control plant growth. Another important factor is the **texture of the soil and its chemical content**. Not even pickleweed will grow "in the rough" on the Devils Golf Course, for example. There is just too much salt for even that salt-tolerant plant to survive.

One reason why botanists find Death Valley National Park of especial interest is the occurrence of a few species that grow there and nowhere else. Others equally interesting are restricted to the Death Valley region, which includes the adjoining counties in California and adjacent Nevada. Those that grow in the region and nowhere else are called *endemics* of that place. A few of the endemics are illustrated in this book. A few of the others that are not pictured are: **hollybush** (*Tetracoccus ilicifolius*), **napkinring eriogonum** (*Eriogonum intrafractum*), **Gilman sandpaper-plant** (*Petalonyx thurberi* subspecies *gilmanii*), and **Panamint lupine** (*Lupinus magnificus*). Some of the endemics are found only in limestone areas.

Trees are scarce in the Park except around the springs and the inhabited areas, though the mountain canyons and higher elevations have suitable habitat and support a number of tree species. **Athel tamarisk** (*Tamarix aphylla*), though it was originally an introduced tree, has made itself quite at home and can be found growing spontaneously around wells and springs on the valley floor. **Cottonwood** (*Populus fremontii*) grows naturally in some of the canyons of the higher ranges and it has also been planted as a shade tree. The **date palm** has been introduced and a fine orchard can be seen at Furnace Creek Ranch. A few of the other trees found in Death Valley are included in this book.

HOW TO USE THIS BOOK

In this book on Death Valley wildflowers we have attempted to make it easy for you to find the name of the plant that arouses your curiosity. Many more plants—be they shrubs, herbs, or even trees—grow in the Park and are not included here. We are limited by space, but we present to you those that you *will* see: because they are so common, or because they are so beautiful, or even some of those you will want to see because they are so interesting (for example, the unique "turtleback," page 178).

For those of you who are not botanists, there are "clues" in the descriptions which should help you identify your plant quickly. Sometimes, just looking at the pictures will suffice. (Please remember you are in a National Park and don't pick the wildflowers.) The first clue is **habitat**—the kind of place where the plant normally grows in Death Valley; the second is the type of plant—**herb, shrub, or tree**; and the third is the **color of the flower** (or at least the predominant color). Flowers are often spotted, lined, or shaded with colors other than their predominant shade. They also may change from youth to age; for example, white evening-primroses often fade to pink. The creamy yellow flowers of desert dandelion and the golden yellow ones of desert-gold are both called yellow. Some plants, the grasses, rushes, and pines, for example, have flowers that are green or brown or absent in a few species (ferns, fungi).

Basic habitat information is provided for

each species, based largely on the descriptions provided in *A California Flora* by Philip A. Munz (first published in 1959). Habitat is a key character used to help you find the kind of place where a plant grows, but may also need qualifying remarks, as with flower color. Creosotebush, for example, is listed under "Valley floor and fans" where, in the Park, it is most abundant. You may see it, too, on the hot southern exposures of the "Upper desert slopes" or even occasionally on the gravel floors of the upper canyons (temperature is an important factor in the distribution of creosotebush). An explanation of what each habitat includes follows.

PLANT HABITATS

• VALLEY FLOOR AND ALLUVIAL FANS
This includes the area from the valley floor to the foot of the steep slopes of the mountains. The elevation is from below sea-level to about 3,500 feet. Within this area are a few other distinctive habitats to which certain plants are restricted. In this case supplementary words are added; for example, Cooper rush would be listed as "Valley floor, marshes." These few supplementary subdivisions are defined below:

  Marshes—Mostly alkaline, and including springs, wells, ditches, and the surrounding drying meadows.

  Salt flats—The floor of Death Valley is often called the "Chemical Desert." Along its edges will be found some salt-tolerant plants.

  Washes—These often extend above the line of alluvial fans into the lower slopes of the mountains.

  Lower canyon walls and cut banks—A few plants grow in this habitat and are found nowhere else.

• UPPER DESERT SLOPES
This includes the densely shrub-covered slopes and broad valleys from approximately 3,500 to 6,000 feet elevation.

  > Stream beds—may or may not have water showing at the surface.

  > Canyon walls—also present and providing unique habitat for plants.

• PINYON-JUNIPER WOODLANDS
This is the area where the trees begin. Shrubs also are present. There is some overlapping of the preceding and the following habitats. The juniper trees begin to appear at a lower elevation than the first pinyon pines. The area occupies elevations between about 6,000 to 8,000 feet.

  > Springs and canyon walls—also present and providing unique habitat for plants.

• LIMBER PINE-BRISTLECONE PINE WOODS
This area includes the scattered stands of pines, and the open flats with low ground cover, some larger shrubs and occasionally cactus. This occupies the area between 8,000 and 11,000 feet.

PLANT NAMES AND PARTS

There are almost no botanical terms included in the "stories" about the plants in this book. It will be helpful to know, however, that plants that are related to one another are grouped into **families**: rose family, sunflower family, and so forth. Within each family are more closely related groups called **genera** (singular, **genus**): for example, in the rose family, rose belongs to the genus *Rosa*, mountain-mahogany to the genus *Cercocarpus*, cliffrose to the genus *Purshia*—and there are about seventy more genera in that plant family in the world. Within each genus are **species** (singular also **species**);

sometimes a genus has only a few species, sometimes many, and sometimes only one: for example, in the sunflower family, **gravelghost** (*Atrichoseris*) has but one species, **rabbitbrush** (*Ericameria*) has several species. Occasionally there will be a third scientific name which is called a **variety** (var.) or **subspecies** (subsp.); for example, **Panamint beardtongue** (*Penstemon floridus*) has two varieties, var. *austinii* (described in this book), and the closely related var. *floridus*. In a more technical publication the scientific name would be more complete—including the name of the botanist who first described it (*Penstemon floridus* var. *austinii* (Eastw.) N. Holmgren).

The word **fruit** in the text may be somewhat confusing. It is used here in the botanical sense, as an organ of the plant in which the seeds ripen. It may be dry or fleshy and may contain one seed or many, or may have several parts each containing seeds, like the fruit of desert fivespot. (There are three plants included that reproduce by spores and therefore do not have seeds: two ferns and one fungal puffball.)

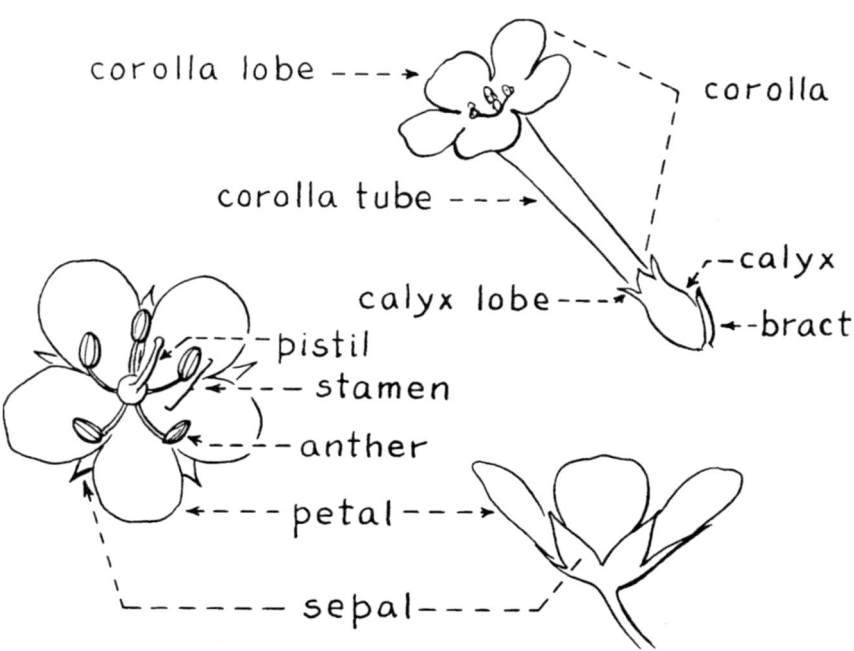

ABOVE Flower part names.

Family list of illustrated species

AMARANTH FAMILY (Amaranthaceae)
Allenrolfea occidentalis, 230
Atriplex hymenelytra, 232
Tidestromia oblongifolia, 148

BLAZINGSTAR FAMILY (Loasaceae)
Eucnide urens, 206
Mentzelia reflexa, 208

BORAGE FAMILY (Boraginaceae)
Cryptantha confertiflora, 180
Cryptantha utahensis, 110
Nama demissa, 18
Phacelia calthifolia, 20
Phacelia perityloides, 112
Phacelia vallis-mortae, 22

BROOM-RAPE FAMILY (Orobanchaceae)
Castilleja chromosa, 90
Castilleja linariifolia, 90
Orobanche cooperi, 52

BUCKWHEAT FAMILY (Polygonaceae)
Chorizanthe rigida, 222
Eriogonum brachypodum, 134
Eriogonum fasciculatum, 136
Eriogonum inflatum, 224
Eriogonum nidularium, 94
Eriogonum panamintense, 82
Gilmania luteola, 226

BUTTERCUP FAMILY (Ranunculaceae)
Aquilegia shockleyi, 96
Delphinium parishii, 60

CACTUS FAMILY (Cactaceae)
Cylindropuntia echinocarpa, 186
Echinocactus polycephalus, 188
Opuntia basilaris, 68
Opuntia polyacantha, 190

CARROT FAMILY (Apiaceae)
Cymopterus gilmanii, 12
Lomatium parryi, 150

CREOSOTE-BUSH FAMILY (Zygophyllaceae)
Larrea tridentata, 228

CYPRESS FAMILY (Cupressaceae)
Juniperus osteosperma, 256

DOGBANE FAMILY (Apocynaceae)
Asclepias erosa, 98

EPHEDRA FAMILY (Ephedraceae)
Ephedra funerea, 242
Ephedra nevadensis, 244
Ephedra viridis, 244

EVENING-PRIMROSE FAMILY (Onagraceae)
Chylismia brevipes, 210
Chylismia claviformis, 120
Eremothera boothii, 122
Oenothera cespitosa, 124

FLAX FAMILY (LINACEAE)
Linum lewisii, 46

FOUR-O'CLOCK FAMILY (Nyctaginaceae)
Abronia villosa, 74
Anulocaulis annulatus, 48

GOURD FAMILY (Cucurbitaceae)
Cucurbita palmata, 196

GRASS FAMILY (POACEAE)
Dasyochloa pulchella, 248
Sporobolus airoides, 250

HONEYSUCKLE FAMILY (Caprifoliaceae)
Symphoricarpos longiflorus, 70

LILY FAMILY (Liliaceae)
Calochortus flexuosus, 116
Calochortus kennedyi, 204

LIZARD'S-TAIL FAMILY (Saururaceae)
Anemopsis californica, 142

LOPSEED FAMILY (Phrymaceae)
Mimulus bigelovii, 54
Mimulus rupicola, 56

MAIDENHAIR FERN FAMILY (Pteridaceae)
Adiantum capillus-veneris, 264
Pellaea breweri, 266

MALLOW FAMILY (Malvaceae)
Eremalche rotundifolia, 72
Sphaeralcea ambigua, 88

MINT FAMILY (Lamiaceae)
Salvia dorrii, 38
Salvia funerea, 40
Salvia pachyphylla, 42
Scutellaria mexicana, 44

MUSTARD FAMILY (Brassicaceae)
Boechera glaucovalvula, 24

Caulanthus crassicaulis, 26
Stanleya elata, 182
Stanleya pinnata, 184

OLIVE FAMILY (Oleaceae)
Menodora spinescens, 118

ORCHID FAMILY (Orchidaceae)
Epipactis gigantea, 50

PEA FAMILY (Fabaceae)
Acmispon rigidus, 198
Astragalus coccineus, 86
Astragalus funereus, 28
Astragalus layneae, 30
Lupinus arizonicus, 32
Lupinus flavoculatus, 34
Prosopis glandulosa, 200
Psorothamnus fremontii, 36
Senna armata, 202

PHLOX FAMILY (Polemoniaceae)
Gilia latiflora, 78
Langloisia setosissima, 130
Linanthus filiformis, 220
Linanthus pungens, 132
Phlox stansburyi, 80

PINE FAMILY (Pinaceae)
Pinus flexilis, 260
Pinus longaeva, 258
Pinus monophylla, 262

PLANTAIN FAMILY (Plantaginaceae)
Holmgrenanthe petrophila, 214
Mohavea breviflora, 216
Neogaerrhinum filipes, 218
Penstemon floridus, 76
Penstemon fruticiformis, 58
Penstemon rostriflorus, 92

POPPY FAMILY (Papaveraceae)
Arctomecon merriamii, 126
Argemone munita, 128
Eschscholzia glyptosperma, 212

POTATO FAMILY (Solanaceae)
Datura wrightii, 144
Nicotiana obtusifolia, 146

PUFFBALL FAMILY (Agaricaceae)
Podaxis farlowii, 268

ROSE FAMILY (Rosaceae)
Cercocarpus ledifolius, 252

Chamaebatiaria millefolium, 138
Purshia mexicana, 140
Rosa woodsii, 84

RUE FAMILY (Rutaceae)
Thamnosma montana, 62

RUSH FAMILY (Juncaceae)
Juncus cooperi, 246

SEDGE FAMILY (Cyperaceae)
Schoenoplectus americanus, 240

SOAPBERRY FAMILY (Sapindaceae)
Acer glabrum, 254

SPIDER-FLOWER FAMILY (Cleomaceae)
Cleomella obtusifolia, 192
Oxystylis lutea, 194

SPURGE FAMILY (Euphorbiaceae)
Euphorbia albomarginata, 114
Euphorbia parishii, 114

SUNFLOWER FAMILY (Asteraceae)
Acamptopappus shockleyi, 152
Ambrosia salsola, 234
Amphipappus fremontii, 154
Anisocoma acaulis, 156
Artemisia tridentata, 236
Atrichoseris platyphylla, 100
Bahiopsis reticulata, 158
Bebbia juncea, 160
Brickellia atractyloides, 102
Calycoseris wrightii, 104
Chaenactis carphoclinia, 106
Cirsium mohavense, 14
Encelia farinosa, 162
Enceliopsis covillei, 164
Ericameria nauseosa, 166
Ericameria paniculata, 168
Geraea canescens, 170
Gutierrezia microcephala, 172
Gutierrezia sarothrae, 172
Malacothrix glabrata, 174
Monoptilon bellioides, 108
Peucephyllum schottii, 176
Picrothamnus desertorum, 238
Pluchea sericea, 64
Psathyrotes ramosissima, 178
Stephanomeria pauciflora, 66
Xylorhiza tortifolia, 16

Plant Descriptions

BROAD-FLOWERED GILIA (*Gilia latiflora*), page 78

BLUE, PURPLE & LAVENDER FLOWERS — Apiaceae

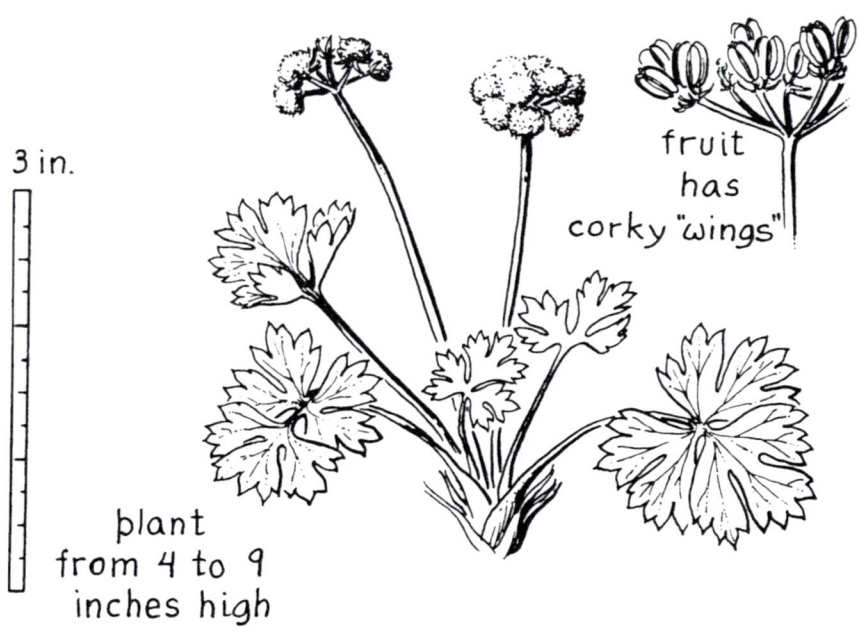

Gilman cymopterus

Cymopterus gilmanii CARROT FAMILY (Apiaceae)

GROWTH FORM Perennial herb

DESCRIPTION Most members of the carrot family have leaves much more finely divided than those of this species. The leaves, which are always basal, are orbicular in outline, and the few divisions are broadly triangular and toothed. The little bractlets around the purplish flowers are longer than the flowers themselves, and the wings on the fruit are wider than the fruit itself. Gilman cymopterus grows only in the canyons in the mountains about Death Valley.

NOTE Often plants are given scientific names to honor the one who first collected them. This was collected by French Gilman, who did so much in the 1930's in finding plants in Death Valley not previously known to occur there.

HABITAT Pinyon-juniper woodland, canyons.

Carrot Family — BLUE, PURPLE & LAVENDER FLOWERS | 13

GILMAN CYMOPTERIS

Mohave thistle
Cirsium mohavense SUNFLOWER FAMILY (Asteraceae)

GROWTH FORM Perennial herb

DESCRIPTION Plants of the **Mohave thistle** grow to a height of about three feet. The stems and leaves are white with a cobwebby covering. The flower heads are lavender to pink and, including the spiny bracts that surround the mass of pink florets, about an inch and a half long.

NOTE The rugged desert bighorn seem to relish the thistles, thorns and all. Plants around the marshy springs where the sheep come for water are always imperfect specimens because of their browsing.

HABITAT Valley floor and fans, marshes. Mohave thistle has been found only in the California deserts and in adjacent Nevada and Arizona. It always grows where water is or has been and can tolerate a great deal of alkalinity in the soil.

Sunflower Family   BLUE, PURPLE & LAVENDER FLOWERS | 15

MOHAVE THISTLE

MOHAVE THISTLE

16 | BLUE, PURPLE & LAVENDER FLOWERS — Asteraceae

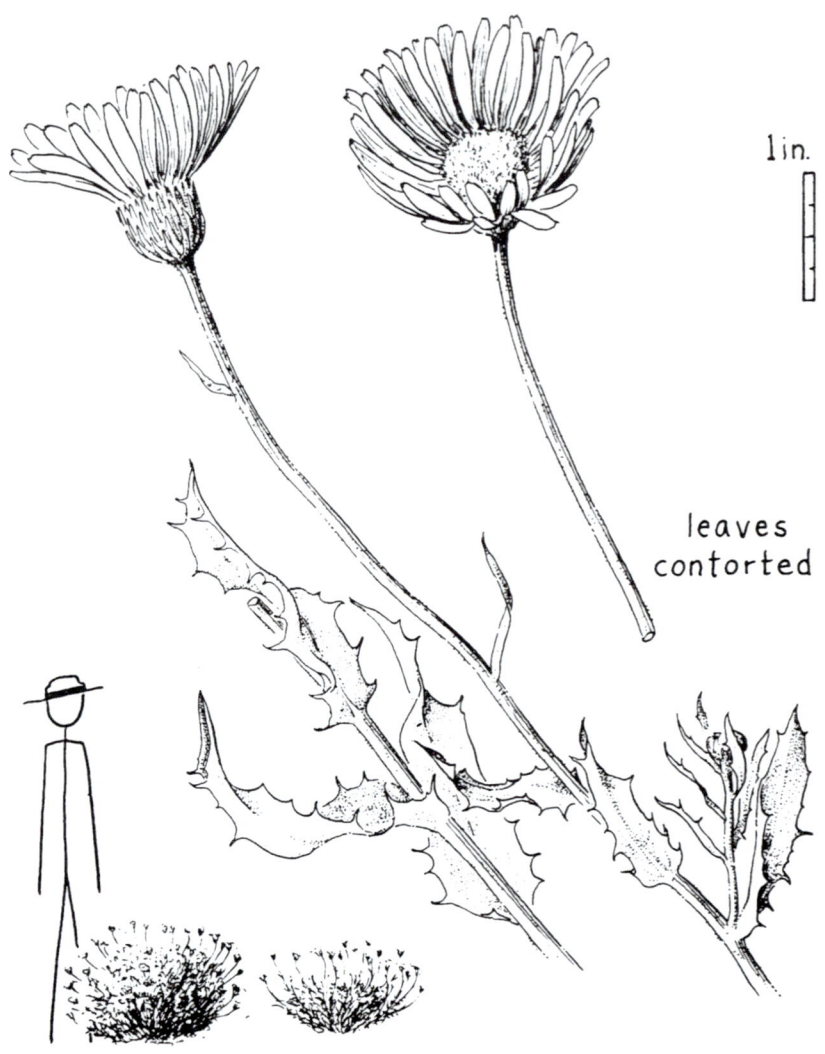

1 in.

leaves contorted

Mohave aster

Xylorhiza tortifolia — SUNFLOWER FAMILY (Asteraceae)

SYNONYM *Aster abatus*

GROWTH FORM Shrub or sub-shrub

DESCRIPTION The flower color of Mohave aster is lavender—quite different from the usual bold colors of most desert wildflowers. The flowers are large, however, and abundant in season, so they are readily seen. The foliage is grayish and the leaves spiny-toothed.

HABITAT Valley floor and fans and upper desert slopes. The plants are quite common in non-alkaline soil and grow all over the western deserts from California to the Mexican border and east to southern Utah.

Sunflower Family | **BLUE, PURPLE & LAVENDER FLOWERS** | **17**

MOHAVE ASTER

MOHAVE ASTER

18 | BLUE, PURPLE & LAVENDER FLOWERS — Boraginaceae

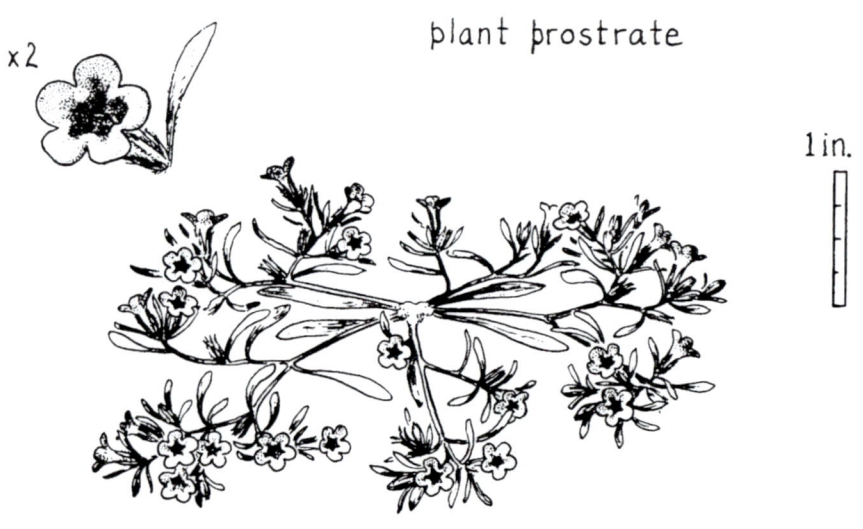

plant prostrate

x2

1 in.

in very dry years or a dry location

Purplemat
Nama demissa — **BORAGE FAMILY** (Boraginaceae)

GROWTH FORM Annual herb

DESCRIPTION The slender stems of **purplemat** spread out as much as ten inches in a green circle on the sand. Of course, in drier years the plants have fewer branches and a much smaller spread. More than one variety grows in the Death Valley region, and another species as well, but both of them have the same habit of growth, and both are annuals. The narrow, tongue-shaped, hairy leaves (about one-half to an inch long) are more or less clustered at the tips of the stems and also at the base of the plants, and set among the leaves are the reddish purple, trumpet-shaped flowers. The flowers are about a half-inch long and are abundant on healthy plants. Where several flowering plants are growing near each other there is a fine splash of purple. Someone has said that purple-mat is just another pretty little "belly plant," but if you get to see it during its short life you will find it very rewarding.

HABITAT Valley floor and fans.

Borage Family — **BLUE, PURPLE & LAVENDER FLOWERS** | 19

PURPLEMAT

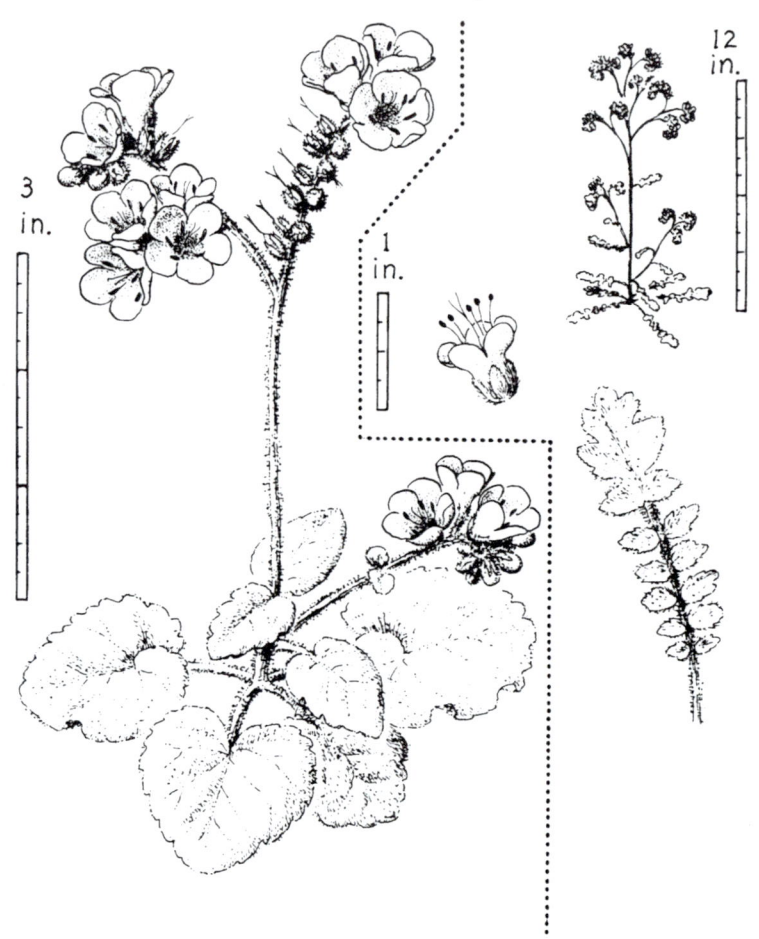

Calthaleaf phacelia

Phacelia calthifolia   BORAGE FAMILY (Boraginaceae)

GROWTH FORM Annual herb

DESCRIPTION The **calthaleaf phacelia** (above left) is a striking violet-flowered annual, six to eighteen inches high, with broad, dull greenish leaves. The whole plant is quite sticky and leaves a brownish stain on the hands which causes an irritating dermatitis on some people. Another violet-flowered phacelia, the **crenate phacelia** (*Phacelia crenulata,* above right) is more widespread than calthaleaf phacelia throughout the desert regions. It, too, has ill-scented glandular foliage but the leaf blades are longer than wide and deeply lobed.

NOTE Phacelias are represented in the west by many species and they grow in all sorts of places—sea coast, valleys, mountains, or deserts. The flowers are either white or various shades of purple, though some kinds are yellowish at the base. Several species, differing greatly in appearance, are found in Death Valley National Park.

HABITAT Valley floor and fans.

Borage Family | **BLUE, PURPLE & LAVENDER FLOWERS** | 21

CALTHALEAF PHACELIA

CALTHALEAF PHACELIA

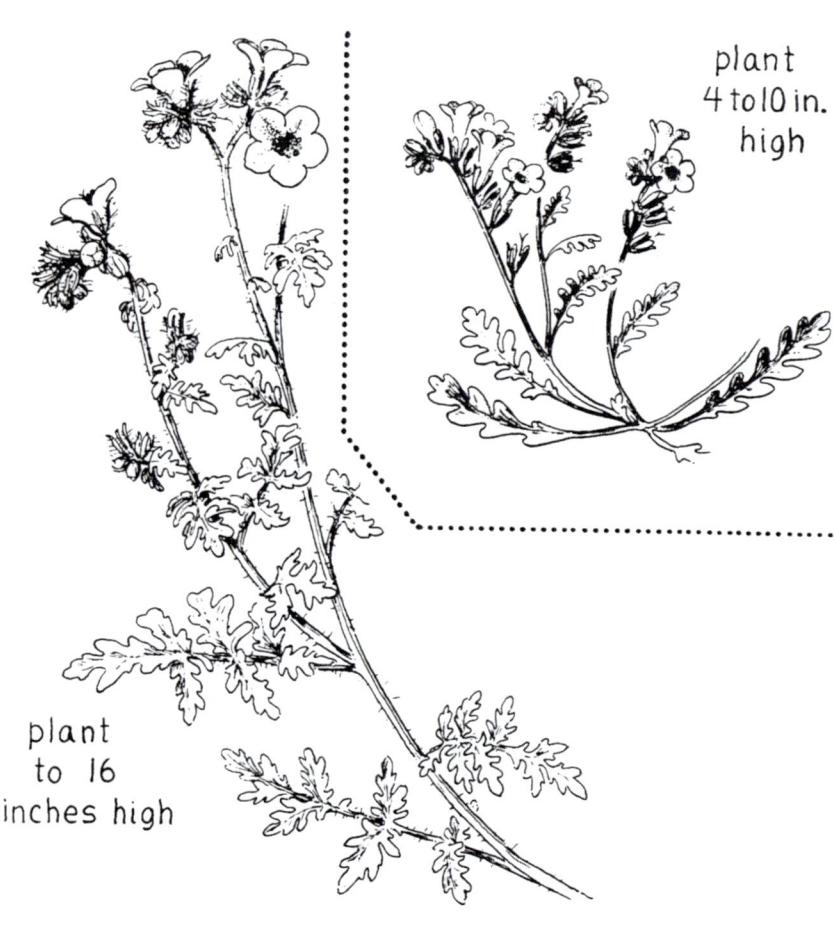

Death Valley phacelia
Phacelia vallis-mortae   **BORAGE FAMILY** (Boraginaceae)

GROWTH FORM Annual herb

DESCRIPTION **Death Valley phacelia** is a weak-stemmed annual growing up among desert shrubs. The leaves are much longer than they are wide and are parted into leaflets, the stem has bristly hairs, and the flowers are lavender. Though it was named for its presence in Death Valley, it is found as far east as southern Utah and south to northern Arizona. **Fremont phacelia** (*Phacelia fremontii*), on the upper right, branches at ground level. The flowers are yellow at the base. These phacelias grow on upper fans and also on upper desert slopes.

HABITAT Valley floor and fans.

Borage Family | **BLUE, PURPLE & LAVENDER FLOWERS** | 23

DEATH VALLEY PHACELIA

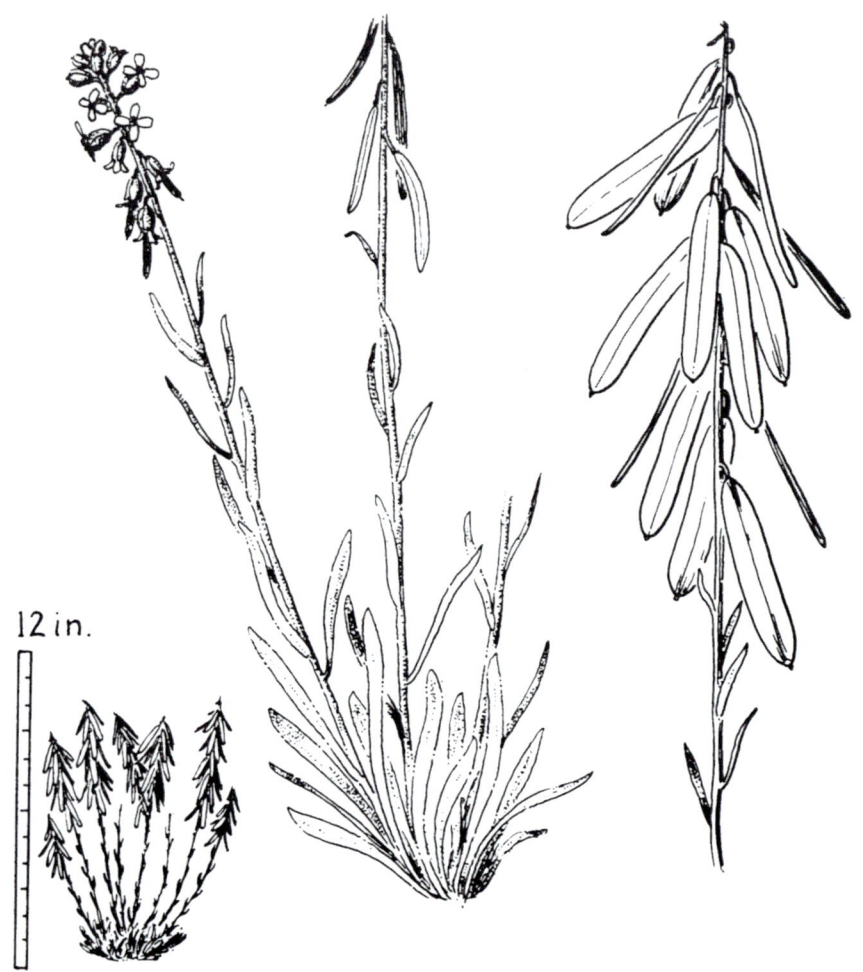

Blue-podded rockcress

Boechera glaucovalvula   MUSTARD FAMILY (Brassicaceae)

SYNONYM *Arabis glaucovalvula*
GROWTH FORM Perennial herb
DESCRIPTION This perennial rockcress is more conspicuous in fruit than in flower. The broad pendent pods are about an inch and one-half long and nearly a quarter of an inch broad, and are of a bluish purple cast in color. The flowers are pale pinkish purple and are sharply reflexed after flowering. The plants are a foot or less in height. They are limited to the Mohave Desert area, but other kinds of rockcress occur in this area. One which may be noticed is the **beautiful rockcress** (*Boechera pulchra*, photo next page). It has bright purple flowers and more slender pods which are much longer and fewer in number than in blue-podded rockcress.
HABITAT Upper desert slopes, pinyon-juniper woodland.

Mustard Family — BLUE, PURPLE & LAVENDER FLOWERS | 25

BLUE-PODDED ROCKCRESS - FRUITS

BLUE-PODDED ROCKCRESS - FLOWERS

BEAUTIFUL ROCKCRESS

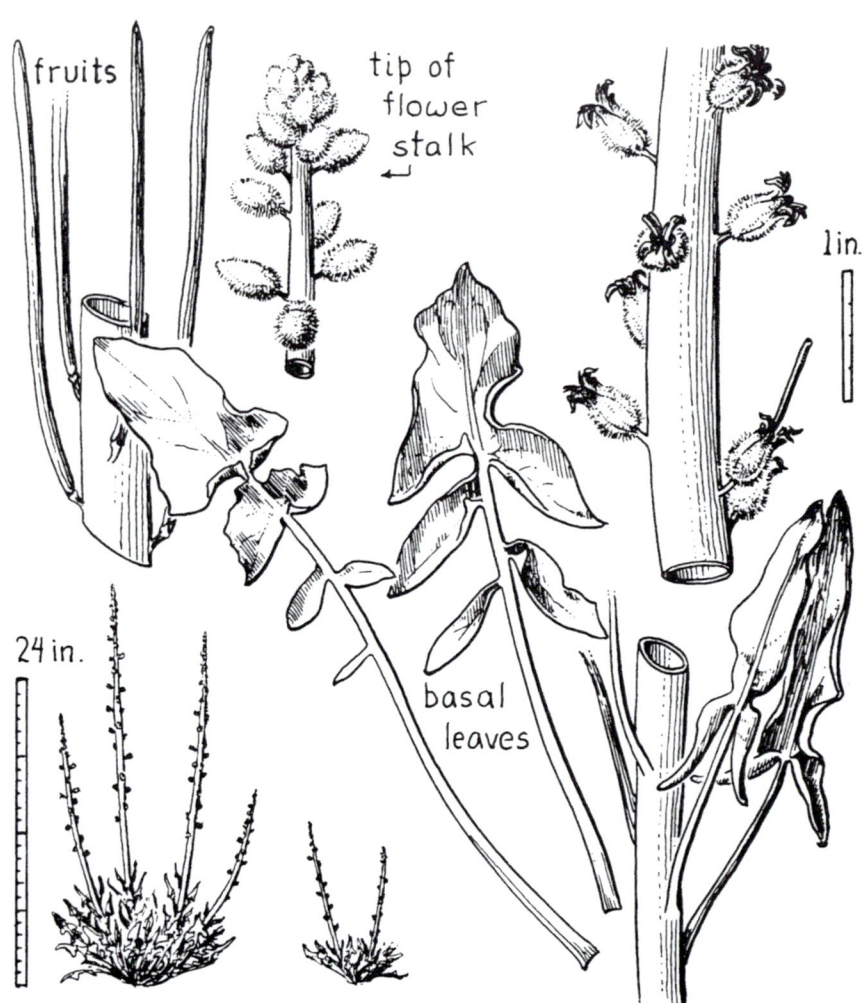

Thick-stem wild-cabbage
Caulanthus crassicaulis MUSTARD FAMILY (Brassicaceae)

GROWTH FORM Biennial to perennial herb

DESCRIPTION Coville reported in notes published on plant materials used by the Panamint Indians, that leaves of this and other plants of the mustard family were first boiled and then re-dried before the Indians considered them ready for eating. Thick-stem wild-cabbage grows one to three feet high and the leaves are bluish green. The flowers, which have hairy purplish sepals and purple petals, are set along the thickened flower stalk and the pods are erect. This is a species of the Great Basin rather than one of the southern deserts. Don't confuse it with **desert-candle** (*Caulanthus inflatus*), which has a very thick flower stalk and grows in the Mohave Desert.

HABITAT Pinyon-juniper woodland.

Mustard Family — BLUE, PURPLE & LAVENDER FLOWERS | 27

THICK-STEM WILD-CABBAGE

Death Valley locoweed
Astragalus funereus   PEA FAMILY (Fabaceae)

GROWTH FORM Perennial herb

DESCRIPTION The growth habit of this species is much like the crimson loco-weed. The pea-shaped flowers are shades of purple mixed with white, and the tubular calyx has an abundance of black hairs which contrast with the white hairs of the rest of the plant. The pods are large and woolly, and when ripe the stalks on which they grow bend over, half concealing the pods in the leaves. As you may guess from the name, this *Astragalus* was described from Death Valley, and is found only in the Funeral Range. There are other locoweeds with woolly pods that have much the same coloring, but they differ from this rare species in length of floral parts and in size of pods.

HABITAT Upper desert slopes.

Pea Family | **BLUE, PURPLE & LAVENDER FLOWERS** | **29**

DEATH VALLEY LOCOWEED

BLUE, PURPLE & LAVENDER FLOWERS — Fabaceae

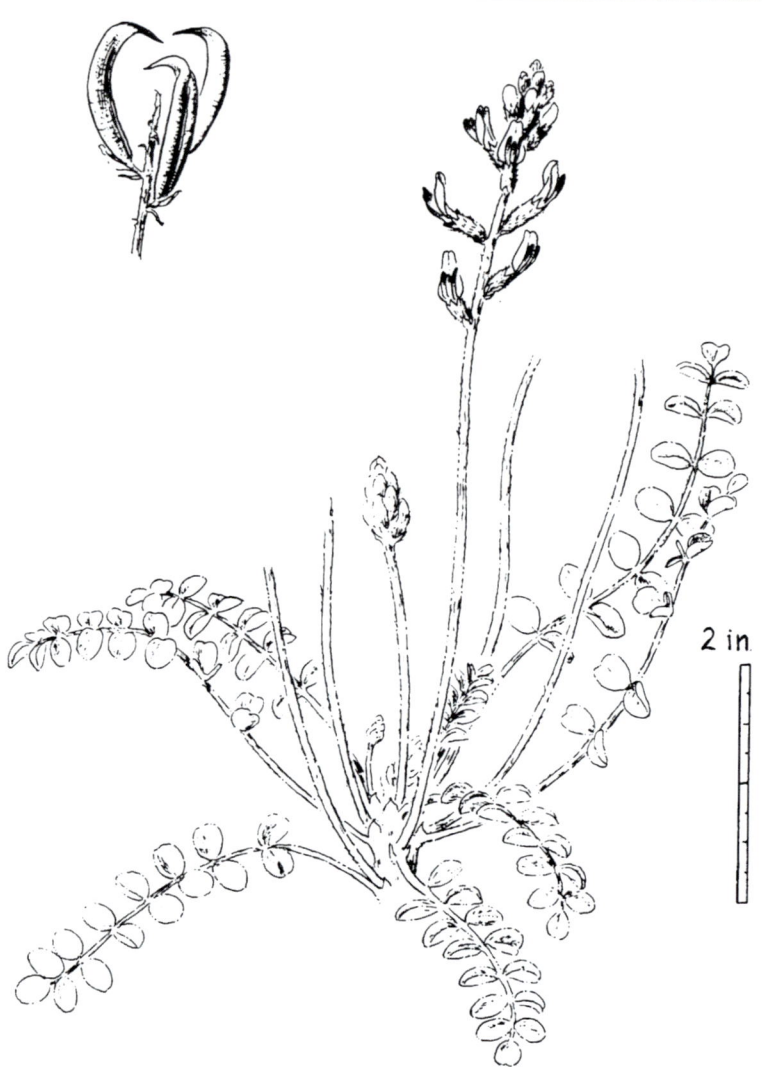

Layne locoweed
Astragalus layneae   PEA FAMILY (Fabaceae)

GROWTH FORM Perennial herb

DESCRIPTION This plant has a creeping rhizome with one or more stems a half a foot or more tall rising erect from the ground. The leaflets are hairy but not so dense as to conceal the green beneath. The flowers spread away from the flower stalk and, though many, are well spaced. They are better than a half-inch long including the dark tubular calyx, and the separate parts of the flower are tipped with purple and are white below. The pods are hard, hairy, narrow and pointed. They are more or less erect and curve inward toward the stalk in a half circle.

HABITAT Upper desert slopes.

Pea Family | **BLUE, PURPLE & LAVENDER FLOWERS** | 31

LAYNE LOCOWEED

LAYNE LOCOWEED

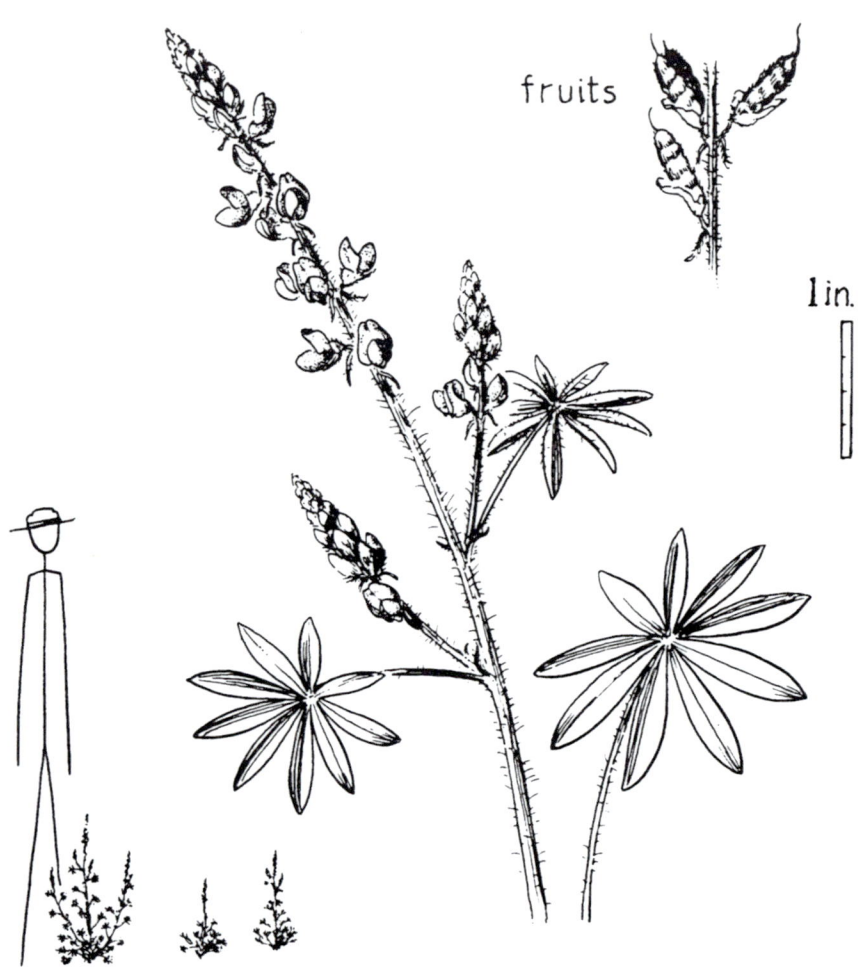

Arizona lupine
Lupinus arizonicus   PEA FAMILY (Fabaceae)

GROWTH FORM Annual herb
DESCRIPTION Arizona lupine, which is widespread elsewhere in the west, is commonly found in sand and gravel at low elevations in Death Valley. It is a leafy-stemmed annual up to three feet high but usually much less. The flowers, though plentiful, are not crowded. They are light blue, often having shades of pink. The oblong pods are nearly an inch long.
NOTE The species of lupines are not as well represented in Death Valley National Park as in wetter or cooler places in the west. Several kinds occur, however, some on the valley floor, others with the limber and bristlecone pines, and still others in the cool, damp, upper canyons.
HABITAT Valley floor and fans.

Pea Family | BLUE, PURPLE & LAVENDER FLOWERS | 33

ARIZONA LUPINE

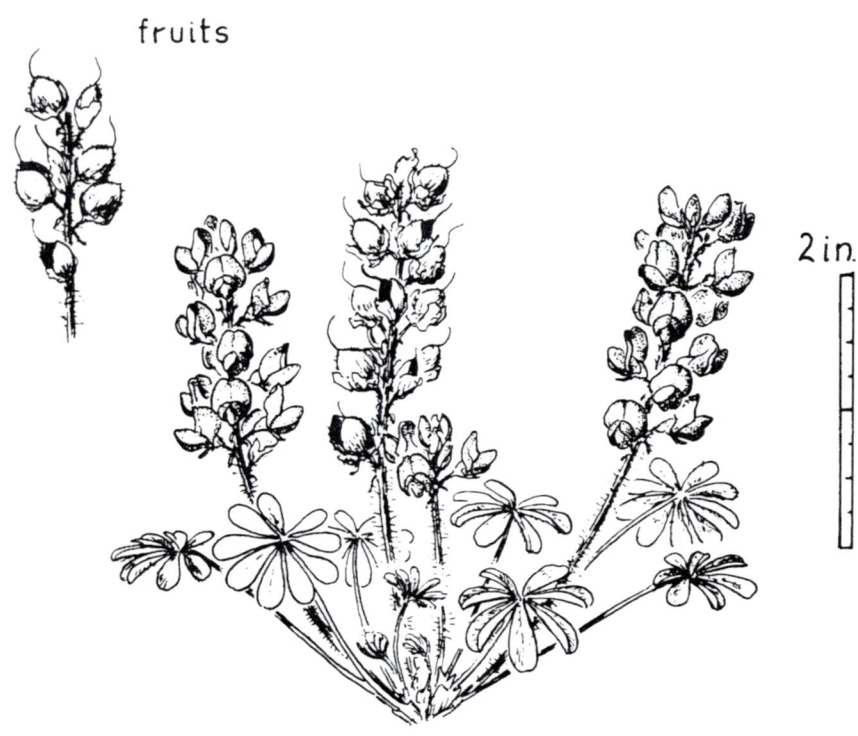

Yelloweye lupine

Lupinus flavoculatus   PEA FAMILY (Fabaceae)

GROWTH FORM Annual herb

DESCRIPTION A splash of blue in loose soil at higher elevations in Inyo and San Bernardino counties and adjacent Nevada will probably turn out to be plants of this species. The sparsely hairy leaves are basal. The flowering stem, three to ten inches high, is densely set with violet-blue, pea-shaped flowers, each of which has a bright yellow spot on the upright banner. The pods are short and almost round.

HABITAT Upper desert slopes, pinyon-juniper woodland.

Pea Family | **BLUE, PURPLE & LAVENDER FLOWERS** | 35

YELLOWEYE LUPINE

YELLOWEYE LUPINE

YELLOWEYE LUPINE

BLUE, PURPLE & LAVENDER FLOWERS — Fabaceae

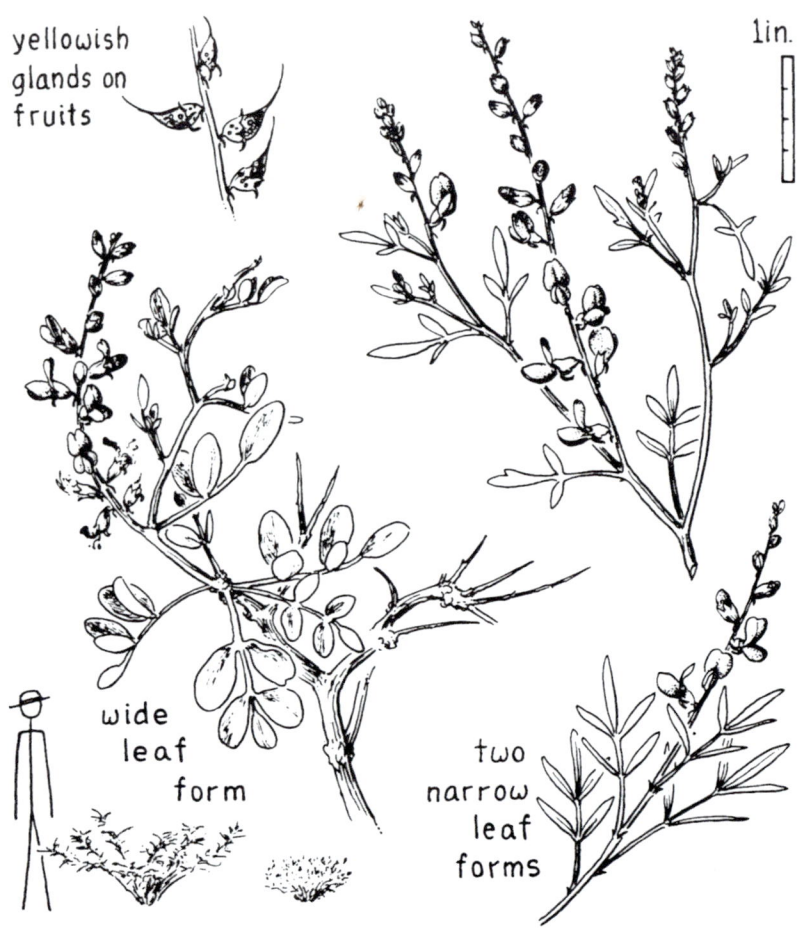

Fremont dalea
Psorothamnus fremontii   PEA FAMILY (Fabaceae)
SYNONYM *Dalea fremontii*
GROWTH FORM Shrub
DESCRIPTION Two forms of this "desert beauty," as the shrub is sometimes called, occur in the Park; both are equally beautiful. They are difficult to tell apart, and part of the difference lies in the width of the leaflets and the pubescence that covers them. Many spikes (two to three inches long) of small, royal blue, pea-shaped flowers rise above the gray leaves. The bushes are much-branched and from one to about three feet high. Those of the upper alluvial fans are conspicuous also in their leafless state. The stems and branches are white and their form is that of a miniature broad-crowned oak tree. The roundish sharp-pointed pods are dotted with brown glands.
NOTE Fremont dalea with its varieties is widely distributed in the southern part of the Great Basin and in the deserts southward.
HABITAT Valley floor and fans.

FREMONT DALEA

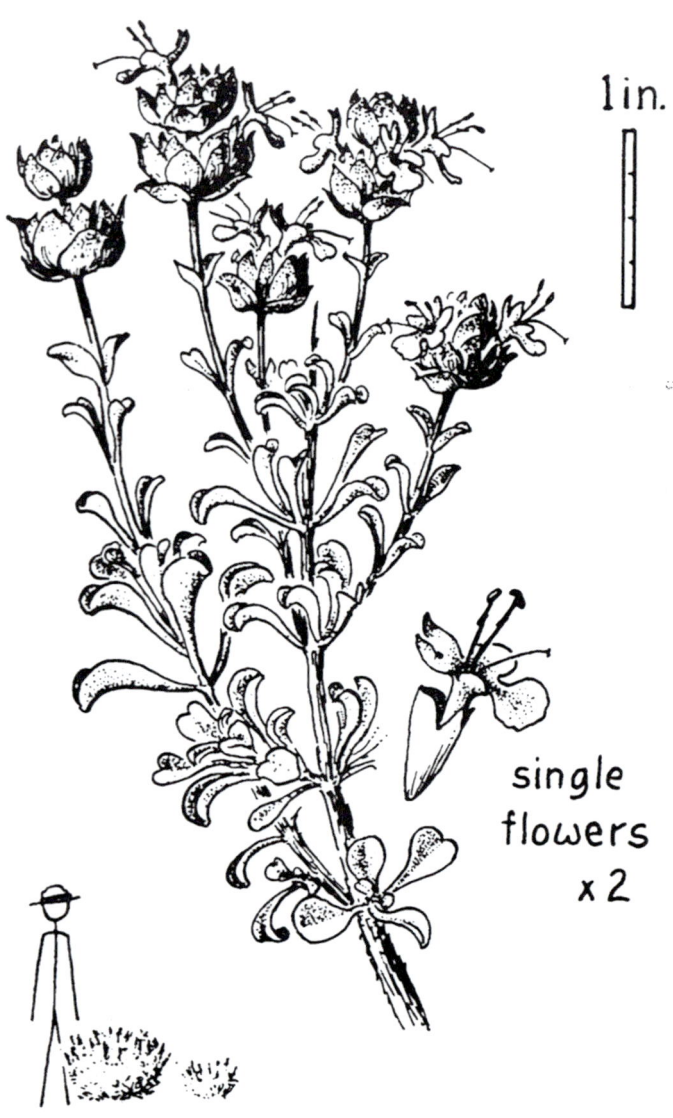

Desert sage (Purple sage)
Salvia dorrii   MINT FAMILY (Lamiaceae)

GROWTH FORM Shrub or sub-shrub
DESCRIPTION The **desert sage** of the higher mesas and canyons of the Death Valley region at elevations of 4,000 to 6,000 feet is a form which differs in some minor technical details from the one Zane Grey probably meant in his "Riders of the Purple Sage." The flowering stems with their purplish bracts and blue flowers surpass the compact whitish leafy bushes, and all parts of the plant give off a very pleasing fragrance.
HABITAT Pinyon-juniper woodland.

Mint Family | **BLUE, PURPLE & LAVENDER FLOWERS** | 39

DESERT SAGE

DESERT SAGE

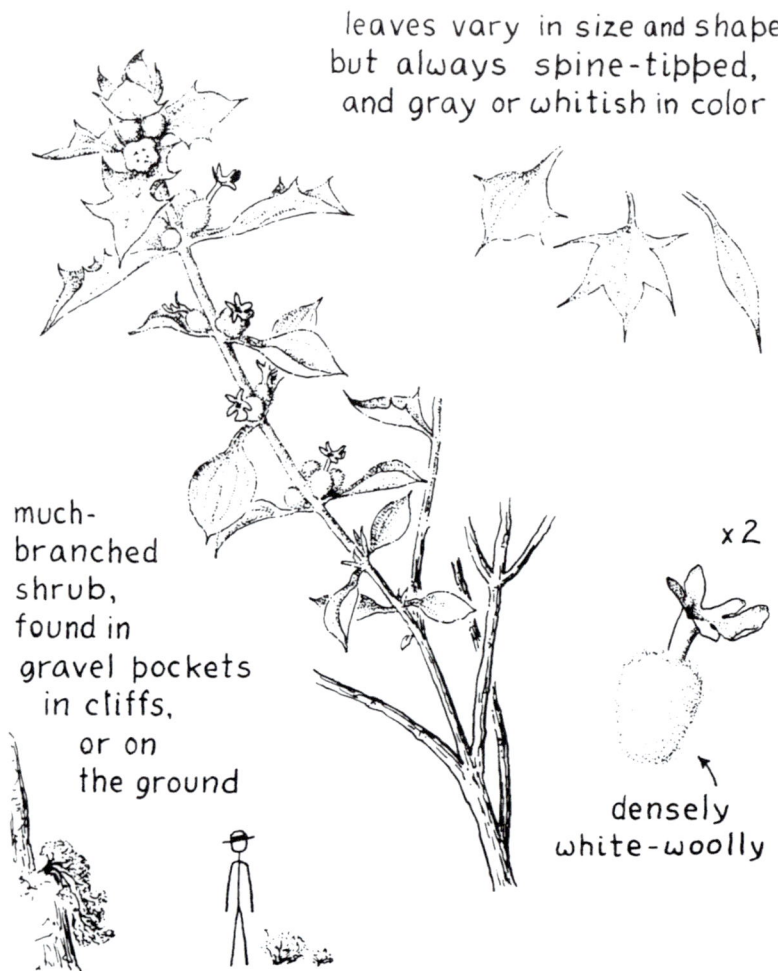

Death Valley sage
Salvia funerea — MINT FAMILY (Lamiaceae)

GROWTH FORM Shrub or sub-shrub

DESCRIPTION **Death Valley sage** is often a straggly shrub two feet or so in height with bright blue or violet-blue flowers which are in clusters in the leaf axils. The flowers themselves are partially embedded in white wool. The young branches and the leaves are white with a covering of very short hair, and the leaves have marginal spines, though these are often reduced to one only at the leaf tip. Death Valley sage grows at low elevations at the bases of canyon walls or in the side gullies draining into the canyons or may hang from cliffs.

NOTE So far as is known, Death Valley sage is found only in the canyons draining into Death Valley and can be considered to be a true endemic of the area.

HABITAT Valley floor and fans, canyon walls.

Mint Family | **BLUE, PURPLE & LAVENDER FLOWERS** | 41

DEATH VALLEY SAGE

DEATH VALLEY SAGE

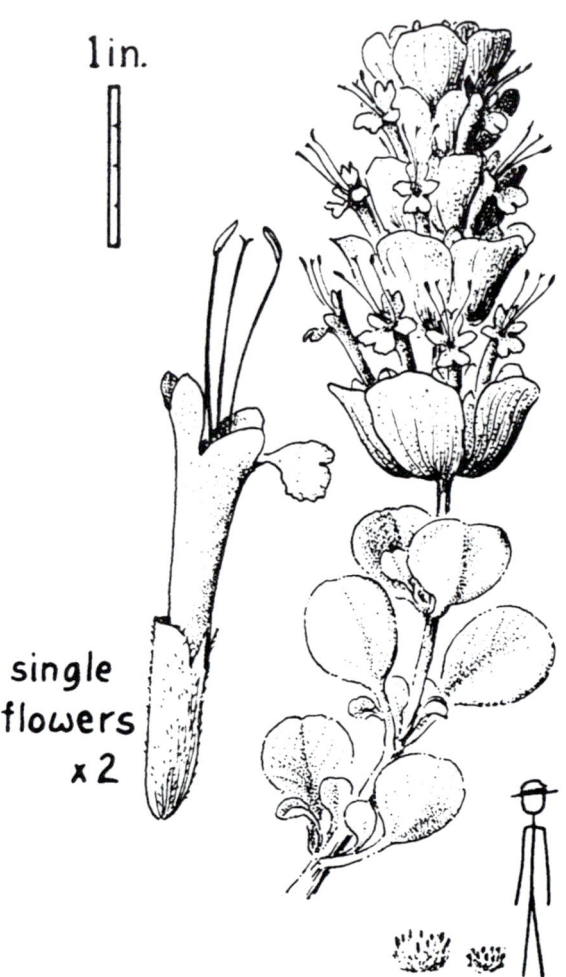

Rose sage

Salvia pachyphylla MINT FAMILY (Lamiaceae)

GROWTH FORM Shrub or sub-shrub

DESCRIPTION **Rose sage** much resembles the **desert sage** in the way it grows and in the shape of the leaves and in the pleasant odor. Though the flowers and bracts are in whorls around the flowering stem, the whorls are very close together and make an oblong head a few inches long. The flower bracts are much larger than those of desert sage and are rose-colored. They remain on the stems until the wind carries them off, long after the inch-long, deep blue flowers have fallen. The low shrubs are found in open places among the mountain-mahoganies and pinyons and also higher in the limber pine woodland, not only in the Death Valley region, but south in desert mountain ranges to northern Baja California.

HABITAT Pinyon-juniper and limber-bristlecone pine woodland.

Mint Family | **BLUE, PURPLE & LAVENDER FLOWERS** | 43

ROSE SAGE

ROSE SAGE

Mexican bladdersage
Scutellaria mexicana — MINT FAMILY (Lamiaceae)

SYNONYM *Salazaria mexicana*
GROWTH FORM Shrub or sub-shrub
DESCRIPTION Perhaps the most interesting thing about this desert shrub is the enlarged papery calyx which encloses the fruit. The fruit actually consists of four little nutlets—four nutlets being a characteristic of the mint family. The shrubs are two to three feet high, and the greenish white, somewhat spiny branches, spreading at almost right angles, make a dense tangle. The leaves are rather sparse. It is common in northern Mexican deserts and grows as far north as Utah and Nevada.
HABITAT Upper desert slopes.

Mint Family | **BLUE, PURPLE & LAVENDER FLOWERS** | 45

MEXICAN BLADDERSAGE

MEXICAN BLADDERSAGE

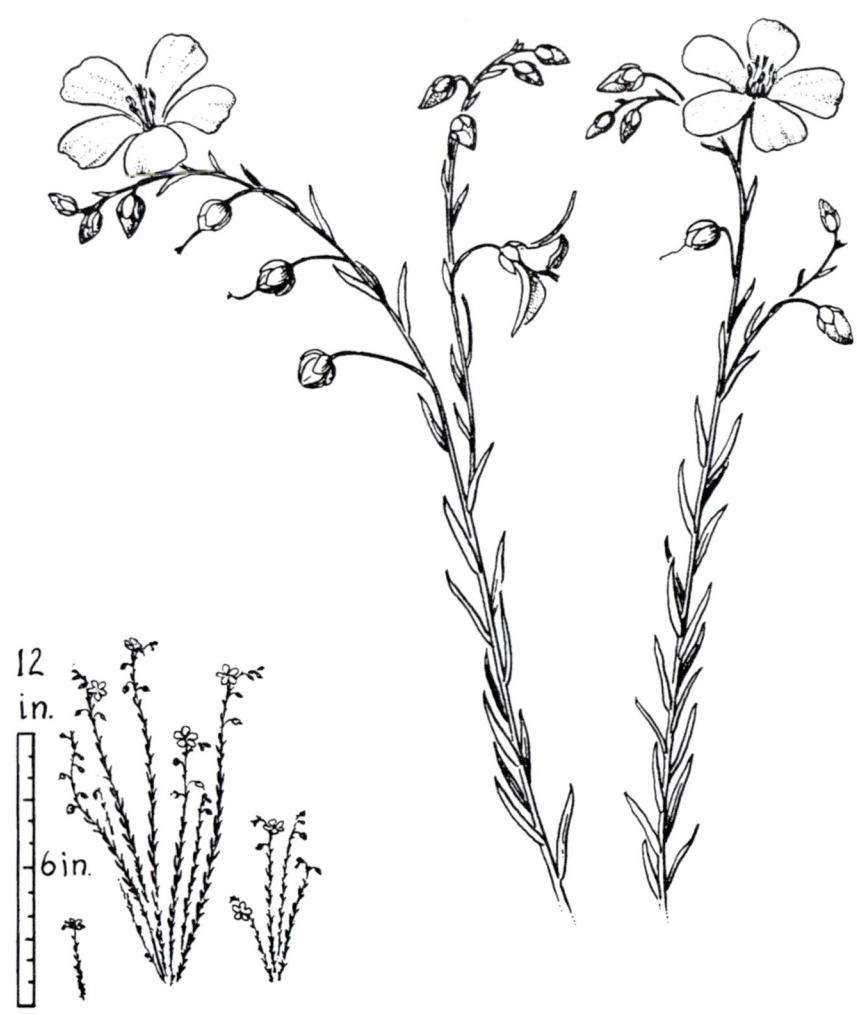

Prairie flax
Linum lewisii
FLAX FAMILY (Linaceae)

GROWTH FORM Perennial herb

DESCRIPTION This blue-flowered flax may be seen in late spring or early summer almost anywhere from the pinyon and juniper groves to the top of Telescope Peak. It will have a familiar look to you, and quite understandably, for this form, or one very similar, is a home garden favorite. The flowers are about an inch across. The leaves are small and bluish green. This widespread plant can be found in mountainous areas from Alaska and the Rocky Mountain region to Mexico.

NOTE *Linum lewisii* is the name that was given to it to honor its first collector, Meriweather Lewis of the Lewis and Clark Expedition.

HABITAT Pinyon-juniper and limber-bristlecone pine woodland.

Flax Family | BLUE, PURPLE & LAVENDER FLOWERS | 47

PRAIRIE FLAX

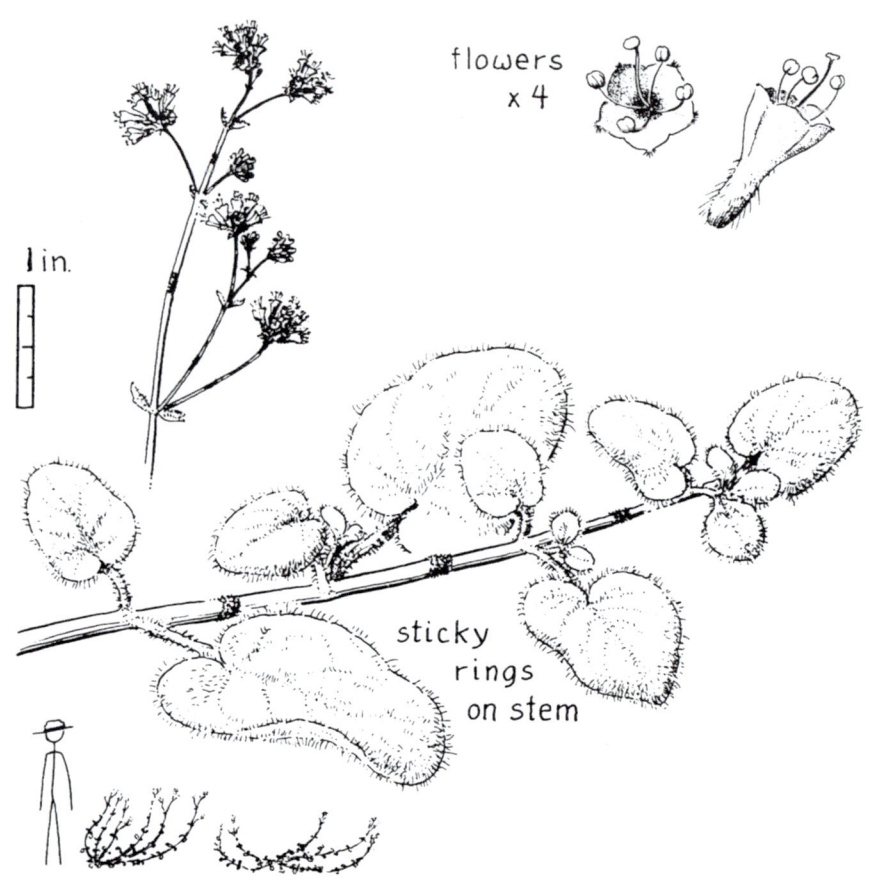

Wetleaf spiderling

Anulocaulis annulatus　　　　FOUR-O'CLOCK FAMILY (Nyctaginaceae)

SYNONYM *Boerhavia annulata*
GROWTH FORM Perennial herb
DESCRIPTION On the floor of the valley and the alluvial fans one sees bunches of large, bright green leaves quite different in appearance from the usual desert plants. Frederick Coville, who made the first collection in 1891 on the Death Valley Expedition, said that before the flowering stems grew up, it looked like a begonia plant. The small lavender flowers, which blossom from March to May, are not as conspicuous as the leaves. The underside of the leaf is wet to the touch, a fact that explains the common name. Sticky reddish brown rings occur on the coarse stems between the few stem-leaves and often trap small insects.
NOTE At one time wetleaf was thought to grow only in Death Valley but has since been found in other desert valleys in the region. Another kind with larger flowers grows in southern Nevada and Utah.
HABITAT Valley floor and fans, washes.

Four-O'Clock Family | **BLUE, PURPLE & LAVENDER FLOWERS** | 49

WETLEAF SPIDERLING

WETLEAF SPIDERLING

WETLEAF SPIDERLING

Giant helleborine

Epipactis gigantea   ORCHID FAMILY (Orchidaceae)

GROWTH FORM Perennial herb

DESCRIPTION You might not expect to find orchids growing in Death Valley, but **giant helleborine** is to be found in wet places in the upper canyons or on the valley floor. It grows to a height of one to three feet and is much more conspicuous for its large clasping leaves than its purplish flowers, which grow in the axils of the smaller upper leaves.

HABITAT Valley floor to pinyon-juniper woodland, marshes.

Orchid Family | BLUE, PURPLE & LAVENDER FLOWERS | 51

GIANT HELLEBORINE

BLUE, PURPLE & LAVENDER FLOWERS — Orobanchaceae

flowers have a delicate, pleasing fragrance

Desert broomrape
Orobanche cooperi   BROOM-RAPE FAMILY (Orobanchaceae)

GROWTH FORM Annual herb

DESCRIPTION All the members of the broomrape family are root parasites without any green at all in the plants. In other words, they cannot manufacture their own food as the green plants do, but get theirs by attachment of their roots to those of other plants. **Desert broomrape** seems to prefer **white bur-sage** (*Ambrosia dumosa*) as a host but "attachments" have been reported for other desert shrubs. The plants are six to twelve inches high and the larger ones occasionally branch. They are dark brown and rather dusty-looking. The flowers are deep purple, with a yellow mark in the throat, and they, too, have a grizzled look because of the very fine hairs on the outside of the corolla. The plant grows in the western deserts wherever its host may grow.

HABITAT Valley floor and fans.

Broom-Rape Family **BLUE, PURPLE & LAVENDER FLOWERS** | 53

DESERT BROOMRAPE

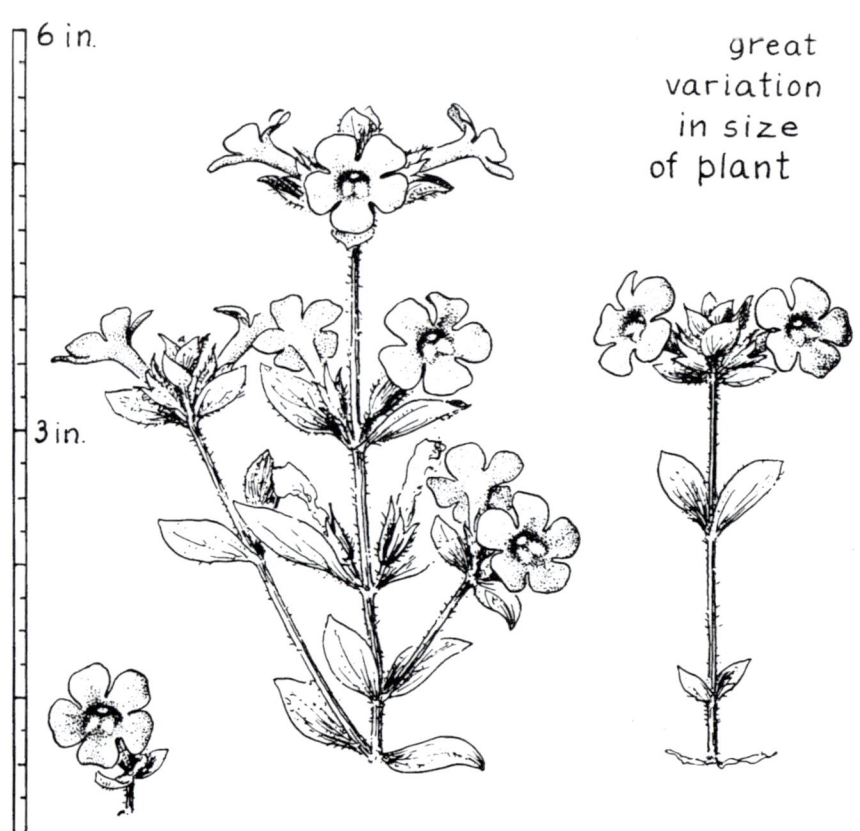

Yellow-throat monkey-flower
Mimulus bigelovii   **LOPSEED FAMILY** (Phrymaceae)

GROWTH FORM Annual to perennial herb

DESCRIPTION This is humorously classified as one of the "belly plants." The reason is obvious when one finds at one's feet in the sand or on the desert pavement a small bouquet of purplish red flowers with yellow centers that are spotted with purple. Flowers are not picked in a National Park, so one gets down to its level for a better look. The flowers are large in relation to the plant and can be easily spotted as one travels around the deserts in early spring.

HABITAT Valley floor and fans.

Lopseed Family | **BLUE, PURPLE & LAVENDER FLOWERS** | 55

YELLOW-THROAT MONKEY-FLOWER

YELLOW-THROAT MONKEY-FLOWER

grows in crevices in cliffs

Death Valley monkey-flower

Mimulus rupicola   **LOPSEED FAMILY** (Phrymaceae)

SYNONYM *Diplacus rupicola*
GROWTH FORM Perennial herb
DESCRIPTION Small plants growing to about six inches tall, with oblanceolate leaves one to two inches long. The pinkish flowers have a magenta or purple spot on each lobe. This *Mimulus* is rarely seen and is found only in some of the deep canyons surrounding the valley in the crevices of steep limestone cliffs.
NOTE Endemic to the Death Valley region.
HABITAT Valley floor and fans, lower canyon walls.

Lopseed Family | **BLUE, PURPLE & LAVENDER FLOWERS** | 57

DEATH VALLEY MONKEY-FLOWER

DEATH VALLEY MONKEY-FLOWER

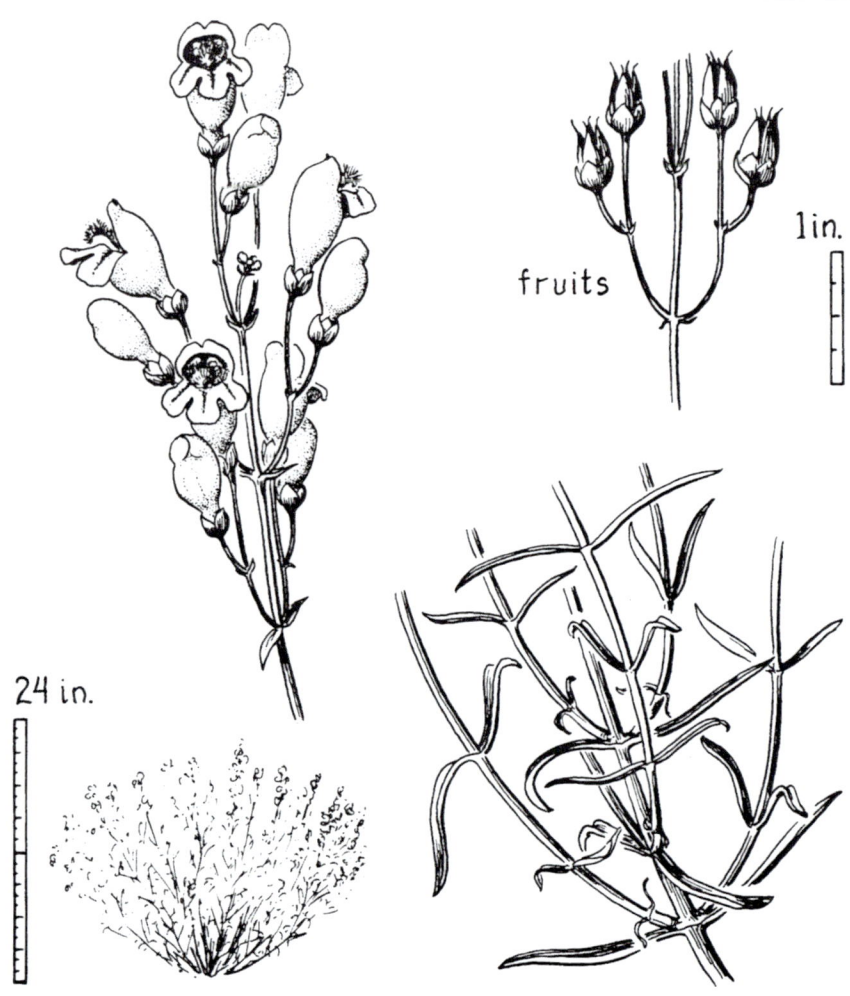

Death Valley Beardtongue

Penstemon fruticiformis   **PLANTAIN FAMILY** (Plantaginaceae)

GROWTH FORM Perennial herb

DESCRIPTION This is another plant that Coville found and later described in his report on the Death Valley Expedition. It grows in the desert mountains adjacent to Death Valley, and a subspecies of it (subsp. *amargosae*) grows as far south as the San Bernardino Mountains. It forms a rounded shrub much branched from the base, but the stems do not make a dense mass. The leaves are narrow and bluish green. The flowers are an inch long and distinctly fat in the middle—a gibbous throat is the technical way of describing it. The flower has been variously described as rose-colored, as white with blue lobes, or as lavender with purplish lobes. The color probably changes with the age of the flower.

HABITAT Pinyon-juniper woodland and upper desert slopes.

Plantain Family | BLUE, PURPLE & LAVENDER FLOWERS | 59

DEATH VALLEY BEARDTONGUE

DEATH VALLEY BEARDTONGUE

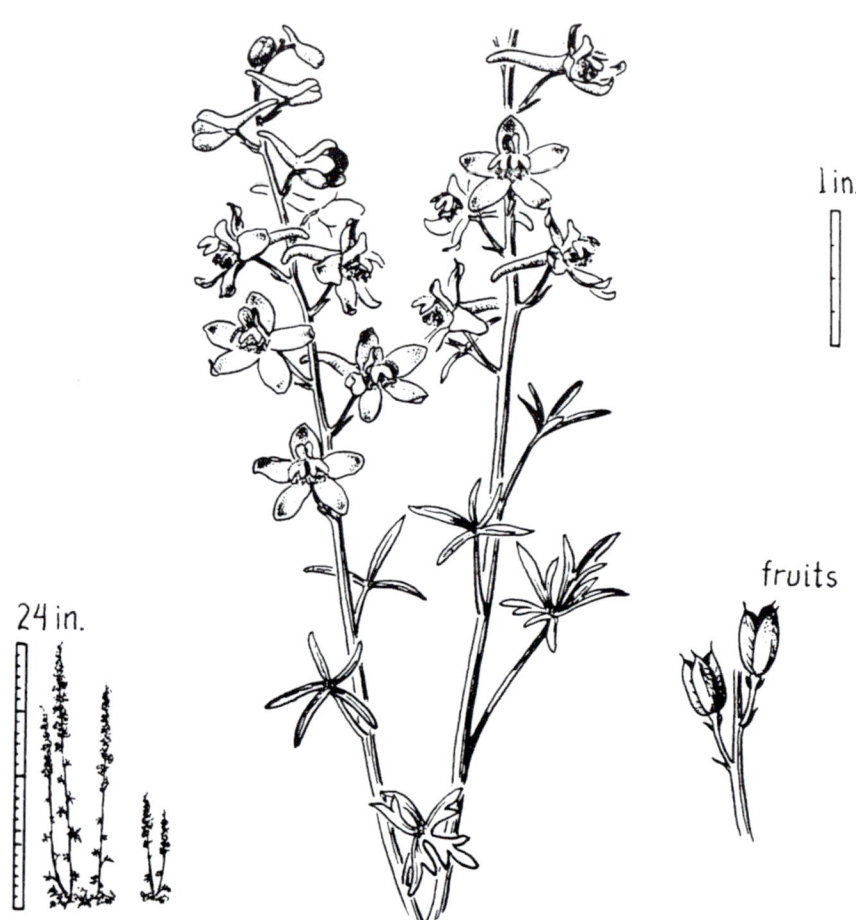

Parish larkspur
Delphinium parishii   **BUTTERCUP FAMILY** (Ranunculaceae)

GROWTH FORM Perennial herb

DESCRIPTION There are several kinds of plants in Death Valley National Park that have blue flowers, but only one other, the blue flax of limber pine-bristlecone pine woodlands, is a similar sky blue to the **Parish larkspur**. The plants are not very tall—usually a foot and a half to two feet high—and grow in a spotty fashion among the gray-green shrubs of sagebrush in the pinyon belt or with other shrubs that grow on the higher desert slopes. It is found in like situations in other desert ranges. It is even sometimes found in the upper limits of the creosotebush scrub.

NOTE This is another example where the species name honors a botanist and collector. Samuel B. Parish contributed much to our knowledge of California desert plants in the days when travel on desert roads was rough. One of his last major trips was to Death Valley in 1915 under the auspices of the Carnegie Institution.

HABITAT Upper desert slopes and pinyon-juniper woodland

Buttercup Family | **BLUE, PURPLE & LAVENDER FLOWERS** | 61

PARISH LARKSPUR

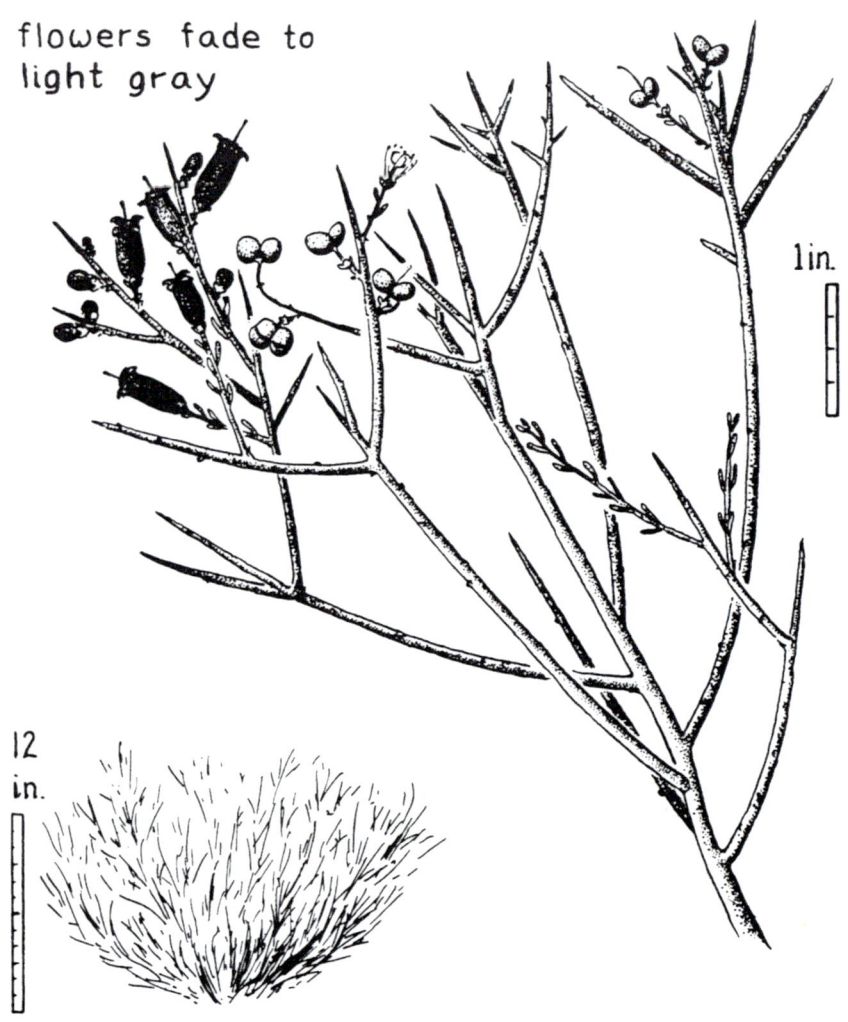

Mohave desert-rue
Thamnosma montana RUE FAMILY (Rutaceae)

GROWTH FORM Shrub or sub-shrub

DESCRIPTION The entire **Mohave desert-rue** plant is dull green and covered with small warty glands, even to the striped two-lobed fruits which remain for a long time on the bushes. The petals of the flower and the narrow leaves, which soon drop off from the round, green, broom-like stems, are less warty. The petals are of so deep a purple color that they appear to be almost black. This species is to be found from southern Utah to California and south into northern Mexico.

NOTE It has been reported that the Panamint Indians thought the crushed stems an aid in healing wounds.

HABITAT Upper desert slopes and pinyon-juniper woodland.

BLUE, PURPLE & LAVENDER FLOWERS | 63

MOHAVE DESERT-RUE

MOHAVE DESERT-RUE

Arrowweed pluchea

Pluchea sericea **SUNFLOWER FAMILY** (Asteraceae)

GROWTH FORM Shrub

DESCRIPTION **Arrowweed pluchea**, here and elsewhere in the west, is never far from water, though the water may be underground quite a few feet. It is more tolerant of alkaline conditions than the mesquite, which also likes an underground water supply. One sees the willow-like growth of arrowweed pluchea throughout the valley around springs and wells and the alkaline marshes and meadows that surround them, and on the broad expanse of valley floor under which water drains from the upper part of the valley to below sea level. Like pickleweed and mesquite, arrowweed is often partially buried in drifting sand. At the southern end of the sand dunes there is a strange assemblage of plants known as the Devil's Corn Field (upper photo, next page). The "shocks" form when soil is blown from around the plants and is caught and held in their roots and branches.

NOTE **Arrowweed pluchea** was not used for arrow shafts according to Coville's report on plants used by the Panamint Indians, but other tribes have used the straight stems for that purpose.

HABITAT Valley floor and fans, marshes.

Sunflower Family — **PINK, ROSE & MAGENTA FLOWERS** | 65

ARROWWEED PLUCHEA

ARROWWEED PLUCHEA

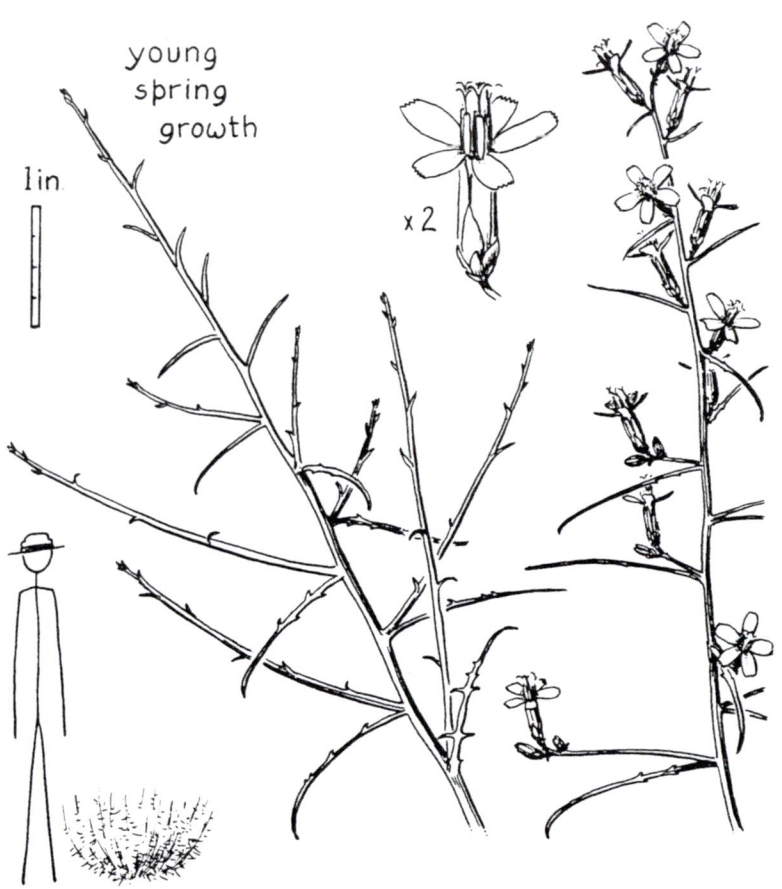

Desert wire-lettuce

Stephanomeria pauciflora SUNFLOWER FAMILY (Asteraceae)

GROWTH FORM Perennial herb or sub-shrub

DESCRIPTION Here is a plant in the sunflower family which has flowers that are pink instead of some shade of yellow. This and other species of the genus are quite common in southwestern deserts. The flowers are small and few, and fade to a buff color. For most of the year, wire-lettuce is a tangled mass of dry, slender, straw-colored stems a foot or so high, which you will probably call just another kind of tumbleweed. In early spring tender stems with milky juice come up from the root, and bear narrow, bluish green leaves with a few toothed lobes on the margins. Desert bighorn eat many different kinds of plants, but this in its spring stage is so attractive to them that they will paw the young shoots out of the soil; they are bitter, but there is no accounting for taste. Another kind of **wire-lettuce** (*Stephanomeria parryii*), just a few inches high and bearing larger and more abundant flowers, is found in the mountains at an elevation of 4,000 or 5,000 feet.

HABITAT Valley floor and fans.

Sunflower Family | **PINK, ROSE & MAGENTA FLOWERS** | 67

DESERT WIRE-LETTUCE

DESERT WIRE-LETTUCE

BEAVERTAIL PRICKLYPEAR

Beavertail pricklypear

Opuntia basilaris CACTUS FAMILY (Cactaceae)

GROWTH FORM Cactus

DESCRIPTION A clump of **beavertail pricklypear** in full bloom is well worth a stop for a picture. You may think you are now seeing a cactus that is safe to touch, as it has no spines, but the small bunches of short hairs that dot the blue-green, sometimes wrinkled pads come off easily and are extremely irritating to the skin. The showy magenta flowers are borne on the margins of the pad-like joints.

NOTE The Panamint Indians are reported to have boiled the joints for food.

HABITAT Valley floor and fans; upper desert slopes.

Cactus Family | **PINK, ROSE & MAGENTA FLOWERS** | 69

BEAVERTAIL PRICKLYPEAR

Desert snowberry

Symphoricarpos longiflorus   HONEYSUCKLE FAMILY (Caprifoliaceae)

GROWTH FORM Shrub

DESCRIPTION This is an open shrub one to four feet high with rather slender erect stems. The bark of the old stems is gray and shreddy, while that of the younger stems and widely spreading branches and branchlets is smooth and brown. The small, pale blue-green leaves are clustered on the branchlets and it is in these clusters that the long-tubed, very fragrant flowers appear. The flower is more deeply colored on the outside than within. In fact the outside is about all one sees, as the flat-spreading lobes are only about one-fifth the length of the tube. The fruits are white and about one-half inch long.

HABITAT Pinyon-juniper woodland, canyons. This snowberry seems to prefer limestone as a place to grow. It is rather common in the desert mountains of the Great Basin.

Honeysuckle Family | **PINK, ROSE & MAGENTA FLOWERS** | 71

DESERT SNOWBERRY

DESERT SNOWBERRY

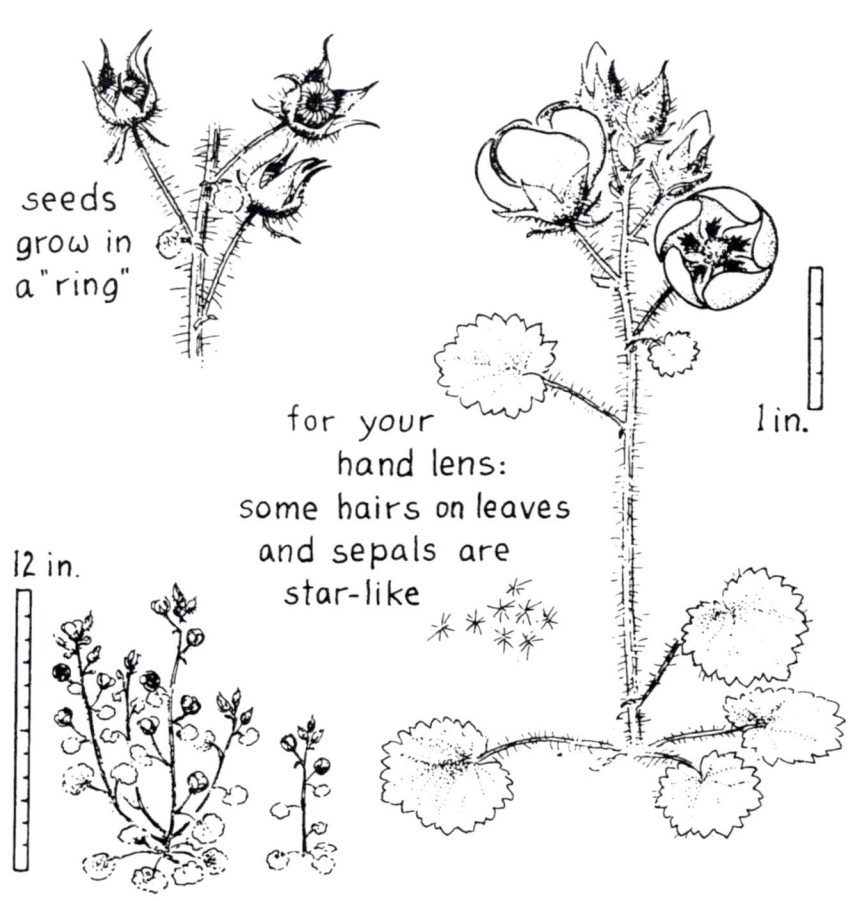

Desert fivespot

Eremalche rotundifolia   **MALLOW FAMILY** (Malvaceae)

SYNONYM *Malvastrum rotundifolium*
GROWTH FORM Annual herb
DESCRIPTION Judging by the number of common names, **desert fivespot** comes near to winning the popularity contest among the local wildflowers. It has been variously called lantern flower, Chinese lantern, and fivespot mallow. The plants are usually less than a foot high, the leaves are round with a toothed margin, and though the plants have a conspicuous hairy covering they are green and not gray. The rose-pink petals of the flowers curve inward, thus suggesting a small lantern, but not enough to conceal the crimson spot at the base pf each of the five petals.
HABITAT Valley floor and fans. This plant will be seen on other deserts in the west, as it occurs as far south as northern Baja California, Mexico and in western Arizona.

Mallow Family | **PINK, ROSE & MAGENTA FLOWERS** | 73

DESERT FIVESPOT

DESERT FIVESPOT

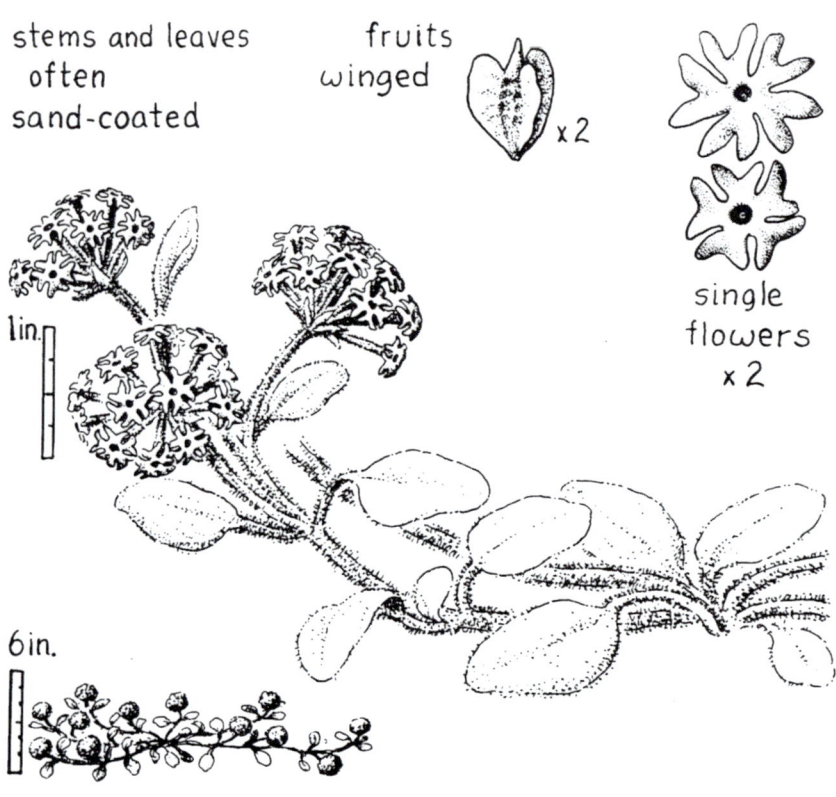

Desert sand-verbena

Abronia villosa   FOUR-O'CLOCK FAMILY (Nyctaginaceae)

GROWTH FORM Annual herb

DESCRIPTION Perhaps this kind of **sand-verbena** has been photographed for picture postcards more than any other desert wildflower. At least the low-growing plants with their heads of fragrant, rose-pink flowers have inspired many an amateur photographer. From a technical point of view the pretty verbena-like flower is not a corolla but a brightly colored calyx; nor is it a true verbena, though the flowers are of much the same shape. The hairs on the leaves are rather sticky and often are partially coated with sand.

HABITAT Valley floor and fans. It is widespread in sandy places throughout the western deserts as far south as Sonora and Baja California, Mexico.

Four-O'Clock Family | **PINK, ROSE & MAGENTA FLOWERS** | 75

DESERT SAND-VERBENA

DESERT SAND-VERBENA

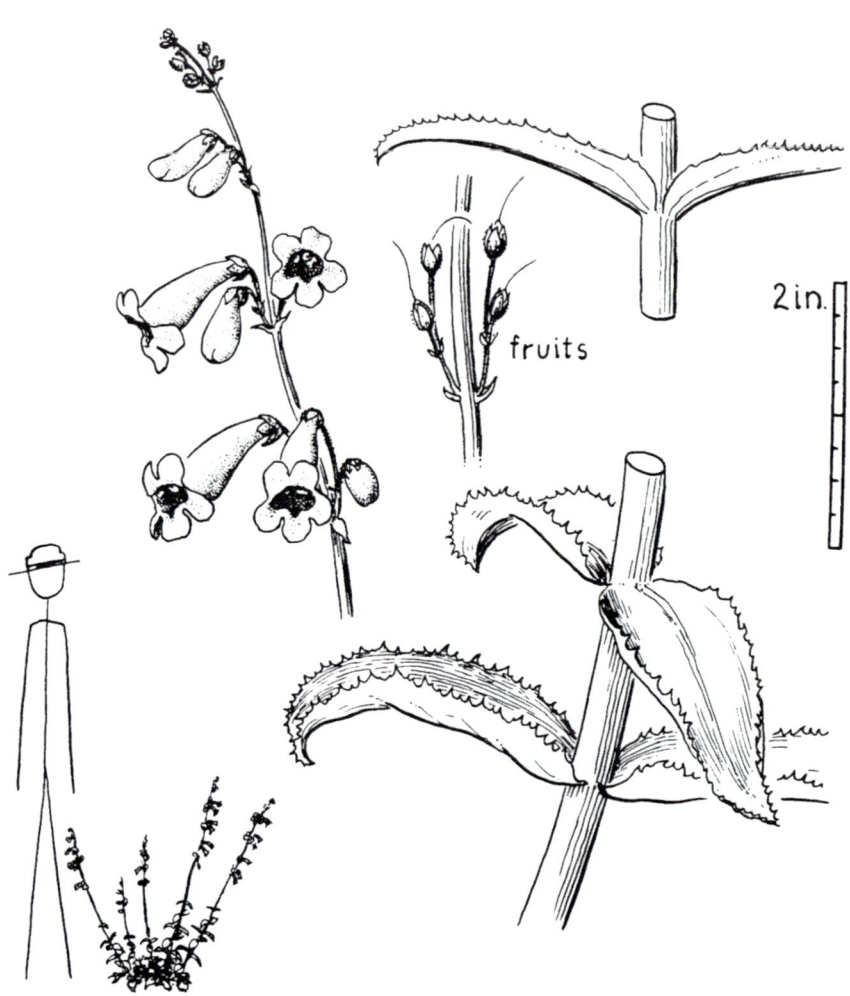

Panamint beardtongue

Penstemon floridus var. *austinii*   **PLANTAIN FAMILY** (Plantaginaceae)

GROWTH FORM Perennial herb

DESCRIPTION This variety has a much less swollen look to the rose-pink corolla than that of the species which is found more commonly in the desert mountains north of Death Valley. Though the plants do not occur in great abundance in any one place, the individual plants one finds have several straight unbranched stems rising from the root to a height of two or three feet. The leaves below the flowers are bluish green and are margined with many small teeth. The flower stalk itself has some glandular hairs.

HABITAT Pinyon-juniper woodland, upper desert slopes.

Plantain Family | **PINK, ROSE & MAGENTA FLOWERS** | 77

PANAMINT BEARDTONGUE

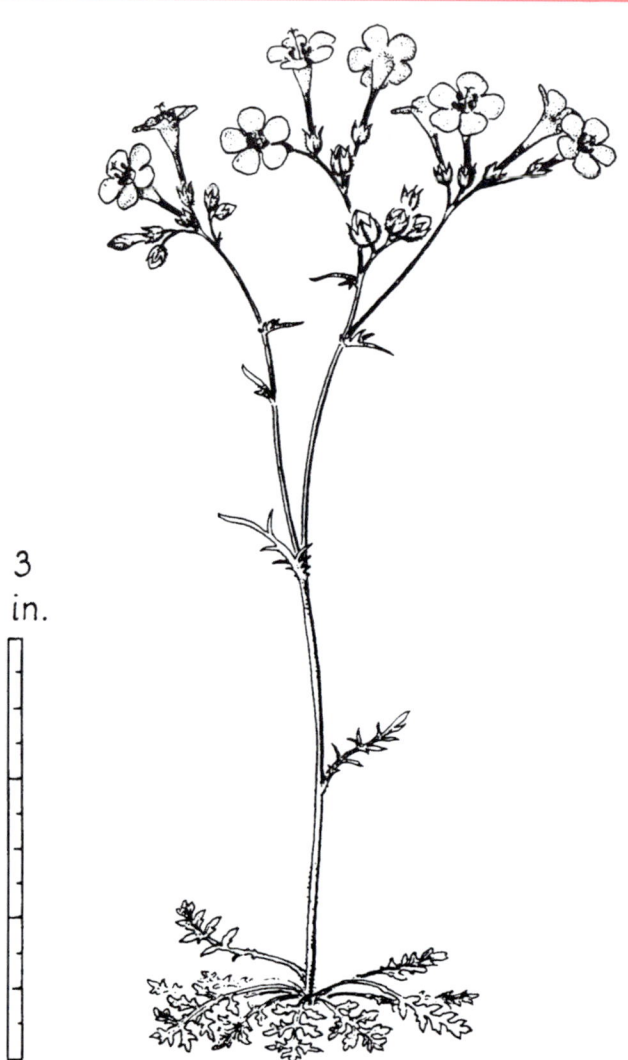

Broad-flowered gilia
Gilia latiflora PHLOX FAMILY (Polemoniaceae)

GROWTH FORM Annual herb

DESCRIPTION In the flowers of the phlox family in general all colors of the rainbow can be found, though the white-violet-blue series is more common. The flowers of the **broad-flowered gilia** have more than their share of color: the lobes are pink-lilac, the throat is blue on the upper part and yellow below, and the tube is deep purple. In addition to this, the stamens, which are to be seen in the top of the throat, are blue. In good years the plants grow to a foot or so in height and the several flowers are nicely displayed on the leafless branching stem.

HABITAT Valley floor and fans.

Phlox Family | **PINK, ROSE & MAGENTA FLOWERS** | 79

BROAD-FLOWERED GILIA

BROAD-FLOWERED GILIA

Stansbury phlox

Phlox stansburyi   **PHLOX FAMILY** (Polemoniaceae)

GROWTH FORM Perennial herb or sub-shrub

DESCRIPTION If you had **Stansbury phlox** in your rock garden, blooming as it does in the stony ground in the pinyon and limber pine forest, you would have something to boast about. However, it probably would not respond favorably to good garden care. The plants are four to eight inches high with several rather woody stems from a stout root. The leaves are narrow, gray-green and hairy. The pink flowers with their long tubes and flaring lobes often cover this small shrublet with a profusion of bloom.

NOTE Here again is another instance where the scientific name gives a hint of the botanical history of the west. Stansbury led an exploring expedition of the Great Salt Lake area about the time of the gold rush.

HABITAT Pinyon-juniper and limber pine-bristlecone pine woodland.

Phlox Family **PINK, ROSE & MAGENTA FLOWERS** | 81

STANSBURY PHLOX

STANSBURY PHLOX

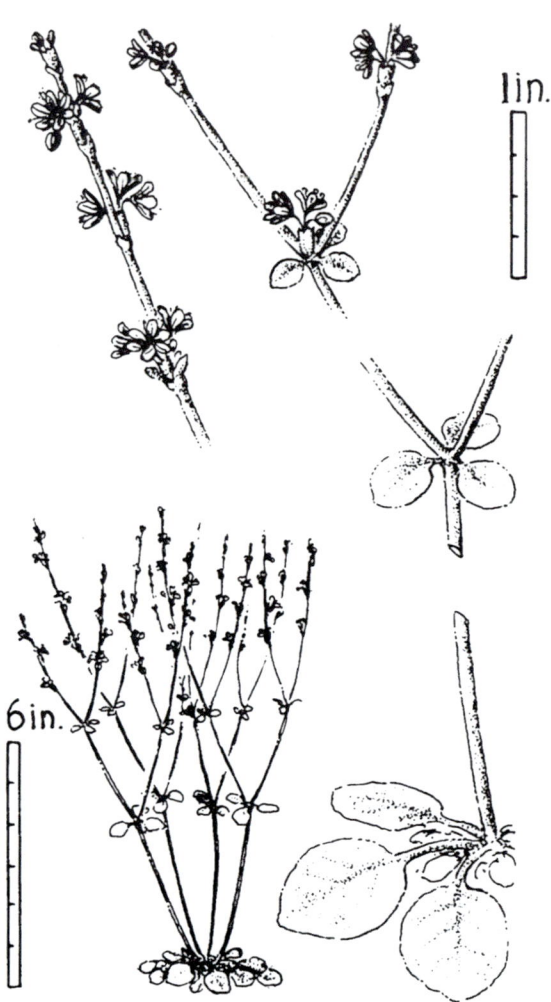

Panamint Mountain eriogonum

Eriogonum panamintense BUCKWHEAT FAMILY (Polygonaceae)

GROWTH FORM Perennial herb

DESCRIPTION Along with the shrubs of rabbitbrush, sagebrush, and other woody growth among the pinyons and junipers, there are many perennial herbs, some of which are eriogonums. This species of *Eriogonum* is found in the mountains of the Park and in the other high desert ranges of Inyo County east of the Sierra Nevada to those of western Nevada. The plants have stalked felty white leaves at the base and at each joint of the stem, and as it divides and redivides there is a collar of round white leaves which reduce in size on the upper joints. The pinkish white flowers are in small clusters fitted tightly to the nearly upright stems.

HABITAT Pinyon-juniper woodland.

Buckwheat Family | **PINK, ROSE & MAGENTA FLOWERS** | 83

PANAMINT MOUNTAIN ERIOGONUM

PINK, ROSE & MAGENTA FLOWERS — Rosaceae

Woods' rose

Rosa woodsii subsp. *gratissima*   ROSE FAMILY (Rosaceae)

GROWTH FORM Shrub

DESCRIPTION **Wood's rose** certainly should be included in a list of Death Valley wildflowers. After all, one of the entrances to the valley goes through a canyon named for a wild rose. Other canyons in the surrounding mountains, where streams flow at least part of the year, also support wild roses which grow among the willow thickets and other shrubs that are companions of streams. Everyone recognizes a wild rose, but telling the difference between the kinds of wild roses poses a real problem; it is a variable genus.

HABITAT Upper slopes and pinyon-juniper woodland.

Rose Family | **PINK, ROSE & MAGENTA FLOWERS** | 85

WOODS' ROSE

WOODS' ROSE

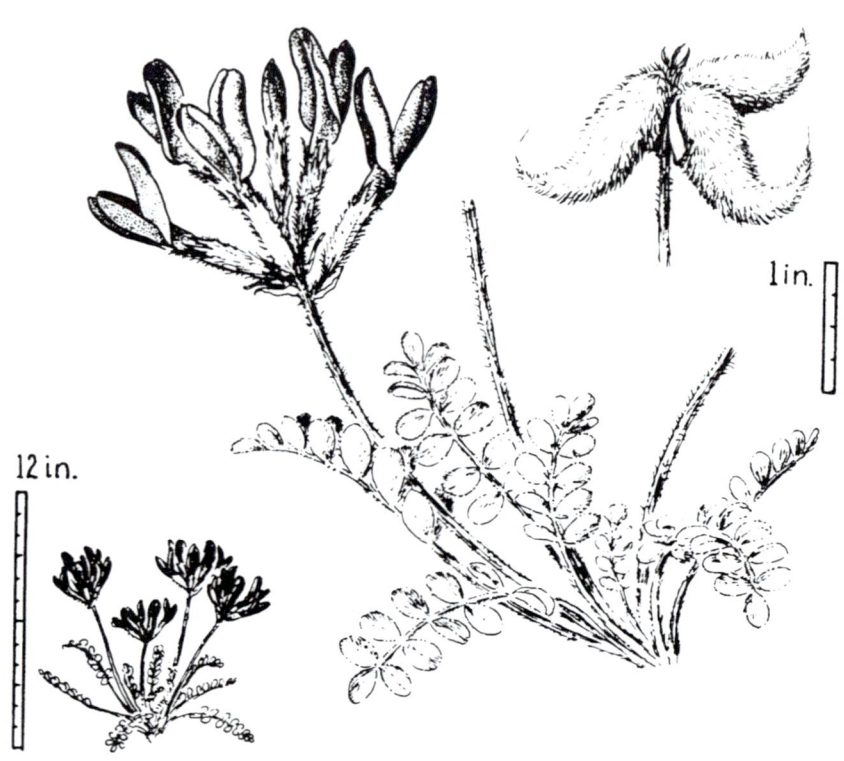

Scarlet locoweed

Astragalus coccineus   **PEA FAMILY** (Fabaceae)

GROWTH FORM Perennial herb

DESCRIPTION When in bloom this is one of the showiest plants that California deserts can offer, even if it is only a low-growing perennial herb. The leaves (divided into several leaflets) are silvery with dense tangled hairs and set off to advantage the large, bright red flowers on the many flower stalks. The stalks rise above the leaves three to five inches. The pea-shaped blossoms are an inch to an inch and one-half long. The pods are somewhat longer and densely clothed with wool.

NOTE There are literally hundreds of species of *Astragalus* in the world. California alone has about a hundred different kinds, and more than fifteen kinds are found in Death Valley and the surrounding desert ranges. Though there is a combination of characters that makes certain plants unmistakably species of the genus *Astragalus,* there are quite a lot of different shapes and sizes in the pods, even in the few kinds in Death Valley. They may be large and woolly, papery and shaped like bladders, narrow and stiffer than parchment, thin-walled and resembling tiny bean pods, and some even like irregular-shaped small nuts.

HABITAT Upper desert slopes and pinyon-juniper woodland.

Pea Family | RED & ORANGE FLOWERS | 87

SCARLET LOCOWEED

SCARLET LOCOWEED

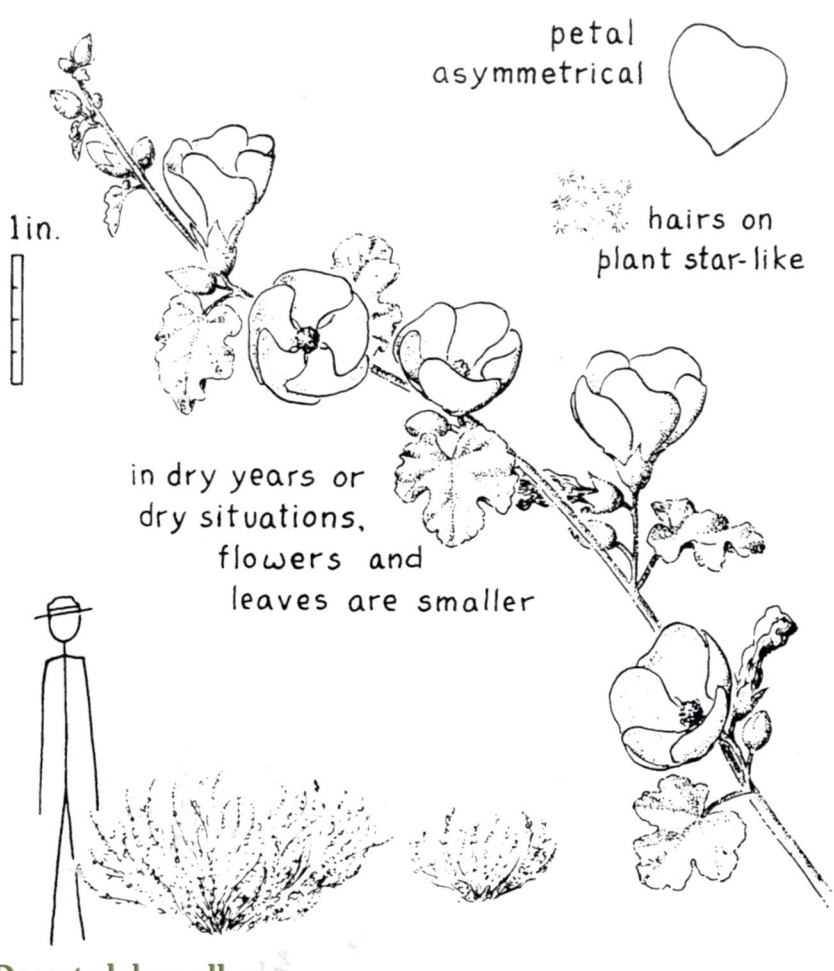

Desert globemallow
Sphaeralcea ambigua   MALLOW FAMILY (Malvaceae)

GROWTH FORM Sub-shrub

DESCRIPTION The woody portion of this plant is mostly limited to the crown and lower branches, while the upper stems and branches are, as a rule, many and pliable. The leaves are an inch or two long, rather broad, and usually three-lobed, and the star-shaped hairs cover them as thickly as they do the other parts of the plant. The flowers are a shade of red not too often seen among the desert wildflowers. It has been designated as "grenadine" but to some it is more nearly the color of a piece of fresh salmon.

NOTE The species is widespread in the southwest and is highly variable. There is a form of **Rusby globemallow** (*Sphaeralcea rusbyi* subsp. *eremicola*) that is an endemic of Death Valley.

HABITAT Valley floor and upper desert slopes.

Mallow Family | RED & ORANGE FLOWERS | 89

DESERT GLOBEMALLOW

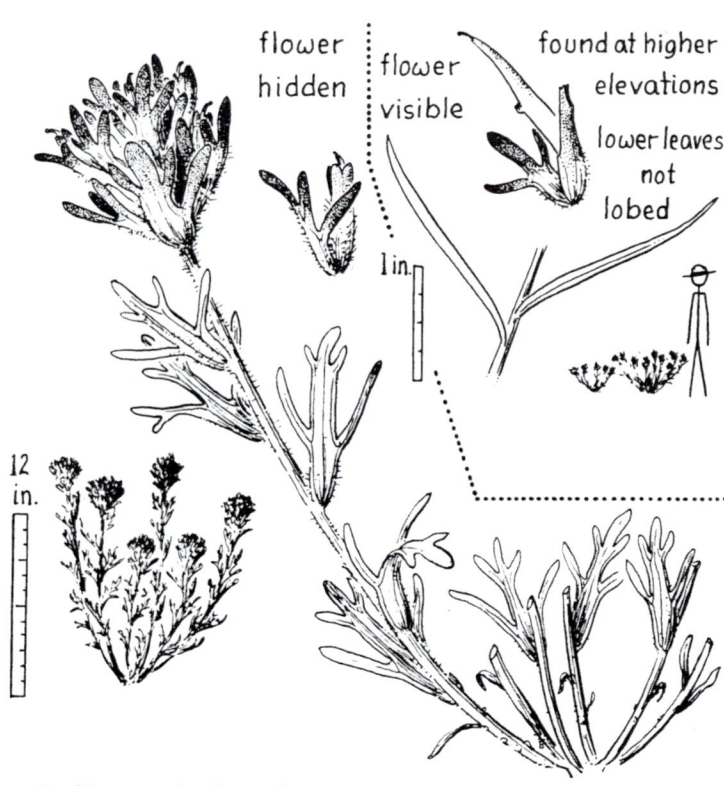

Desert Indian-paintbrush

Castilleja chromosa   BROOM-RAPE FAMILY (Orobanchaceae)

GROWTH FORM Perennial herb

DESCRIPTION This is a desert wildflower than can be accurately identified from a moving automobile. Even the driver with his eyes on the road will catch the flash of scarlet from the occasional plants of **desert Indian-paintbrush** growing up among the low shrubs along the road. The actual flowers are scarcely visible, as they are hidden in the scarlet-tipped calyx, but the several stems end in a "brush" of scarlet-tipped leafy bracts. The plants are not only natives of southwestern deserts but also of the sagebrush plains as far north as Wyoming.

Wyoming Indian-paintbrush

Castilleja linariifolia   BROOM-RAPE FAMILY (Orobanchaceae)

GROWTH FORM Perennial herb

DESCRIPTION This Indian-paintbrush (*Castilleja linariifolia*) is found in Death Valley but often at higher elevations than the desert Indian-paintbrush. The plants are much taller (up to three feet) and not so brilliantly colored as the desert Indian-paintbrush, and the red and green flowers are longer than the bracts and calyx (illustrated above on the upper right).

HABITAT Upper desert slopes.

Broom-Rape Family   RED & ORANGE FLOWERS | 91

DESERT INDIAN-PAINTBRUSH

Beaked penstemon
Penstemon rostriflorus   **PLANTAIN FAMILY** (Plantaginaceae)

GROWTH FORM Perennial herb

DESCRIPTION This scarlet penstemon is found in rocky ground where the pine trees grow, among the pinyons as well as those of higher elevations. The plants are a foot or two high. The yellow-green leaves are narrow and more abundant at the base of the plant. The flowers, of which there are several on the flower stalk, are an inch or an inch and one-half long and rather narrow, and the lower lip is sharply rolled back and split into three lobes. **Beaked penstemon** is widespread in the mountains of the west.

NOTE Penstemons are natives of the northern hemisphere but the greatest number of species is to be found in western North America. Many kinds are grown in gardens, as they are hardy perennials (rarely shrubs) with attractively colored flowers of many different shades. The desert is not without its quota of species, though more are found in wetter climes.

HABITAT Limber pine-bristlecone pine and pinyon-juniper woodland.

Plantain Family | **RED & ORANGE FLOWERS** | 93

BEAKED PENSTEMON

BEAKED PENSTEMON

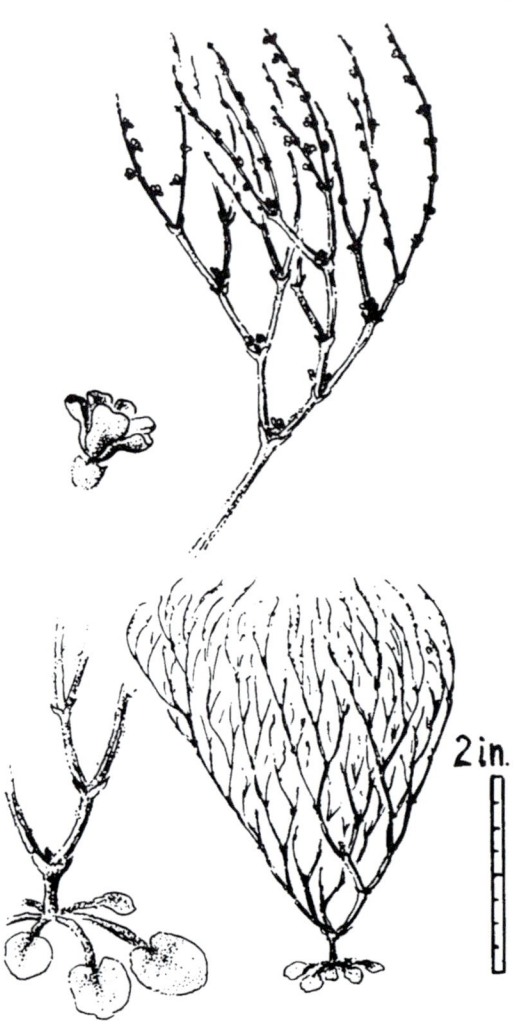

Birdnest eriogonum (Whiskbroom)
Eriogonum nidularium BUCKWHEAT FAMILY (Polygonaceae)

GROWTH FORM Annual herb

DESCRIPTION **Birdnest eriogonum** is found in other places in the Mohave Desert, but in the Park it is found in late summer in canyons and on upper desert slopes and with the junipers and pinyons. The small reddish (sometimes yellowish) flowers are set at regular intervals along the somewhat cobwebby stems, which branch and rebranch as this small annual (three to six inches high) lives out its short life span. The dried-up plants persist until the wind blows them away. They are readily recognizable by the dense mass of incurved branches which rather resembles old birds' nests. The scientific name given to this eriogonum is based on this resemblance.

HABITAT Pinyon-juniper woodland and upper desert slopes.

Buckwheat Family | RED & ORANGE FLOWERS | 95

BIRDNEST ERIOGONUM

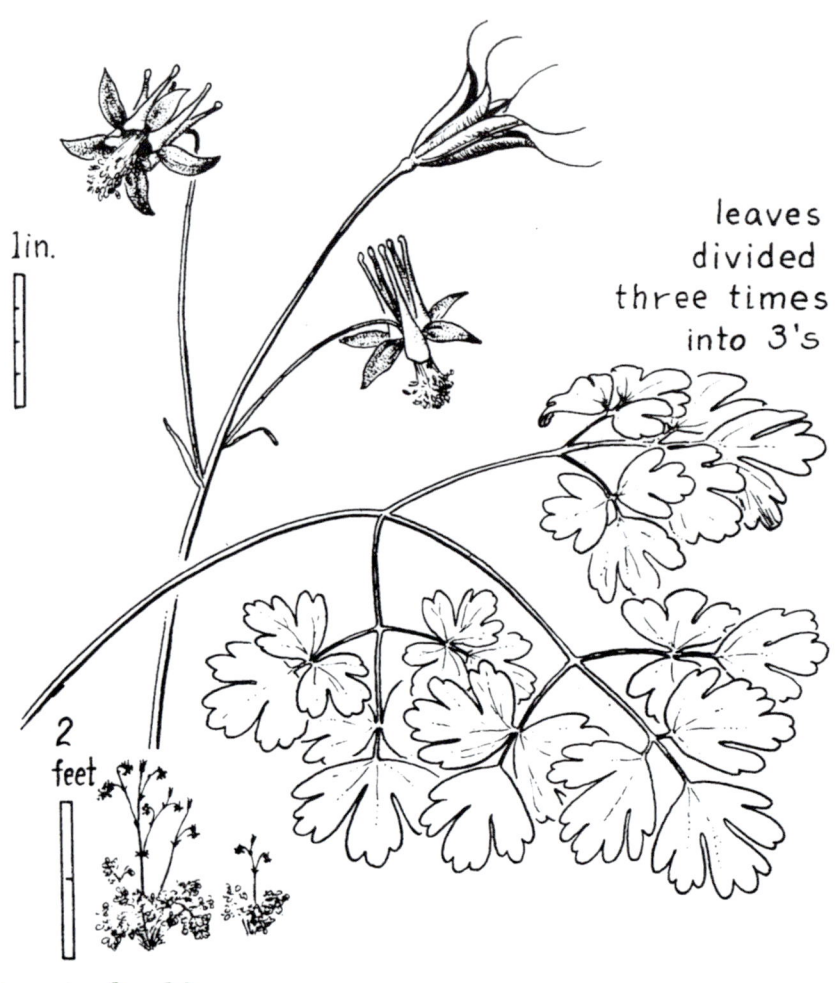

Desert columbine
Aquilegia shockleyi   BUTTERCUP FAMILY (Ranunculaceae)

GROWTH FORM Perennial herb

DESCRIPTION If you should be fortunate enough to see this red and yellow columbine by some spring or running stream in the canyons of mountains around Death Valley, you will probably think you have seen the same columbine before in other mountains in the west far removed from the desert area. The coloring of the drooping flowers is much the same as those, but the red or yellowish red spurs are more slender. A more obvious difference is in the faintly bluish basal leaves, which are tritemate instead of biternate; in other words, they are divided three times into threes instead of two times into threes. The plants grow to a height of one and one-half to two and one-half feet.

HABITAT Upper desert slopes, pinyon-juniper woodland, streambanks. Desert columbine is not uncommon in desert ranges in Nevada and eastern California.

Buttercup Family — RED & ORANGE FLOWERS | 97

DESERT COLUMBINE

DESERT COLUMBINE

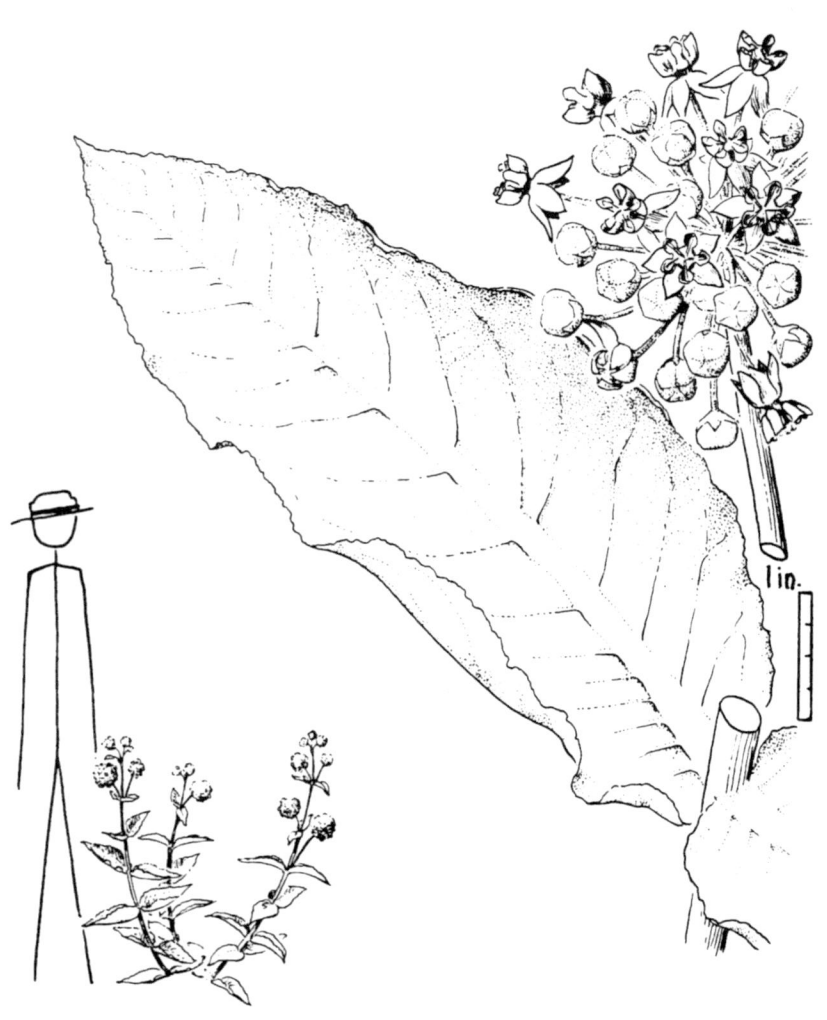

Desert milkweed

Asclepias erosa   DOGBANE FAMILY (Apocynaceae)

GROWTH FORM Perennial herb

DESCRIPTION The tall dead stalks (two to four feet or more) of the **desert milkweed** remain standing after the leaves, flowers and fruits have blown away with the desert wind. The plants grow in the loose soil of the washes and, at least in the desert, never occur in large stands but as scattered groups of plants. The large leaves are broad, whitish green, rather thick in texture, and grow opposite each other, fitting closely against the stem. The whole plant appears to be covered with a loose white lint which rubs off as the plant grows older. The flower clusters grow from the axils of the upper leaves.

HABITAT Valley floor and fans, washes. The species is widespread in western desert regions, and is found occasionally on the seaward side of the mountain ranges.

Dogbane Family — WHITE & CREAM FLOWERS | 99

DESERT MILKWEED

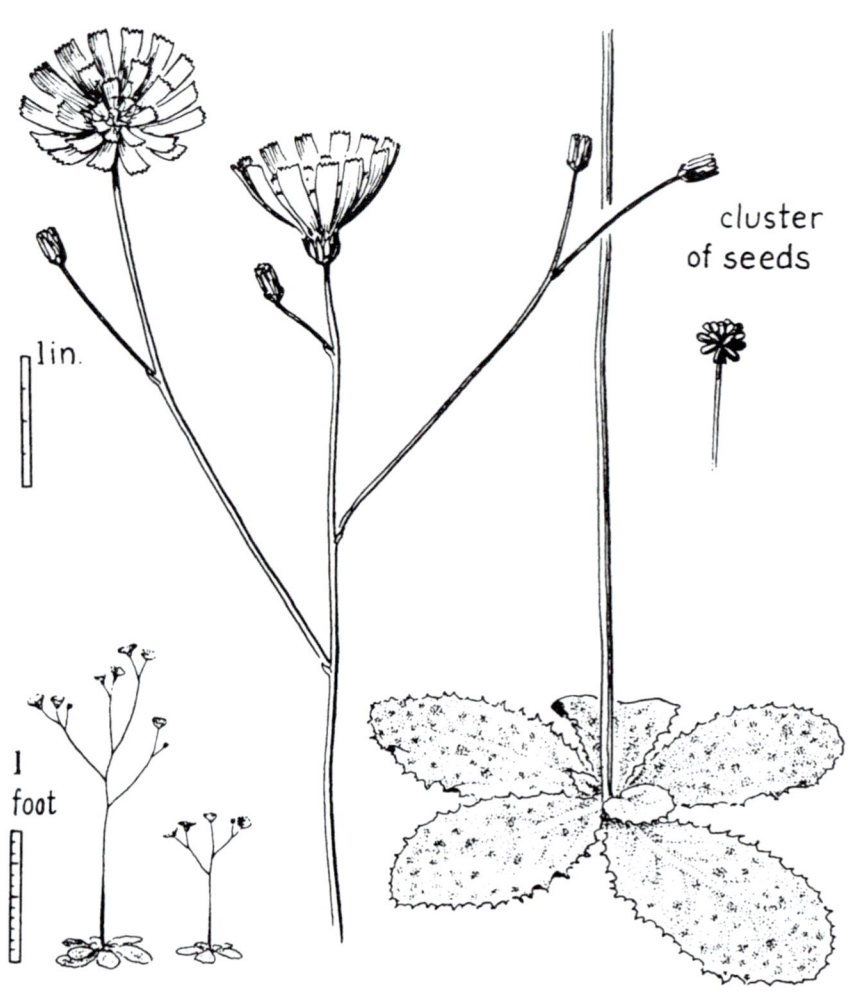

Gravelghost (Tobaccoweed)

Atrichoseris platyphylla **SUNFLOWER FAMILY** (Asteraceae)

GROWTH FORM Annual herb

DESCRIPTION There is only one species or kind of **gravelghost**, and it grows on low washes and rocky slopes all over the western deserts. The broad bluish brown-spotted leaves make flat rosettes on the ground which blend with the sand and gravel, and the leafless stems rise from them to the height of one foot to two and one-half feet. The white or purplish-tinged, fragrant flower heads are borne on the upper part of the stem. They are about one inch across and make an attractive sight from February to May (or later if the rains come late) waving in the desert wind. If you are far enough away, the flowers on the slender stems seem to float in the air—and so the name "gravelghost" has been given to it.

HABITAT Valley floor and fans, washes.

Sunflower Family · WHITE & CREAM FLOWERS | 101

GRAVELGHOST

GRAVELGHOST

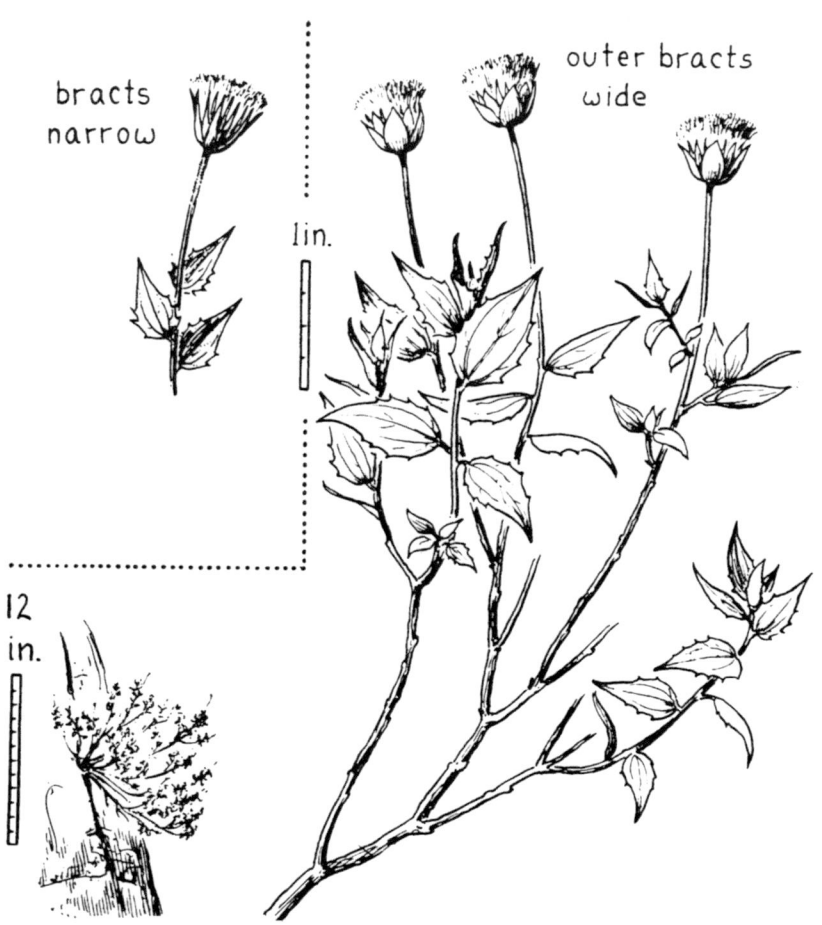

Spearleaved brickellia

Brickellia atractyloides   SUNFLOWER FAMILY (Asteraceae)

GROWTH FORM Shrub

DESCRIPTION Some plants that grow on canyon walls may grow in other habitats as well but this one, to grow at all, must have its roots buried in cracks and crevices of the rocks here in Death Valley or in other southwest desert ranges. Perhaps it needs the additional shade that it will get some part of the day on the cliffs of the canyon. The plant grows in loose clumps. The flower heads are few and creamy white, but the leaves are its most interesting feature. These are an inch or less long, very firm and rather shiny, and sharply toothed around the margin. Just to show that you need an observing eye and a hand lens as well to tell some species apart, the flower head and the flower stalk of the **pungent brickellia** (*Brickellia atractyloides* var. *arguta*) are illustrated at upper left. Both brickellias grow in the same kinds of places in Death Valley National Park.

HABITAT Valley floor and fans, canyon walls.

Sunflower Family | WHITE & CREAM FLOWERS | 103

SPEARLEAVED BRICKELLIA

SPEARLEAVED BRICKELLIA

Asteraceae

White tackstem
Calycoseris wrightii   SUNFLOWER FAMILY (Asteraceae)

GROWTH FORM Annual herb

DESCRIPTION In the chicory tribe of the Sunflower Family (Asteraceae) the flower heads, which look like ordinary flowers, are made up of many strap-shaped florets. The dandelion in your lawn is an excellent example of this type. Several members of this tribe occur in Death Valley: **desert dandelion** (*Malacothrix glabrata*), **desert wirelettuce** (*Stephanomeria pauciflora*), **New Mexican rafinesquia** (*Rafinesquia neomexicana*), and others. One of the others is **white tackstem**, which can be seen quite often growing in loose, sandy soil. The flower heads of this annual are white with the back of the rays brushed with pink. The leaves are much divided and the "tacks" which give the plant its common name are the pale stalked glands on the upper stem. There is another species (*Calycoseris parryi*) with yellow flower heads and darker tack-shaped glands. Both kinds occur in southwestern deserts.

HABITAT Valley floor and fans.

WHITE TACKSTEM

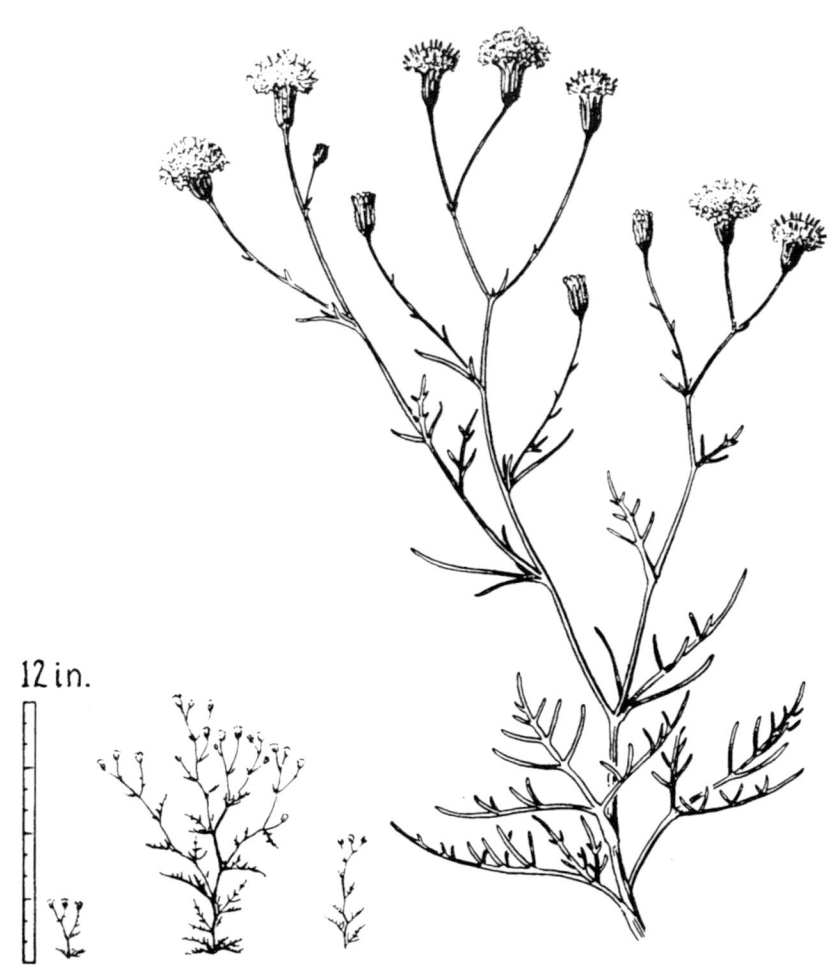

Pebble chaenactis

Chaenactis carphoclinia SUNFLOWER FAMILY (Asteraceae)

GROWTH FORM Annual herb

DESCRIPTION Several kinds of chaenactis grow in this area. One kind is found on Telescope Peak, others in various lower habitats down to the **pebble chaenactis**, which seems to prefer one of the hottest spots of all in the valley—the desert pavement. It grows from here southward to western Arizona and northern Mexico. As it is an annual it has a short life span. The water supply its short roots can reach soon evaporates in the desert heat and it dies. Its height and the number of branches from the main axis, of course, depend on the water supply. If it is a year of several winter rains, the plants may be over a foot high, with several stems from the base, and bear many white flower heads over which the stamens stand up like little pins. In dry years, the plants are tiny and can support only a few flower heads.

HABITAT Valley floor and fans.

Sunflower Family · WHITE & CREAM FLOWERS | 107

PEBBLE CHAENACTIS

WHITE & CREAM FLOWERS — Asteraceae

white, stiff hairs on stems and leaves

1 in.

facetiously called a "belly flower"

one bends low to see them

MOHAVE DESERT-STAR

Mohave desert-star
Monoptilon bellioides — SUNFLOWER FAMILY (Asteraceae)

GROWTH FORM Annual herb

DESCRIPTION **Desert star** is another annual of the area that well deserves to be called a "belly plant." The branches with their scattered, dull green, hairy leaves flatten in the gravel in a circle three to six inches wide. The flowers look much like daisies—those pleasant little weeds of our lawns—in size and color. They cling as closely to the soil as do the stems and leaves. A close-up color photo of desert star is well worth the time spent in taking it.

HABITAT Valley floor and fans.

Sunflower Family WHITE & CREAM FLOWERS | 109

MOHAVE DESERT-STAR

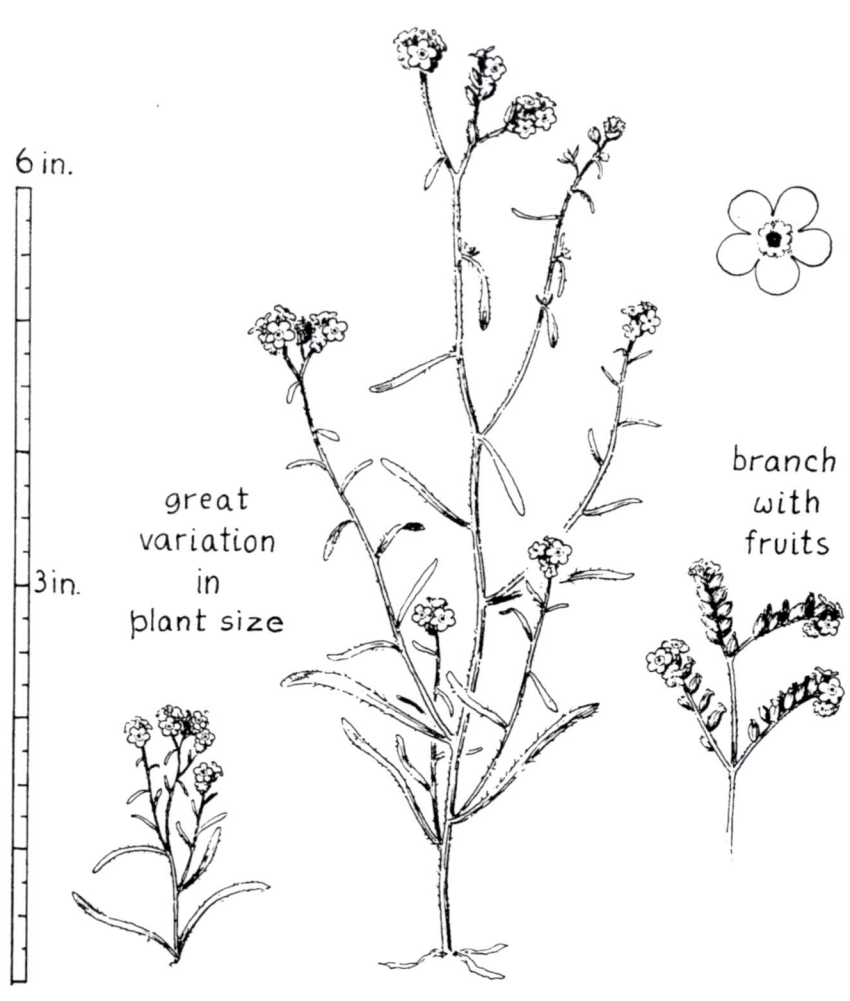

Scented cryptantha

Cryptantha utahensis   BORAGE FAMILY (Boraginaceae)

GROWTH FORM Annual herb

DESCRIPTION There are several species of *Cryptantha* in various places in the Park and all are rather small annual plants with white flowers which are very tiny to small. The flowers of many of them are half concealed in stiff spreading hairs. The hairs around the flowers of the **scented cryptantha** are smoothly pressed flat and give a silky appearance to the inflorescence. The flowers have the odor of heliotrope. The plants are usually six to ten inches high and are commonly found at elevations of from 2,000 to 3,500 feet. They are seldom sufficiently abundant to give color at flowering time to the area in which they grow. They are found growing in similar places as far east as southern Utah.

HABITAT Valley floor and fans.

Borage Family | WHITE & CREAM FLOWERS | 111

SCENTED CRYPTANTHA

SCENTED CRYPTANTHA

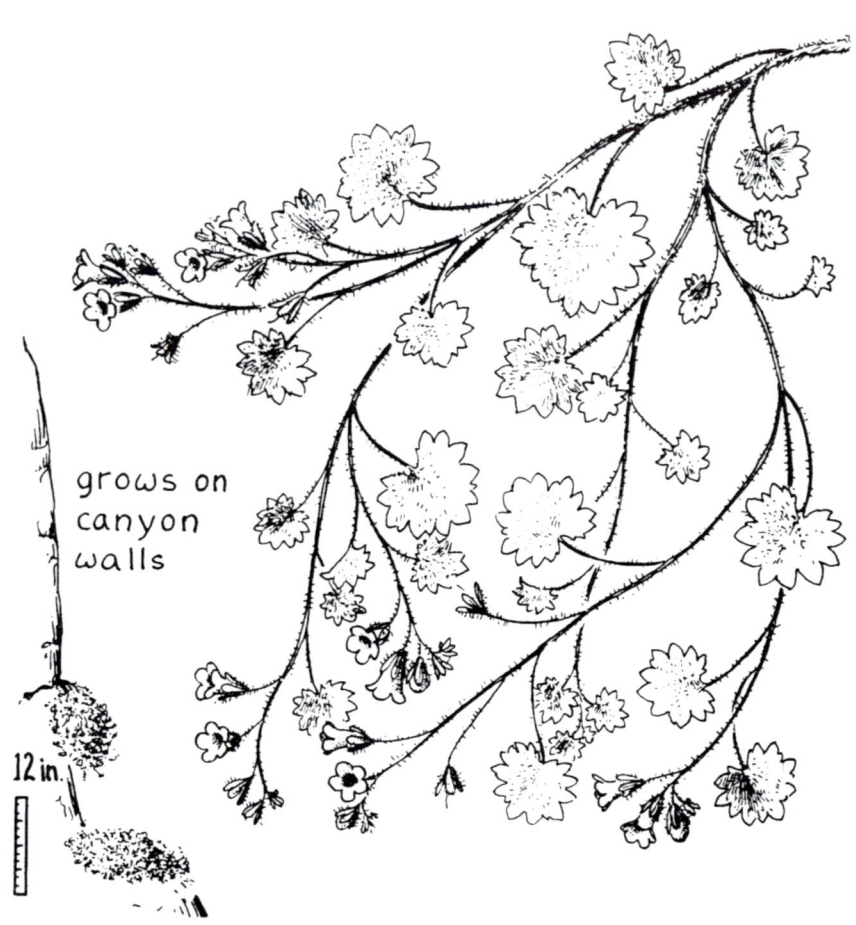

Panamint phacelia
Phacelia perityloides
BORAGE FAMILY (Boraginaceae)

GROWTH FORM Perennial herb

DESCRIPTION This phacelia looks very different from those more commonly seen about the Park. It grows only in crevices or cracks on canyon walls, mostly of limestone, at elevations of about 3,000 to 4,500 feet. The plants form densely leafy mounds or may, where water drips down the vertical cliffs, be seen in pendent masses hanging for a foot or more. The plant is a very showy thing if one is fortunate enough to see it in bloom. The small, rather short-stalked, white (with a purplish base) flowers are set off against the background of the small, round, sticky leaves.

NOTE This is another plant that was first collected on the Death Valley Expedition in 1891, but it is also found in similar places in the limestone canyons of desert ranges in this general area.

HABITAT Pinyon-juniper woodland, canyons.

Borage Family | WHITE & CREAM FLOWERS | 113

PANAMINT PHACELIA

PANAMINT PHACELIA

White-margin euphorbia
Euphorbia albomarginata SPURGE FAMILY (Euphorbiaceae)

GROWTH FORM Perennial herb

DESCRIPTION In washes and in smaller watercourses there are mats six to ten inches wide flattened against the sand and gravel. The tiny leaves are bluish green and glabrous and are covered with seemingly white-petaled flowers that nestle among the leaves. The tiny male flowers and the single female flower are set in a small green cup. This in turn is rimmed by dark maroon glands to which are fastened white petal-like appendages, thus making the best imitation "flower" known (except of course for the plants of the sunflower family, where the individual flowers or florets are clustered into heads that appear to be distinct flowers, such as daisies, dandelions, sunflowers, and many others).

HABITAT Valley floor and fans, washes.

Parish euphorbia
Euphorbia parishii SPURGE FAMILY (Euphorbiaceae)

GROWTH FORM Perennial herb

DESCRIPTION Though not as attractive as the preceding species, **Parish euphorbia** is more conspicuous. It grows where plants are few and widely spaced in alkaline soils and its tangled flattened reddish stems are bare most of the year. It is primarily a prostrate plant like the preceding but often is set up an inch or so above the ground on its woody root because the wind blows the soil away from its base. The tangled branches are inclined to turn up at the tips as if they could not endure the terrifically high temperatures of the ground level. The leaves are smaller than white-margin euphorbia and the "flowers" have no white appendages.

HABITAT Valley floor and fans, washes.

Spurge Family — WHITE & CREAM FLOWERS | 115

WHITE-MARGIN EUPHORBIA

PARISH EUPHORBIA

WHITE & CREAM FLOWERS — Liliaceae

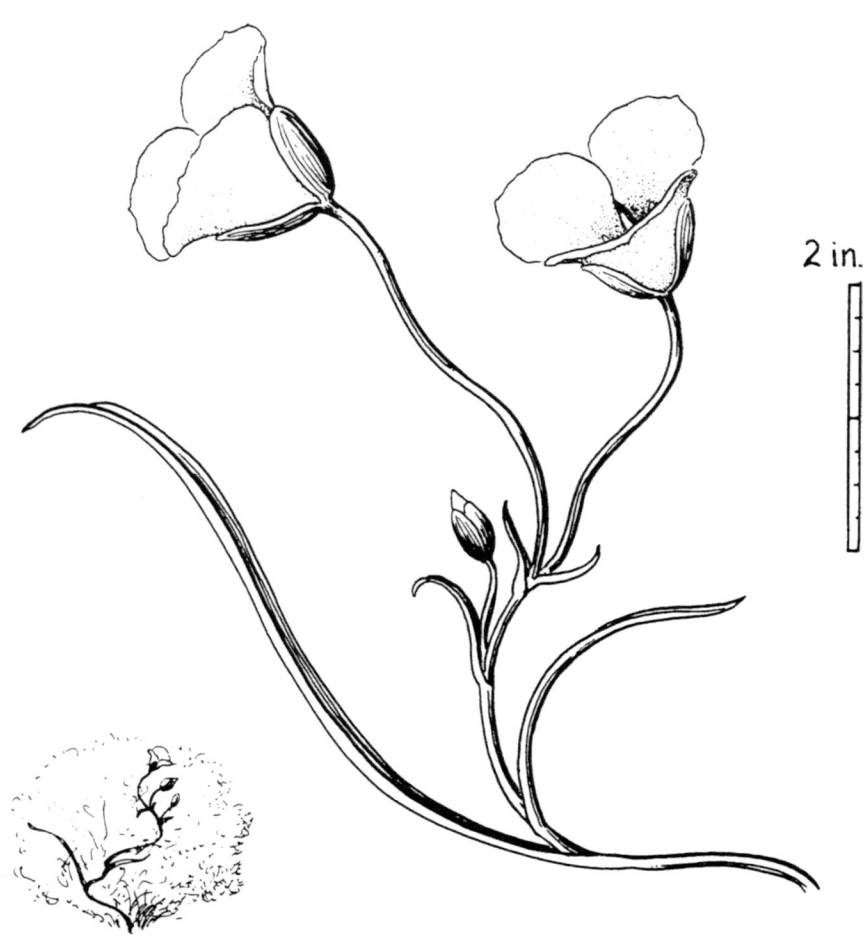

Weakstem mariposa
Calochortus flexuosus   LILY FAMILY (Liliaceae)

GROWTH FORM Perennial herb

DESCRIPTION For a mariposa this one has an unusual habit of growth. The stems are not erect but they more or less twine on the branches of shrubs or merely lean over on the rocky ground. The plants can reach a length of eighteen inches. The flowers are few, not more than four as a rule. The petals, which are one to two inches long, are white tinged with lilac and are beautifully marked basally with a yellow band and a purple spot.

HABITAT Upper desert slopes. This is typically a plant of the Great Basin area and is found from the eastern part of the California deserts to southwestern Colorado. It grows in the upper reaches of the creosotebush belt into the higher areas where big sagebrush grows.

Lily Family WHITE & CREAM FLOWERS | 117

WEAKSTEM MARIPOSA

WEAKSTEM MARIPOSA

WHITE & CREAM FLOWERS — Oleaceae

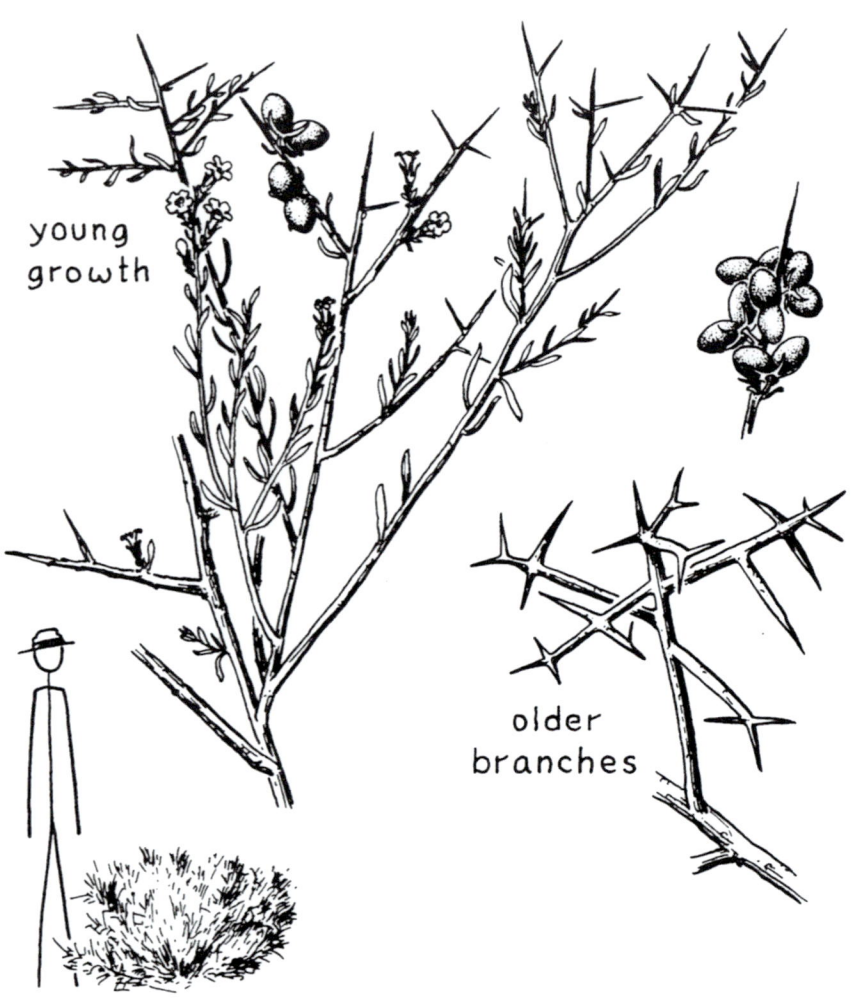

Spiny menodora
Menodora spinescens OLIVE FAMILY (Oleaceae)

GROWTH FORM Shrub

DESCRIPTION Spiny menodora grows on desert slopes of the Mohave Desert northward and eastward to Nevada and Arizona at elevations of 3,500 to about 6,500 feet. Many of the desert plants have spines, stinging hairs or branches ending in spines. Of the last category, spiny menodora is one of the more formidable. The stout green branches of the bushes spread at angles, and each of the many branches ends in a sharp point. Only the young, not yet thickened branches are covered with the small leaves. The small tubular flowers are white with a tinge of pink, and the two-lobed fruits are covered with a translucent coat.

HABITAT Upper desert slopes.

Olive Family WHITE & CREAM FLOWERS | 119

SPINY MENODORA

WHITE & CREAM FLOWERS

Onagraceae

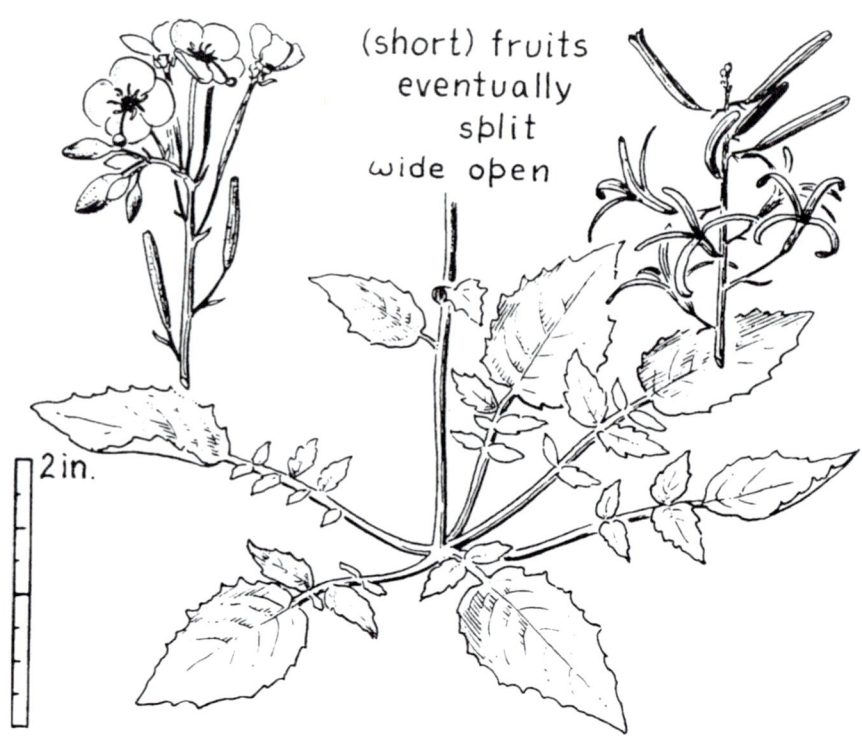

Browneyes

Chylismia claviformis **EVENING-PRIMROSE FAMILY** (Onagraceae)

SYNONYM *Oenothera claviformis*
GROWTH FORM Annual herb
DESCRIPTION When you buy a seed packet of annual larkspur to plant in your garden you expect to get white or pink flowered plants as well as blue—and maybe ones with other minor differences—from the seeds of this one species. This seems normal to you in cultivated garden plants, but you may be surprised that, in some groups at least, this sort of thing goes on all the time in nature. This is very true of the evening-primrose pictured here. All over our western deserts named forms of this species occur; ones with green or grayish leaves, or ones with flowers without a dark spot on each petal and with colors that range through white, cream, buff, and pale yellow. Death Valley has at least two of these variants. This plant has the growth habit of the golden evening-primrose but is shorter than that plant usually is, and the flowers are smaller. The stalked capsules are about an inch long, narrow and blunt at the top.
NOTE This is one of the most abundant flowering plants to be found on the valley floor.
HABITAT Valley floor and fans.

Evening-Primrose Family WHITE & CREAM FLOWERS | 121

BROWNEYES

BROWNEYES

Onagraceae

Shredding evening-primrose
Eremothera boothii   EVENING-PRIMROSE FAMILY (Onagraceae)
SYNONYMS *Camissonia boothii, Oenothera decorticans* var. *condensata*
GROWTH FORM Annual herb
DESCRIPTION The woody skeleton of this desert annual will remain for more than one season unless it is dragged away by some desert rodent for home-building purposes. The stems of the flowering plants are stout, and as they age the loose papery bark of the stems comes off. The white flowers, which become pinkish as they wither, are densely set along the stem and have a definitely one-sided appearance as the stems lengthen. The smaller plants may be unbranched, but more often one sees plants with a few curved branches rising from the base. The bases of the narrow capsules are woody and remain on the spreading dead branches. There are several other species of evening-primrose with small to tiny flowers found within the Park, but they are much more slender and fragile in appearance than this one. All have the typical four-petaled, slightly cupped flowers which are characteristic of this genus.
HABITAT Valley floor and fans.

Evening-Primrose Family · WHITE & CREAM FLOWERS | 123

SHREDDING EVENING-PRIMROSE

SHREDDING EVENING-PRIMROSE - 'SKELETON'

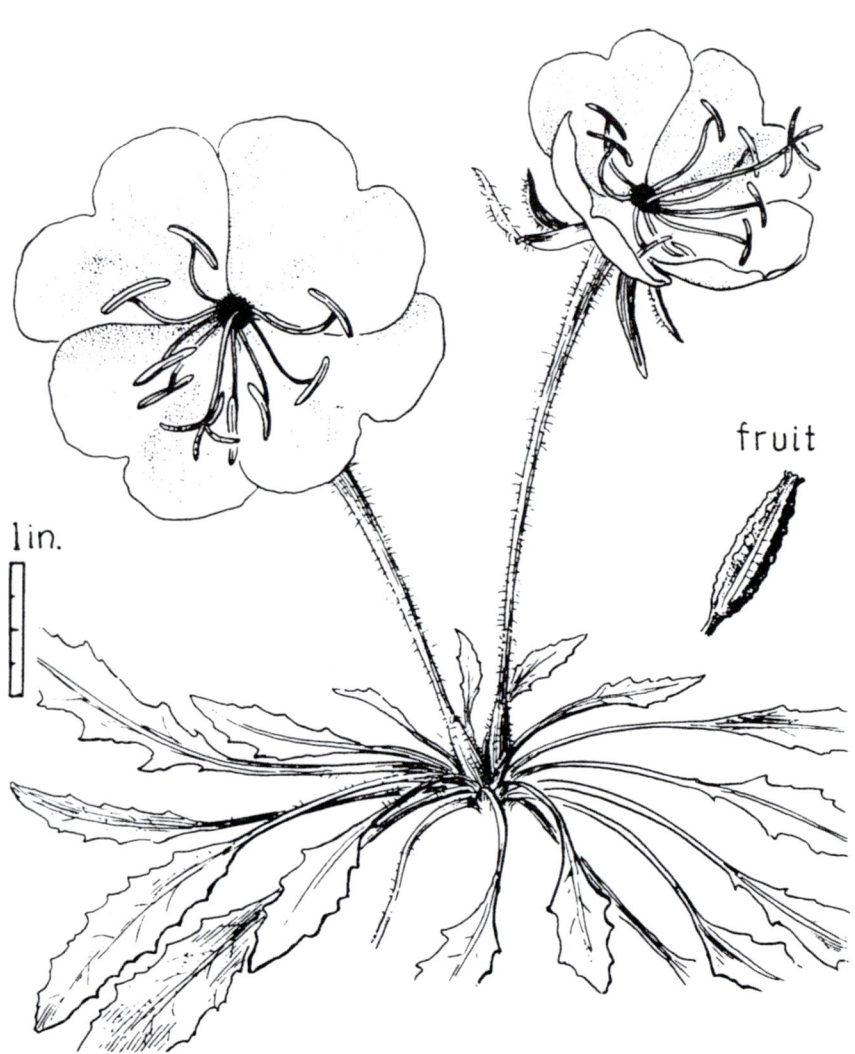

Tufted evening-primrose

Oenothera cespitosa subsp. *marginata*   EVENING-PRIMROSE FAMILY (Onagraceae)

GROWTH FORM Perennial herb

DESCRIPTION Many kinds of evening-primroses with flowers large and small grow in the Park but this is one of the largest. This perennial, found at high elevations, has no stem at all, only a flat cluster of leaves with toothed edges from which rise the fragrant white (sometimes pink-tinged) flowers which are at least two inches broad. They appear to be growing on stalks, but what seems to be a stalk is only the tube of the flower, which is attached to the woody oval seed-bearing capsule down on the ground in the rosette of leaves. It grows in similar places in the west.

HABITAT Limber pine-bristlecone pine and pinyon-juniper woodland.

Evening-Primrose Family   **WHITE & CREAM FLOWERS** | 125

TUFTED EVENING-PRIMROSE

TUFTED EVENING-PRIMROSE

WHITE & CREAM FLOWERS — Popaveraceae

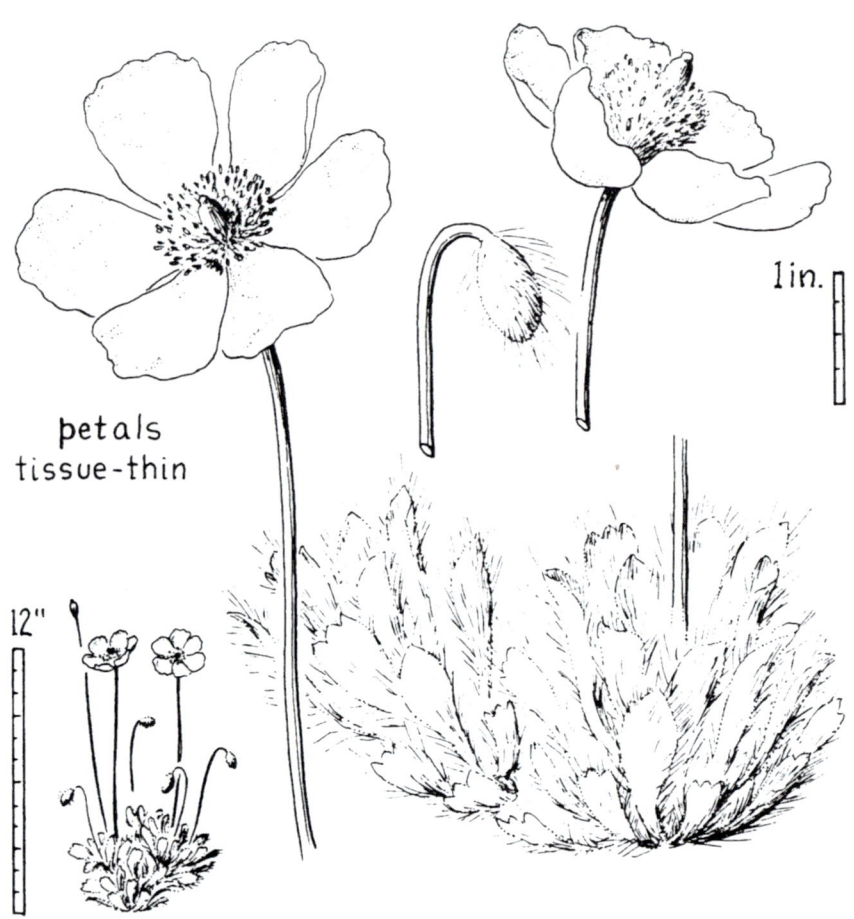

petals tissue-thin

1 in.

12"

Desert bearpoppy

Arctomecon merriamii   POPPY FAMILY (Papaveraceae)

GROWTH FORM Perennial herb

DESCRIPTION The **desert bearpoppy** is a member of the poppy family that grows only in the Death Valley region and southern Nevada. If one excludes the Panamint daisy, it is perhaps the most strikingly beautiful plant in the Park. The large white flowers appear singly on the tall naked stems. The bluish green leaves are fan-shaped and often toothed at the top, and the buds are densely covered with long straight silver hairs. It is called "bearpoppy" because of this covering of hair. It is rarely seen, as it grows only occasionally in the higher washes and canyons. Another kind of bear-poppy with several yellow flowers on a single stem grows in southern Nevada. Though this one has the scientific name *Arctomecon californica,* it has not yet been collected within the state's boundary.

HABITAT Upper desert slopes.

Poppy Family — WHITE & CREAM FLOWERS

DESERT BEARPOPPY

DESERT BEARPOPPY

DESERT BEARPOPPY

Popaveraceae

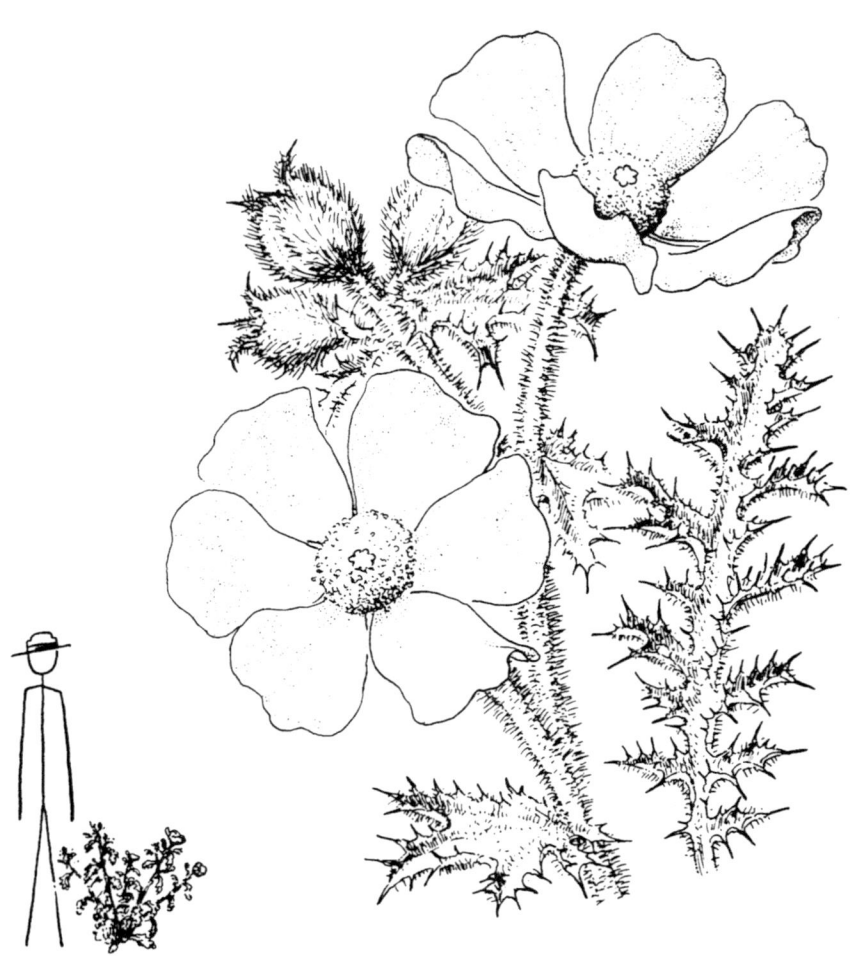

Desert pricklepoppy

Argemone munita subsp. *argentea*   POPPY FAMILY (Papaveraceae)

GROWTH FORM Annual to perennial herb

DESCRIPTION **Pricklepoppies** of some kind or other grow all over the arid southwest and Mexico. Superficially they look much alike in growth form and flowers but differ by such characters as the kinds of hairs and spines on the foliage, the arrangement of spines on the hard fruits, and so forth. The plant is beautiful to look at, but you will regret touching it because of the spines. The large flowers are about four inches broad and the white petals are textured like tissue paper. The flowers of other species and subspecies of the southwestern states look much like ours. The lobed large spiny leaves are bluish white. The plants are two or three feet tall and unbranched. It is mostly found on flats and washes around the 3,000 or 4,500 foot level.

HABITAT Upper desert slopes, washes.

Poppy Family — WHITE & CREAM FLOWERS | 129

DESERT PRICKLEPOPPY

DESERT PRICKLEPOPPY

for your hand lens,

single petal

long white bristles on leaves

2 in.

Spotted langloisia (Lilac sunbonnet)
Langloisia setosissima   **PHLOX FAMILY** (Polemoniaceae)

GROWTH FORM Annual herb

DESCRIPTION Get down on your knees for a good look at this plant, which is only one to three inches tall. It is quite noticeable, though, for it is a perfect bouquet of five-lobed white (or lilac-tinted) flowers spotted with dark purple, and each lobe has in addition a central line. The leaves, which are large for a plant so small, are three-toothed at the tip and furnished with a few long white bristles on the margin. It grows in the Mohave Desert east to Arizona and Nevada.

HABITAT Valley floor and fans, upper desert slopes.

Phlox Family WHITE & CREAM FLOWERS | 131

SPOTTED LANGLOISIA

SPOTTED LANGLOISIA

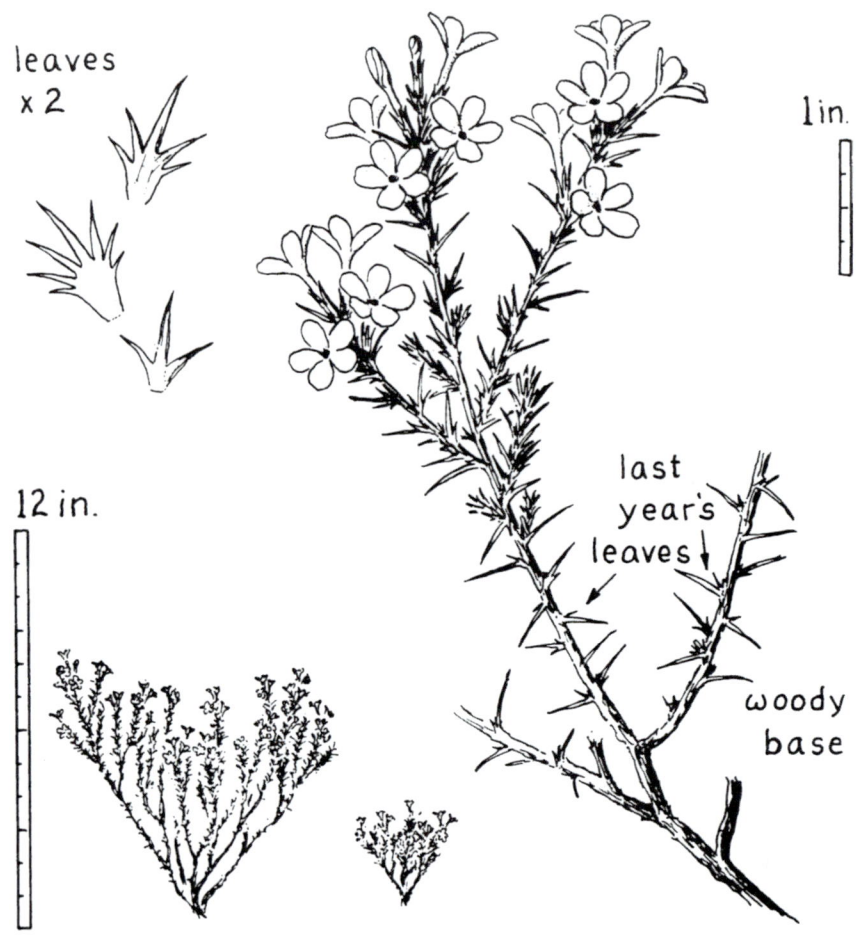

Granite gilia

Linanthus pungens   **PHLOX FAMILY** (Polemoniaceae)

SYNONYM *Leptodactylon pungens*

GROWTH FORM Perennial herb

DESCRIPTION Granite gilia reminds one of the prostrate phloxes of the alpine areas of the western mountains, but it has a more nearly bushy habit, and the lobes of the white corollas spread like a funnel instead of spreading at right angles as do those of the phloxes. The leaves are small and needle-sharp and are set densely along the stems. This variant of granite gilia is found among the pinyon pines and is perhaps more common even at higher elevations where the limber and bristlecone pines are at home.

NOTE At least two other genera and many other Phlox family species occur in Death Valley but are not included here.

HABITAT Limber pine-bristlecone pine and pinyon-juniper woodland.

GRANITE GILIA

FLAT-CROWN ERIOGONUM

ERIOGONUM

There are more kinds of eriogonums growing in Death Valley National Monument than of any other genus of plant, though in number of species, the evening-primrose and gilia are close rivals. Among the many kinds, there is much variety in shape or form of the plant itself; in flower color, which may be white, shades of pink, yellow, or even red; in places where the different species grow, which may be from below sea level to the top of Telescope Peak.

Flat-crown eriogonum

Eriogonum brachypodum   BUCKWHEAT FAMILY (Polygonaceae)

GROWTH FORM Annual herb

DESCRIPTION In summer in the disturbed soil along the roadsides and in the run-off stream beds in the alluvial fans, one sees many plants of the annual **flat-crown eriogonum** (and other related plants). Similar to the flat-topped trees so characteristic of the African veldt, you will find the same shape repeated in this desert plant which is only a few inches high and normally well over a foot broad, and with all the branches in one plane. The small white flowers are clustered in glandular involucres which are attached to the underside of the branches. The most striking of the related kinds is the **Rixford eriogonum** (*Eriogonum rixfordii*). In this species, the plants may be six inches to a foot or more in height, depending upon how much water it has had that season. The round basal leaves and the flowers are much the same as those of the flat-crown erigonum. The branches, however, are not in one plane but several and rise in stories like a pagoda. This species is limited to Death Valley and the area adjacent to it.

HABITAT Valley floor and fans.

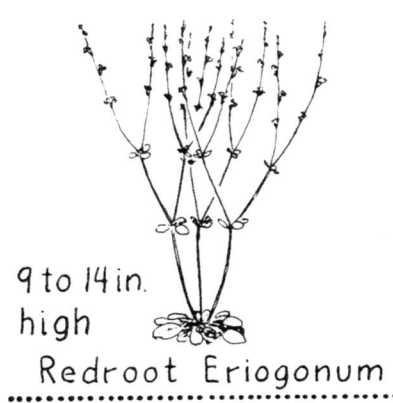

9 to 14 in. high
Redroot Eriogonum

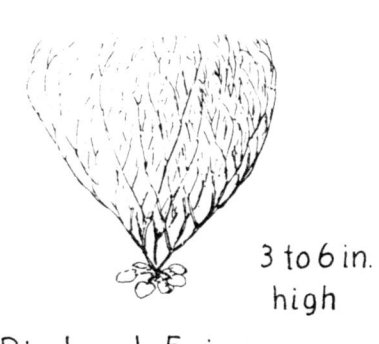

3 to 6 in. high
Birdnest Eriogonum

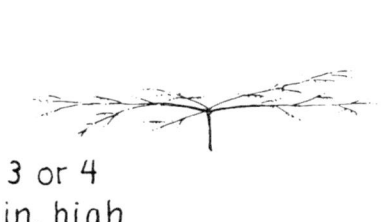

3 or 4 in. high
Flat-crown Eriogonum

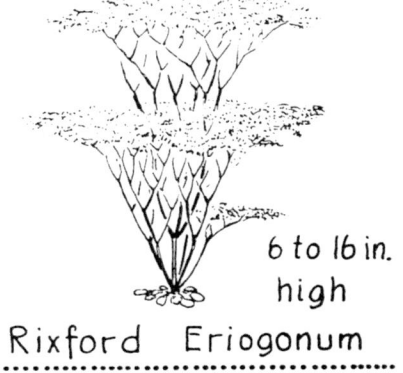

6 to 16 in. high
Rixford Eriogonum

shrub 2 to 4 feet high
(Rosemary Eriogonum)

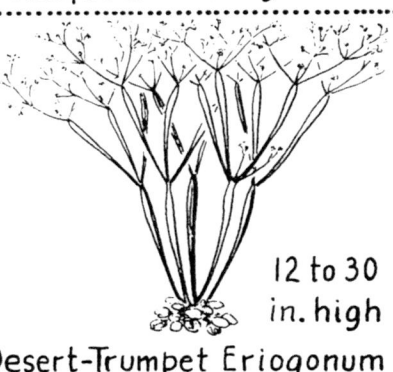

12 to 30 in. high
Desert-Trumpet Eriogonum

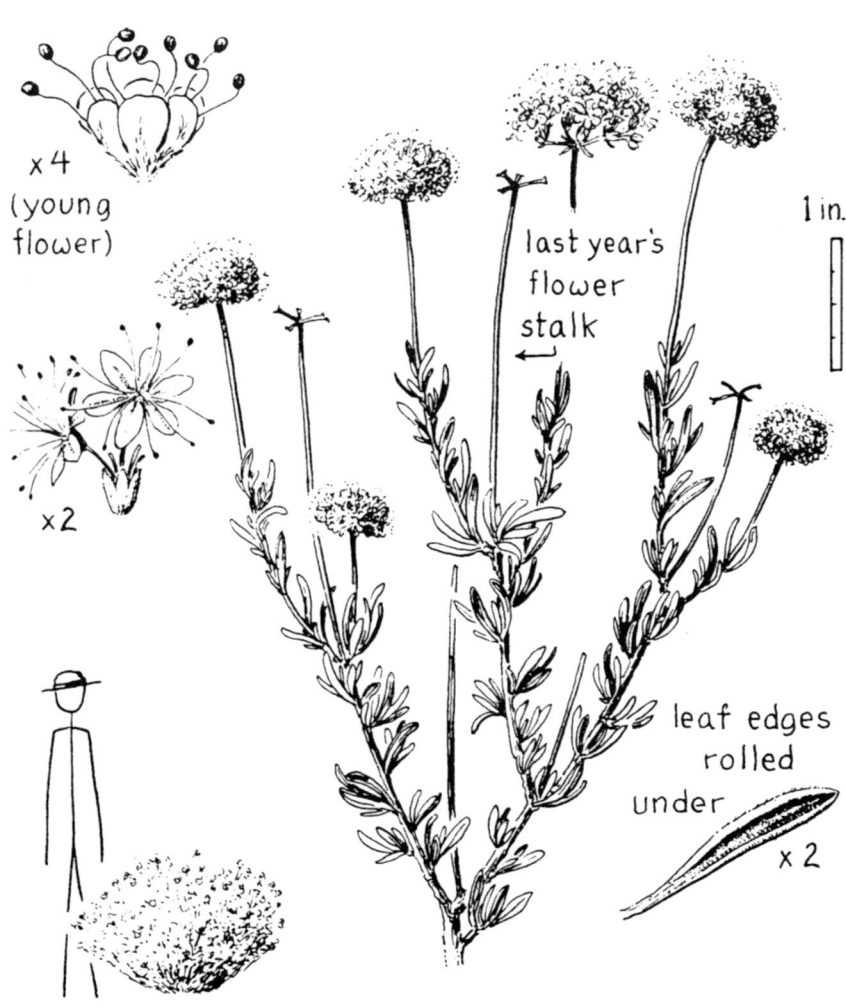

Rosemary eriogonum

Eriogonum fasciculatum var. *polifolium*   BUCKWHEAT FAMILY (Polygonaceae)

GROWTH FORM Shrub

DESCRIPTION There are many varieties of this species of *Eriogonum,* some of them occurring on the ocean side of the mountains. This evergreen shrub has small, narrow, grayish green leaves set closely in bunches along the stems with the leafless flower stalks surpassing the leafy stems. The whitish flowers are tiny but conspicuous by their abundance in the flower heads.

HABITAT Upper desert slopes.

Buckwheat Family   WHITE & CREAM FLOWERS | 137

ROSEMARY ERIOGONUM

ROSEMARY ERIOGONUM

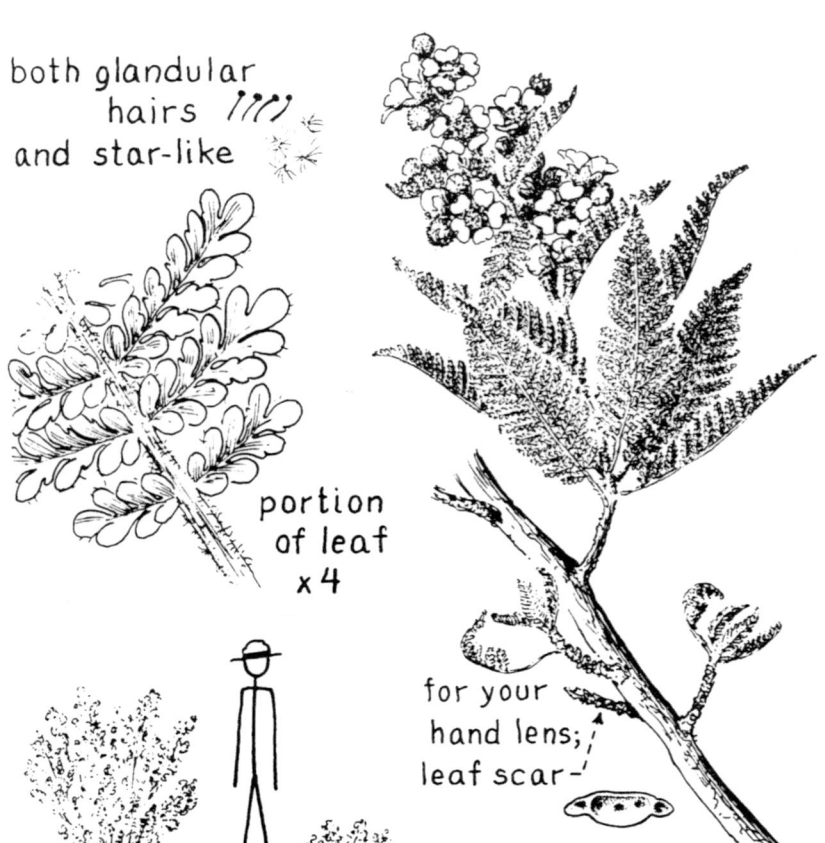

Tansybush (Desertsweet)
Chamaebatiaria millefolium   ROSE FAMILY (Rosaceae)

GROWTH FORM Shrub

DESCRIPTION Shrubs or trees of the rose family are well represented in the pinyon-juniper and limber-bristlecone pine areas. Within an altitudinal range of 5,000 feet, at least a dozen different shrubs belonging to the rose family have been collected in the Park. Some occur commonly; others are rarely seen—serviceberry, for example. About the line where the limber pines begin, and also in the pinyon belt, the erect several-stemmed bushes of the **tansybush** are to be found. The bushes are two and a half to five feet high, with several erect stems which are copiously clothed with thickened, somewhat sticky, fernlike leaves that exude a pleasant aromatic fragrance. The white flowers, though small (about one-half inch broad), grow in clusters on the tops of the branches and are conspicuous by their abundance. It is interesting to note that another good-sized shrub of the rose family, the **rock spiraea** (*Holodiscus discolor*) is often found growing with it.

HABITAT Limber pine-bristlecone pine woodland.

Rose Family | WHITE & CREAM FLOWERS | 139

TANSYBUSH

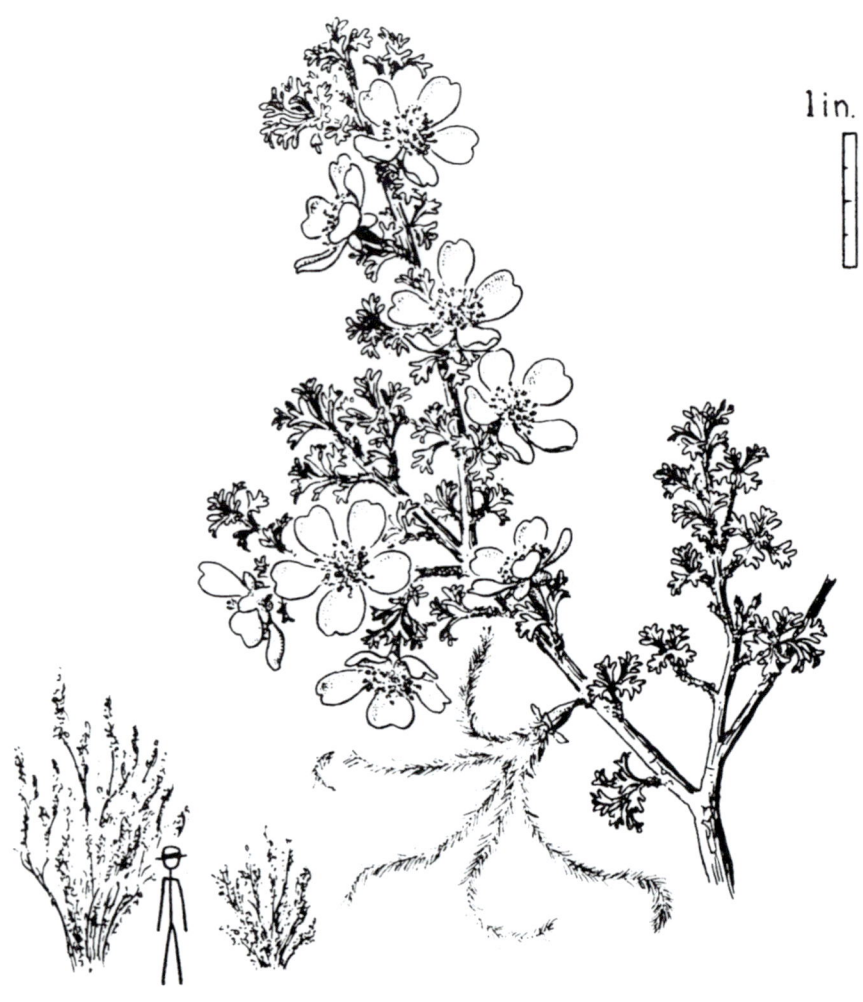

Stansbury cliffrose

Purshia mexicana var. *stansburyana*   ROSE FAMILY (Rosaceae)

SYNONYM *Cowania stansburiana*
GROWTH FORM Shrub
DESCRIPTION Gnarled and wide-branching and shaggy-barked though this eight to ten foot evergreen shrub is, it nevertheless is a wonderful sight to see when covered with cream-colored rose-like flowers. It is almost as attractive in fruit, when each seed in a single flower develops a plumy tail one or two inches long. These plumes resemble those of its relative, the **mountain-mahogany** (*Cercocarpus*), with which it grows, but that small tree has but one plumed tail per flower and no petals at all. The small hard leaves are three- to five-parted.
HABITAT Pinyon-juniper woodland.

Rose Family WHITE & CREAM FLOWERS | 141

STANSBURY CLIFFROSE

STANSBURY CLIFFROSE

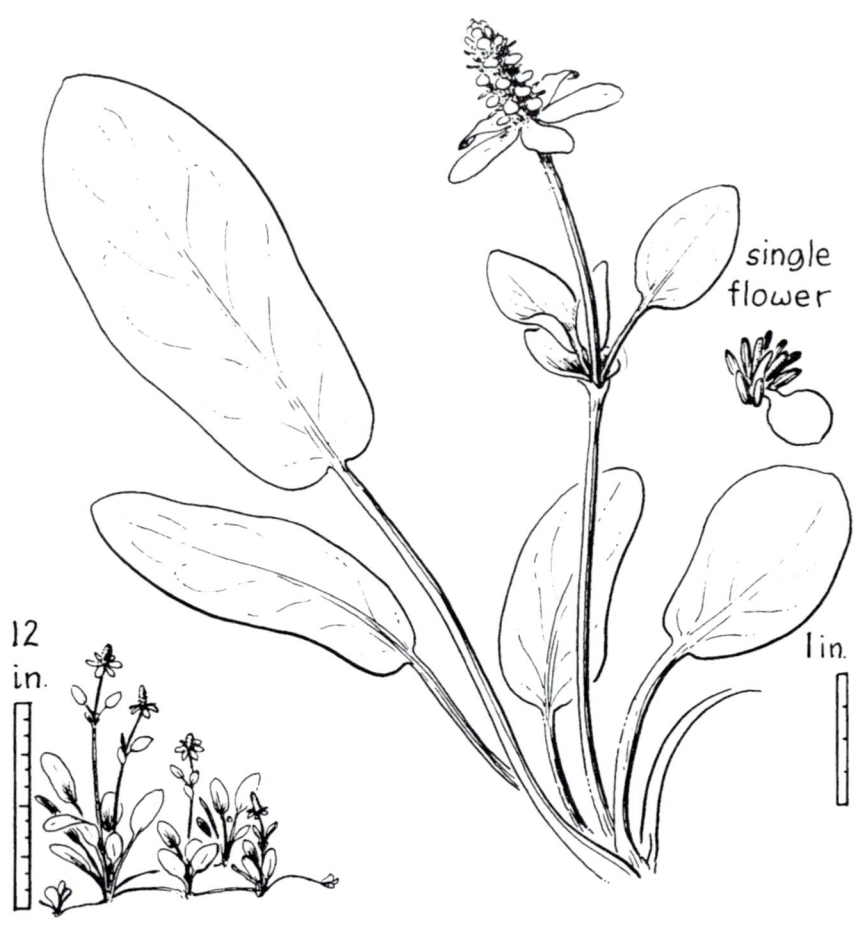

Yerba-mansa

Anemopsis californica   LIZARD'S-TAIL FAMILY (Saururaceae)

GROWTH FORM Perennial herb

DESCRIPTION **Yerba-mansa** is the only native representative of the lizards-tail family in the west, but it is widespread and grows as far east as Colorado and Texas and south into Mexico. It always grows near water, and in Death Valley it is commonly seen around seeps and springs. There, it forms mats that are made by its creeping stems or runners, which root and form new plants in the same manner as the common strawberry. The large oblong leaves are attractive, but its chief attractions are the flowers. What you think is one flower is really many. Each inconspicuous flower is set above a tiny white bract and arranged in spikes, and what appear to be petals are large white bracts set below the spike. It is much like an anemone in appearance, and its scientific name means anemone-like. The plants are aromatic, and the root is peppery in taste. Supposedly the whole plant has some medicinal virtue.

HABITAT Valley floor and fans, marshes.

Lizard's-Tail Family — WHITE & CREAM FLOWERS | 143

YERBA-MANSA

YERBA-MANSA

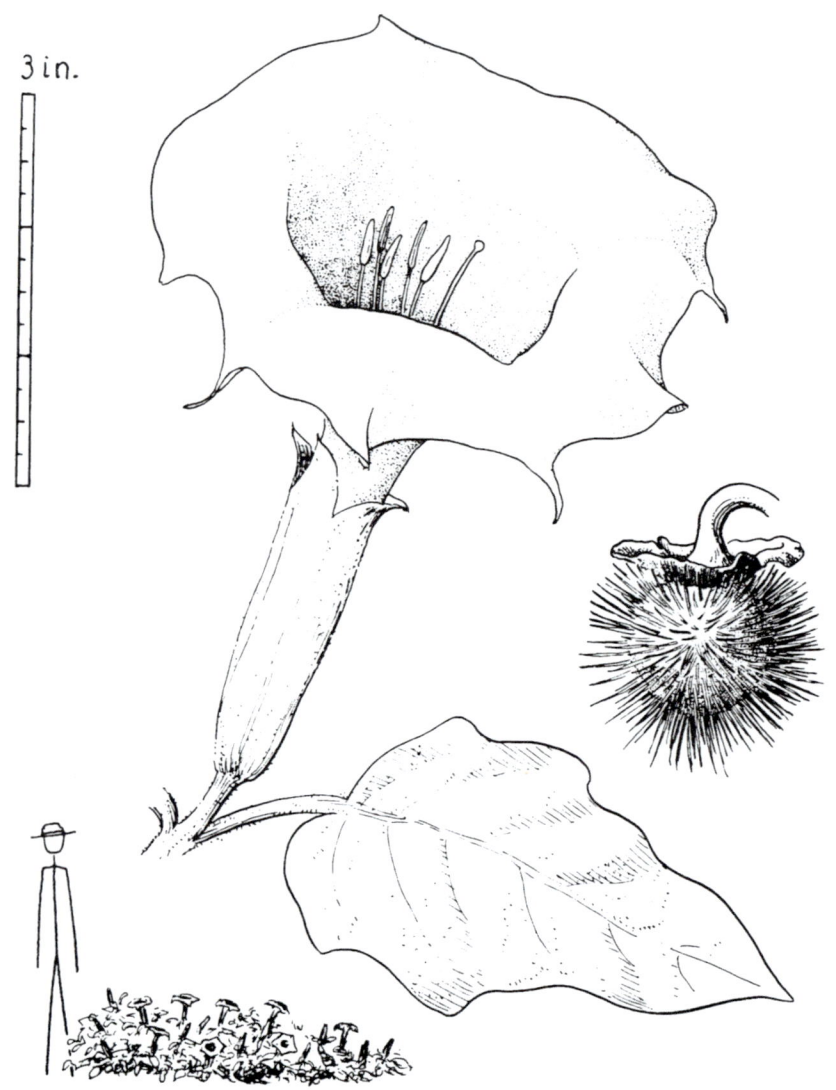

Sacred datura
Datura wrightii POTATO FAMILY (Solanaceae)

SYNONYM *Datura inoxia*
GROWTH FORM Annual to perennial herb
DESCRIPTION This large herb grows in canyon washes but is never common. The herbage is grayish green and ill-smelling. The abundant flowers are as large as Easter lilies and fragrant. It grows from Mexico northward and its occurrence here may have been encouraged by early Indian tribes who used the plant in religious rites to induce visions.
HABITAT Valley floor, fans and washes.

Potato Family — WHITE & CREAM FLOWERS | 145

SACRED DATURA

SACRED DATURA - FRUIT

WHITE & CREAM FLOWERS

Solanaceae

Desert tobacco
Nicotiana obtusifolia   POTATO FAMILY (Solanaceae)

GROWTH FORM Annual or perennial herb

DESCRIPTION The herbage of this ill-smelling sticky member of the potato family is more conspicuous than its tubular, greenish white flowers which grow among the shorter leaves on the tops of the stems of this sprawling many-stemmed plant. The natural habitat here as well as elsewhere in the southwestern deserts is at the bases of cliffs and banks of canyons and washes. If you see it in other places it will undoubtedly be in the shade of some big boulder on an alluvial fan. Even in the driest season the dull, dark green leaves catch the eye. Other kinds of wild tobacco in the west have been used by various Indian tribes for smoking and probably this one was smoked by the local tribes in the Death Valley region.

HABITAT Valley floor and fans, lower canyon walls.

Potato Family　　　WHITE & CREAM FLOWERS | 147

DESERT TOBACCO

DESERT TOBACCO

YELLOW FLOWERS — Amaranthaceae

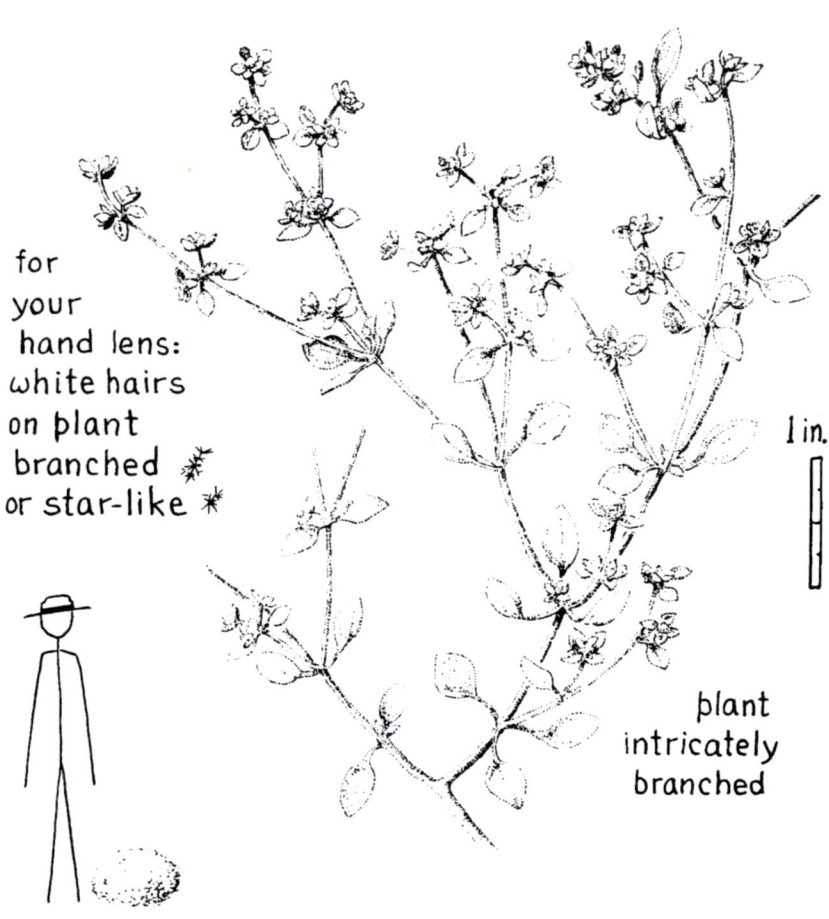

for your hand lens: white hairs on plant branched or star-like

plant intricately branched

1 in.

Honeysweet tidestromia
Tidestromia oblongifolia   **AMARANTH FAMILY** (Amaranthaceae)

GROWTH FORM Perennial herb, sub-shrub

DESCRIPTION This is a plant that thrives under really difficult conditions. These rounded gray-green perennial herbs are found with **desert-holly saltbush** at the lower edge of the creosotebush scrub where it meets the alkali sink of the salt pan area. In fact it will grow on the salt flats to some extent. The foot-high plants, broader even than high, are conspicuous more because of the complete lack of other plants in these hot bare places than from their own attractiveness. The flowers are tiny and clustered in the axils of the leaves. They deserve their common name because they are fragrant. That fragrance, though, is mostly wasted on the desert air as the flowers normally bloom in late summer when few visitors are in the area.

HABITAT Valley floor and fans.

Amaranth Family YELLOW FLOWERS | 149

HONEYSWEET TIDESTROMIA

HONEYSWEET TIDESTROMIA

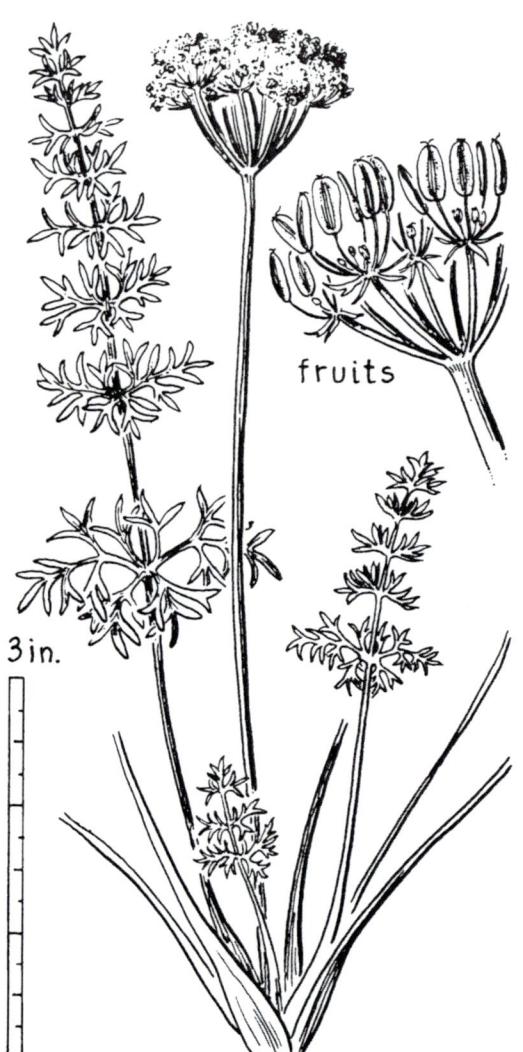

Parry lomatium

Lomatium parryi   CARROT FAMILY (Apiaceae)

GROWTH FORM Perennial herb

DESCRIPTION There are many species of *Lomatium* in the west, but **Parry lomatium** occurs only in the desert ranges from the Death Valley region to southeastern Utah. It grows in rocky draws and around boulders in the pinyons and junipers. The leaves, though much divided, are long and rather narrow in outline and are all basal. The flowering stems are about as tall as the basal leaves, and bear the small yellow flowers clustered at the ends of stalks, which radiate from the main stem like the ribs of an umbrella.

HABITAT Pinyon-juniper woodland, canyons.

Carrot Family — YELLOW FLOWERS | 151

PARRY LOMATIUM

PARRY LOMATIUM

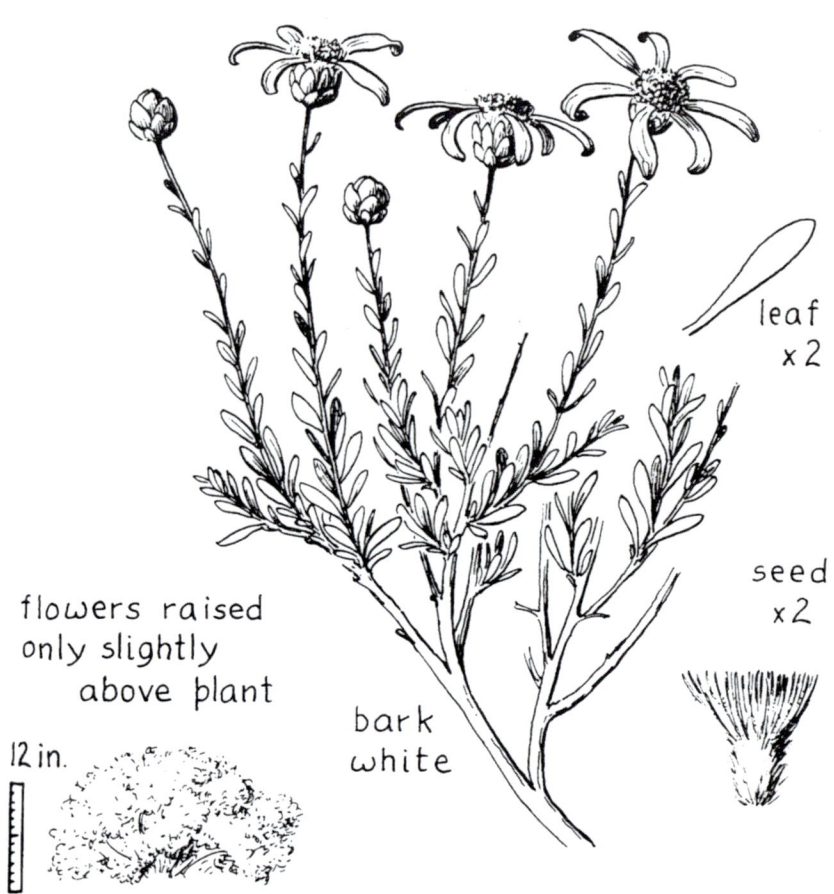

Shockley goldenhead

Acamptopappus shockleyi   SUNFLOWER FAMILY (Asteraceae)

GROWTH FORM Shrub

DESCRIPTION **Shockley goldenhead** would be an ideal plant in a cactus garden if it could be made to grow in cultivation. It is a spreading shrub with woody stems rising to a height of one-half foot to about two feet. The tongue-shaped leaves are small and grayish green. The yellow flower heads are often two inches broad, and are borne on slender stalks above the leaves, making quite a show in spring. Like so many desert shrubs it will respond to late summer rain, and one may have the pleasure of seeing it in flower again in early fall. It grows in southwestern Nevada and eastern California.

HABITAT Upper desert slopes.

Sunflower Family | **YELLOW FLOWERS** | 153

SHOCKLEY GOLDENHEAD

SHOCKLEY GOLDENHEAD

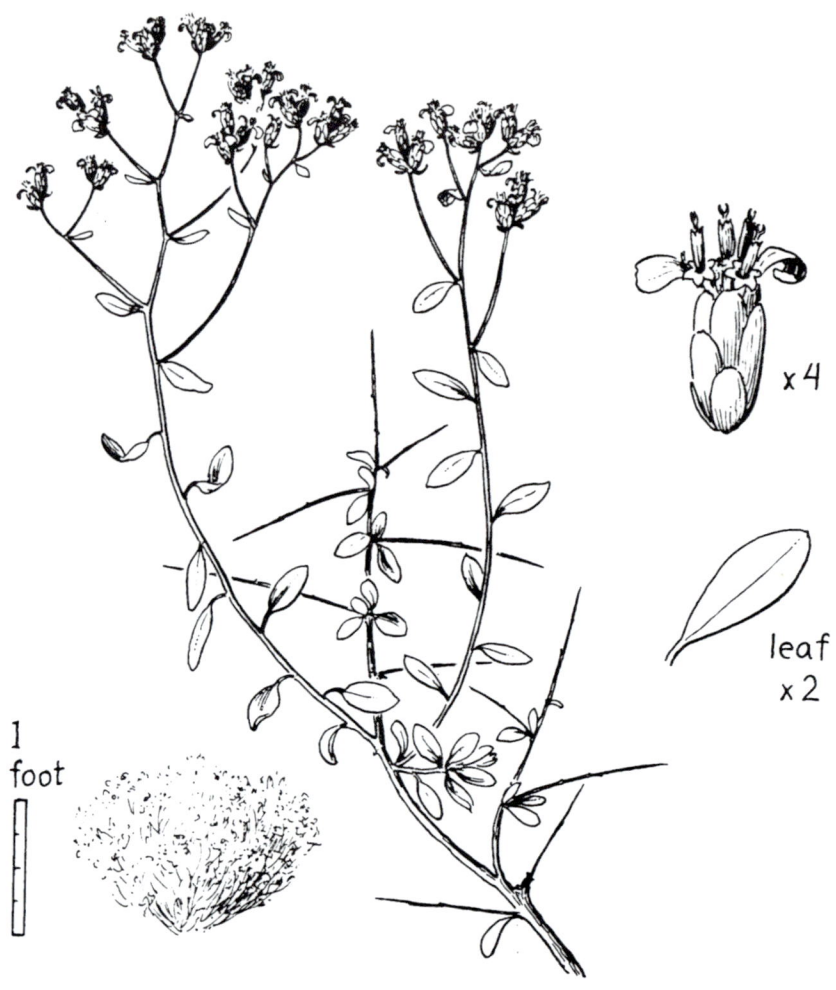

Amphipappus (Chaff-bush)

Amphipappus fremontii SUNFLOWER FAMILY (Asteraceae)
GROWTH FORM Shrub
DESCRIPTION This, as well as the many other plants of the sunflower family (Asteraceae) included in this book, has yellow flowers. The shrubs are not more than a foot in height but are often much wider, as the slender whitish branches and branchlets curve outward and then upward from the main axils. The oblong leaves, which are one-half an inch or less long, are scattered, and the small flowering heads are clustered at the tips of the many branchlets. The whole aspect of the plant is yellow-green. **Amphipappus** grows in rocky canyons or alluvial fans or rocky mesas, often to an elevation of 5,000 feet. It can be found in similar places in the desert areas of California, northern Arizona, and southern Nevada east to southwestern Utah.
HABITAT Valley floor and fans, upper desert slopes.

Sunflower Family | YELLOW FLOWERS | 155

AMPHIPAPPUS

AMPHIPAPPUS

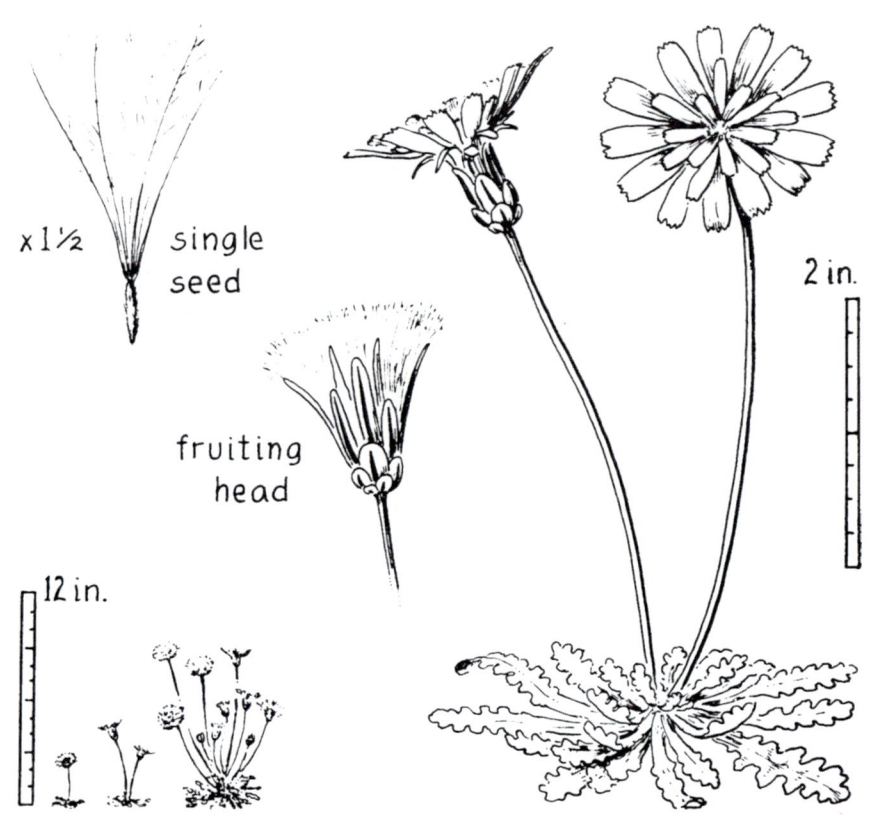

Anisocoma

Anisocoma acaulis   SUNFLOWER FAMILY (Asteraceae)

GROWTH FORM Annual herb

DESCRIPTION This small desert annual (three to eight inches high) grows in both California deserts and in the desert areas of Nevada and Arizona. It grows in sand or gravelly soil mostly at lower elevations, but it also can be found at elevations up to 6,000 feet if conditions are right for its growth. Few to several naked stalks rise from the close rosette of divided leaves with a single, pale yellow flower head on each stalk. **Anisocoma** is at its best in fruit. The bracts under the heads are papery and strawcolored. Each one (both the short rounded lower ones and the narrow upper ones) is marked with a conspicuous maroon line and sometimes, in addition, maroon dots. The feathered fluff on the seeds is longer than the bracts, so that the whole flower head may be an inch or an inch and a half long.

HABITAT Upper desert slopes.

Sunflower Family | **YELLOW FLOWERS** | **157**

ANISOCOMA

ANISOCOMA

YELLOW FLOWERS — Asteraceae

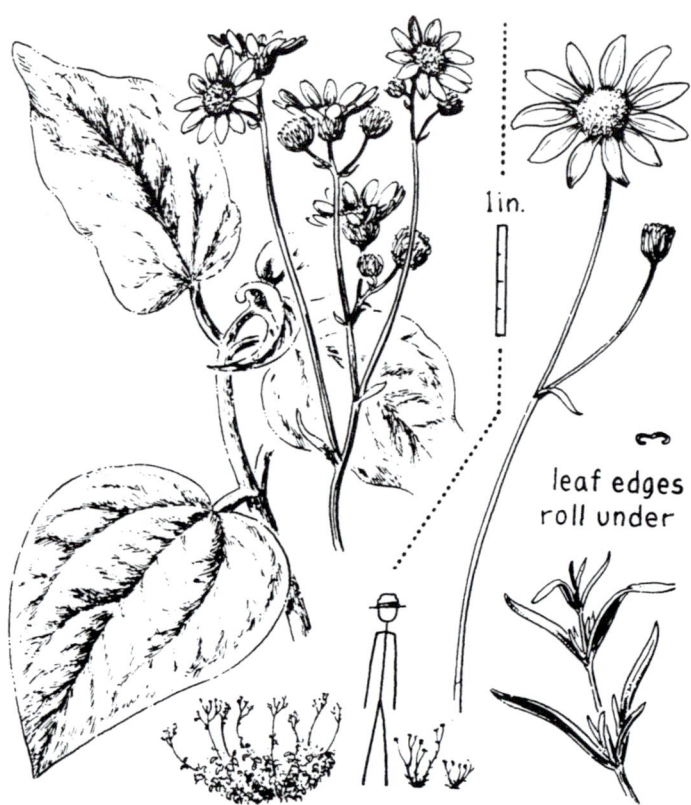

Death Valley goldeneye

Bahiopsis reticulata SUNFLOWER FAMILY (Asteraceae)

SYNONYM *Viguiera reticulata*

GROWTH FORM Shrub

DESCRIPTION **Death Valley goldeneye**, as its name implies, is restricted to the Death Valley region though it is found in adjacent ranges outside of the Park borders. The flowers of this shrub are yellow, are several to many, and are borne in long-stemmed clusters well above the mound of leafy stems. It is not to be confused with **brittlebush** (*Encelia farinosa*) which it much resembles in habit. One look at the leaves will end the confusion, for though the leaves are white they are quite broad and the leaf blades do not taper into the stems as do those of brittlebush. In addition, the veinlets as well as the veins of the leaves are prominent and give a net-like appearance especially on the underside of the leaf, which is harsh to the touch in age. Though the shrub is evergreen, the skeleton leaves of earlier growth stay on the plant dead white among the greenish white of the living leaves. **Nevada showy goldeneye** (*Heliomeris multiflora* var. *nevadensis*) is more common in the southern Great Basin than here. This narrow-leaved herb (shown above at right) grows on the pinyon-juniper slopes.

HABITAT Upper desert slopes and pinyon-juniper woodland.

Sunflower Family   YELLOW FLOWERS | 159

DEATH VALLEY GOLDENEYE

DEATH VALLEY GOLDENEYE

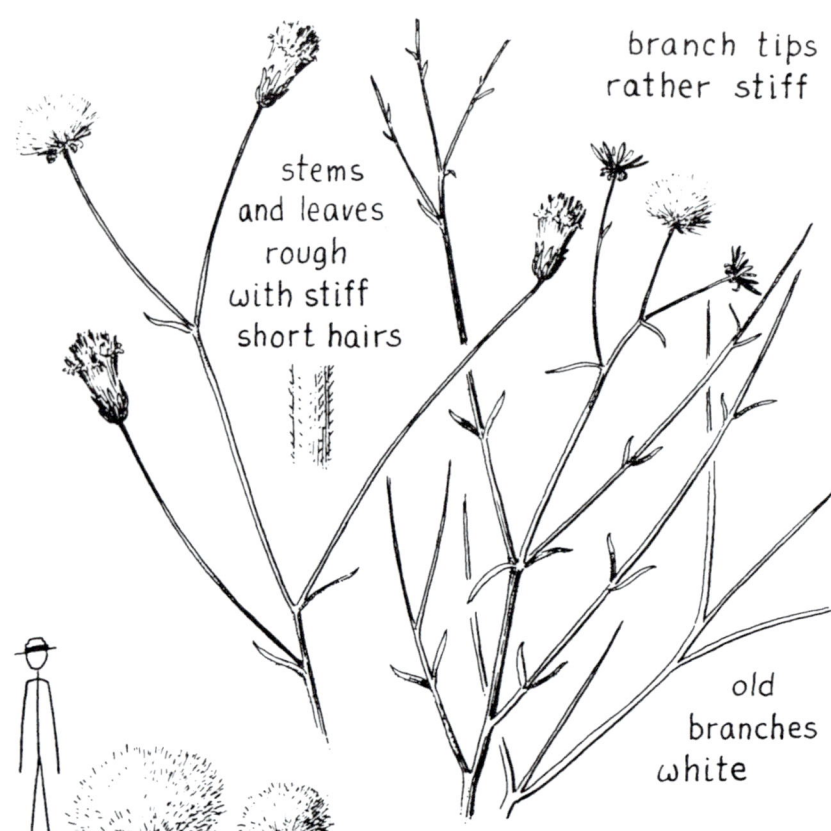

Sweetbush bebbia (Sweetbush)

Bebbia juncea SUNFLOWER FAMILY (Asteraceae)

GROWTH FORM Shrub

DESCRIPTION This is far from being one of the more beautiful shrubs of the area, but it is often seen in trips around the valley. The rounded dense masses of small green, usually leafless twigs, which are rough to the touch, grow sometimes to a height and breadth of three feet or more. The fragrant flower heads, which have no petal-like rays, are orange-yellow and scattered all over the outer twigs. They appear almost anytime that moisture and temperature are favorable for them. At least the chuckwallas like this shrub, as one of the common names that has been given to it implies, and the desert bighorn find it an excellent browse plant. It is not restricted to this part of the country and is found as far south as Baja California, Mexico.

HABITAT Valley floor and fans.

Sunflower Family | YELLOW FLOWERS | 161

SWEETBUSH BEBBIA

SWEETBUSH BEBBIA

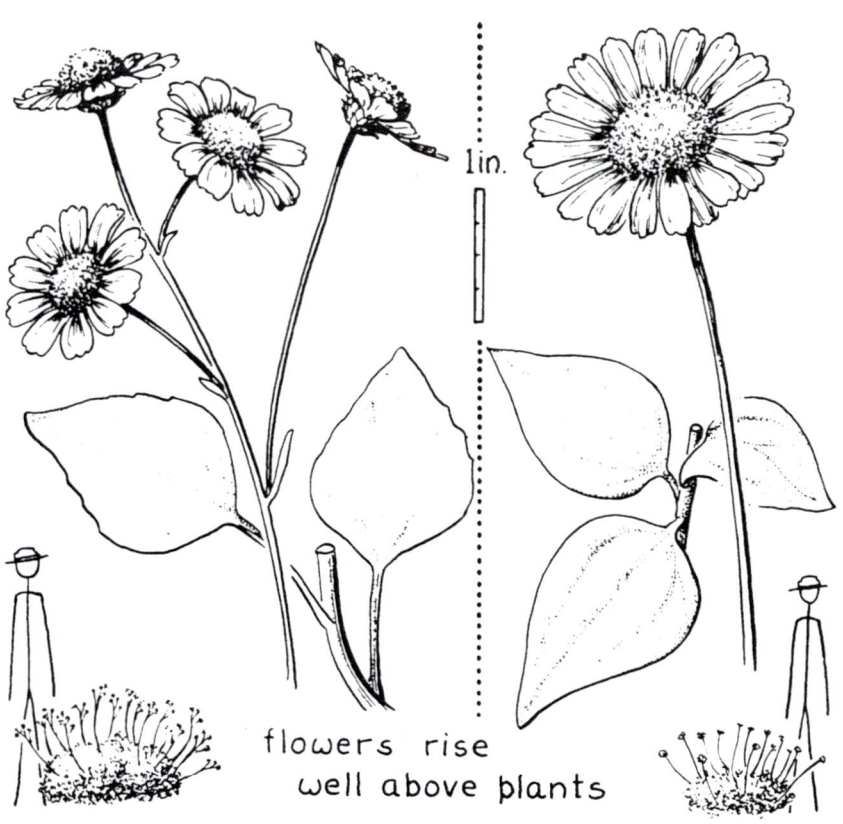

flowers rise well above plants

White brittlebush (Incienso)

Encelia farinosa   **SUNFLOWER FAMILY** (Asteraceae)

GROWTH FORM Shrub

DESCRIPTION White brittlebush is one of the more striking shrubs of the Park. The symmetrical plants, densely clothed with leaves, grow on the basal slopes of the ranges, in the small draws and canyons, and less commonly in the washes. Even in leaf it is conspicuous among the dark rocks; doubly so when covered with a mass of small sunflowers about an inch broad, borne on flower stalks that much surpass the leaves. Both the common names that have been applied to this desert shrub are appropriate. The leaves are silvery white and the stems extremely brittle. Although **Acton encelia** (*Encelia actonii*), on the right, much resembles white brittlebrush, each flower stalk in this species bears only a single flower head instead of bearing several to a stalk, which is characteristic of the brittlebush. It grows more commonly in washes and is not distributed as widely as the white brittlebush.

HABITAT Upper desert slopes and valley floor and fans.

Sunflower Family | YELLOW FLOWERS | 163

WHITE BRITTLEBUSH

WHITE BRITTLEBUSH

Panamint daisy

Enceliopsis covillei **SUNFLOWER FAMILY** (Asteraceae)

GROWTH FORM Perennial herb

DESCRIPTION *Enceliopsis* is known locally as the **Panamint daisy**. "Daisy" is far too modest a name for this magnificent flower, which can be four to five inches across. The flowers rise a foot or more above the basal tufts of large silvery leaves. The plants grow on dry rocky ledges, probably in soil in which there is gypsum, because its closest relative (*Enceliopsis argophylla*) is known to grow only in gypsum deposits in southern Nevada and Utah.

HABITAT Upper desert slopes.

Sunflower Family • YELLOW FLOWERS | 165

PANAMINT DAISY

PANAMINT DAISY

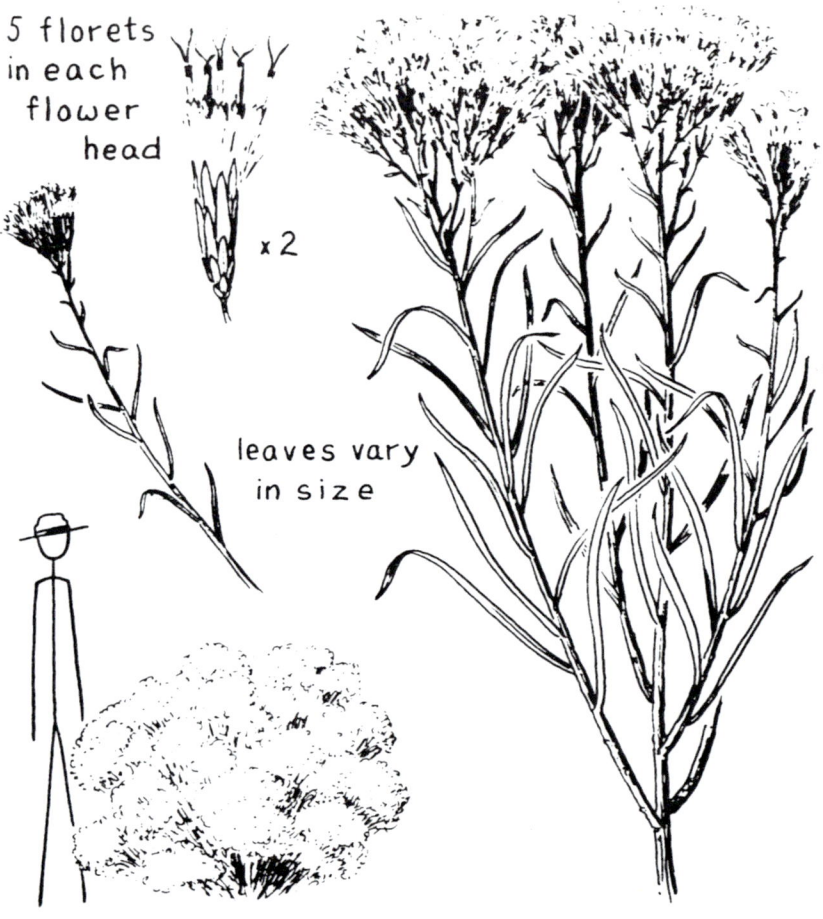

Rubber rabbitbrush

Ericameria nauseosa   **SUNFLOWER FAMILY** (Asteraceae)

SYNONYM *Chrysothamnus nauseosus*
GROWTH FORM Shrub
DESCRIPTION More than one variety or subspecies of **rubber rabbitbrush** is to be found in the Park, as well as five or six other species which look very different in size, leaves and growth habit from the gray-leaved, fall-flowering one you see pictured. The shrubs of the rubber rabbitbrush are three or four feet high, are bushy, and the branches are quite flexible and leafy, though the plants have a tendency to drop their leaves early. The scientific name "nauseosa" is a misnomer, for the plant has a not unpleasant aromatic odor. It grows on flats and along broad watercourses in loose soil, often with sagebrush, and it, or its several subspecies, occurs commonly in the west.
NOTE Some forms of it have been found to produce some rubber, but for various practical reasons it has not been worthwhile to obtain rubber from it commercially.
HABITAT Upper desert slopes and pinyon-juniper woodland.

Sunflower Family | YELLOW FLOWERS | 167

RUBBER RABBITBRUSH

RUBBER RABBITBRUSH

168 | YELLOW FLOWERS — Asteraceae

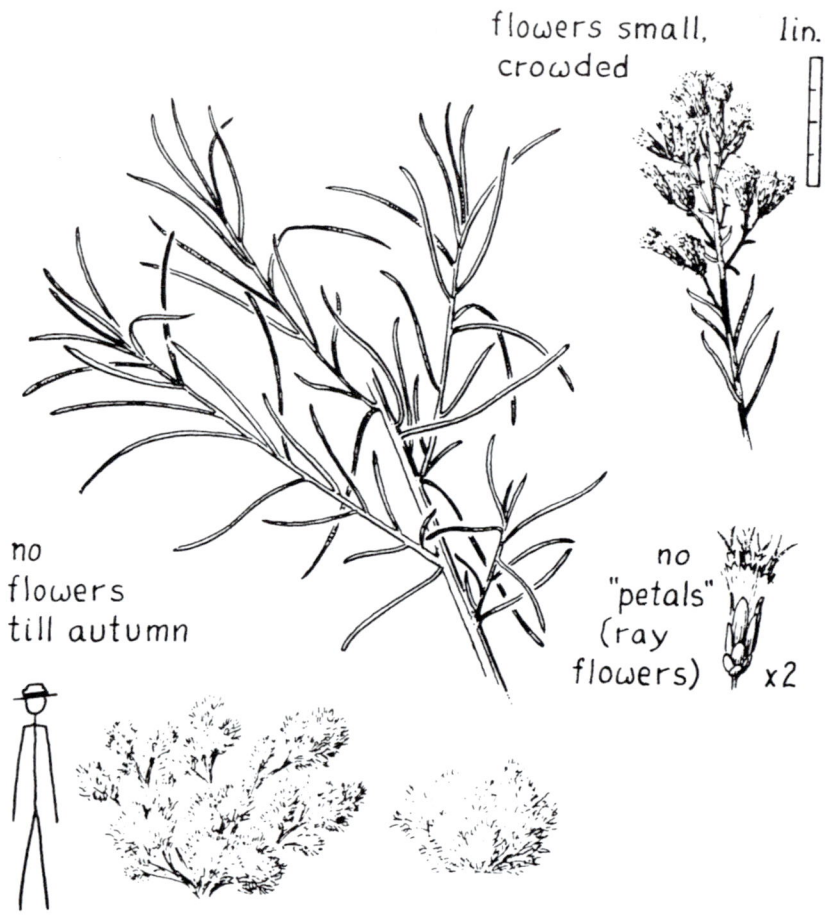

Desert rabbitbrush

Ericameria paniculata   SUNFLOWER FAMILY (Asteraceae)

SYNONYM *Chrysothamnus paniculatus*
GROWTH FORM Shrub
DESCRIPTION **Desert rabbitbrush** is a branching shrub usually five to six feet high with aromatic needlelike green leaves and rather stout, straight, tan-colored, trunklike stems. It grows in the sand and gravel of the canyon washes or even on the fans in the stream courses. It is nearly always infected with a fungus disease that makes black bands around the young growth. It is not to be confused with the **sprucebush** (*Peucephyllum schottii*), a darker-stemmed, open shrub with a treelike growth, which flowers early and grows in the same places. The desert rabbitbrush and all the many other kinds of rabbitbrush, both tall and short, that grow around the Death Valley area bloom in the early fall and their masses of yellow flowers furnish color at that time of the year.
HABITAT Upper desert slopes, washes.

Sunflower Family | YELLOW FLOWERS | 169

DESERT RABBITBRUSH

DESERT RABBITBRUSH

YELLOW FLOWERS — Asteraceae

"bracts" around flower head white-hairy

1 in.

white hairs on leaves

12 in.

Desert sunflower (Desert gold)

Geraea canescens — SUNFLOWER FAMILY (Asteraceae)

GROWTH FORM Annual herb

DESCRIPTION Even in years when there is not much rainfall, this showy sunflower can be found in the first spring blooming period, on rock-covered flats or in sandy places above the low white alkaline stretches of the valley. It grows rather commonly throughout the deserts of the southwest. The **desert sunflower** is an annual six inches to two feet tall with a rather harsh feel to the stems and leaves and fuzzy white bracts at the base of the attractive fragrant yellow-flowered heads, which are much visited by insects. Because the plants occur so commonly, the seeds serve as a dependable crop for small rodents to harvest for food. Many other common names have been used for this widespread desert species.

HABITAT Valley floor and fans.

Sunflower Family | YELLOW FLOWERS | 171

DESERTGOLD

DESERTGOLD

Broom snakeweed, Threadleaf snakeweed

Gutierrezia sarothrae, Gutierrezia microcephala **SUNFLOWER FAMILY** (Asteraceae)

GROWTH FORM Shrubs

DESCRIPTION When you are traveling in the southwest in the late summer months, some species of snakeweed will make their presence known to you by the large areas covered with golden yellow. Though the flower heads are tiny, literally hundreds may cover the bushy perennial herbs or small shrubs. Two kinds grow in Death Valley. The **threadleaf snakeweed** (*Gutierrezia microcephala,* above left) forms a small, slender-stemmed, rounded bush on which the flower heads are clustered in tight little bunches at the ends of the branchlets. Sometimes only one ray floret occurs on each head. The flower heads of **broom snakeweed** (*Gutierrezia sarothrae, above* right) usually have four or five rays each, and are not so tightly clustered. One form of broom snakeweed is only five or six inches high and may have only a single flower head at the ends of the branches.

HABITAT Upper desert slopes to limber pine-bristlecone pine woodland.

Sunflower Family | YELLOW FLOWERS | 173

BROOM SNAKEWEED

THREADLEAF SNAKEWEED

each ray is a perfect flower

Desert dandelion

Malacothrix glabrata **SUNFLOWER FAMILY** (Asteraceae)

GROWTH FORM Annual herb

DESCRIPTION Of the plant families that grow in Death Valley, the sunflower family (Asteraceae) is represented by the greatest number of different kinds of plants. This is hardly surprising, however, when it is remembered that the Sunflower Family (Asteraceae) is the largest one among the flowering plants, and that representatives of it grow all over the world from the tropics to arctic regions. **Desert dandelion** grows in sandy places in the Great Basin region southward through the deserts to northern Mexico. This annual is quite conspicuous in good years. The pale yellow flower heads contrast with the lush, dark green, finely divided leaves. As usual, it is quite a different story in the all-too-frequent dry years. Then, the small plants can support only two or three flower heads.

HABITAT Valley floor and fans, washes.

Sunflower Family — YELLOW FLOWERS | 175

DESERT DANDELION

Sprucebush (Pygmy cedar)
Peucephyllum schottii   SUNFLOWER FAMILY (Asteraceae)

GROWTH FORM Shrub

DESCRIPTION Whether it is called **sprucebush** or **pygmy cedar** this shrub has a good descriptive name, as the dark but vivid green needle-like leaves are reminiscent of conifers. Even in a half-dead state after a long stretch of drought, the branches that are still alive are conspicuously leafy. The shrubs (three to six feet high) are shaped like small juniper trees. The yellow flower heads are apt to appear after the winter rains. **Sprucebush** is common in the broad washes in the ranges and occasionally even grows on the canyon walls.

NOTE Sprucebush was first collected by Arthur Schott along the Colorado River during the Mexican Boundary Survey in the early 1850's; the species name of this widespread plant was given in his honor.

HABITAT Valley floor and fans, washes.

Sunflower Family | YELLOW FLOWERS | 177

SPRUCEBUSH

SPRUCEBUSH

Asteraceae

Turtleback
Psathyrotes ramosissima   SUNFLOWER FAMILY (Asteraceae)

GROWTH FORM Perennial herb, sub-shrub

DESCRIPTION There are few common names among the wildflowers that are as descriptive as "**turtleback**" is for this gray-leaved member of the sunflower family. Along the roadsides, and in other places if you care to walk, you will see rounded mounds of leaves growing from a woody root, just about the size and shape of a desert tortoise shell. As the size of a desert herb is always dependent on the water it receives, in some years your "turtles" may be small indeed. The flower heads are yellow; the leaves are thickish and wrinkled and give off an odor much like turpentine; the plants will grow in loose sand or gravel or the more compacted soils of the desert pavement. Turtleback is a native of the western desert regions.

HABITAT Valley floor and fans.

Sunflower Family | YELLOW FLOWERS | 179

TURTLEBACK

TURTLEBACK

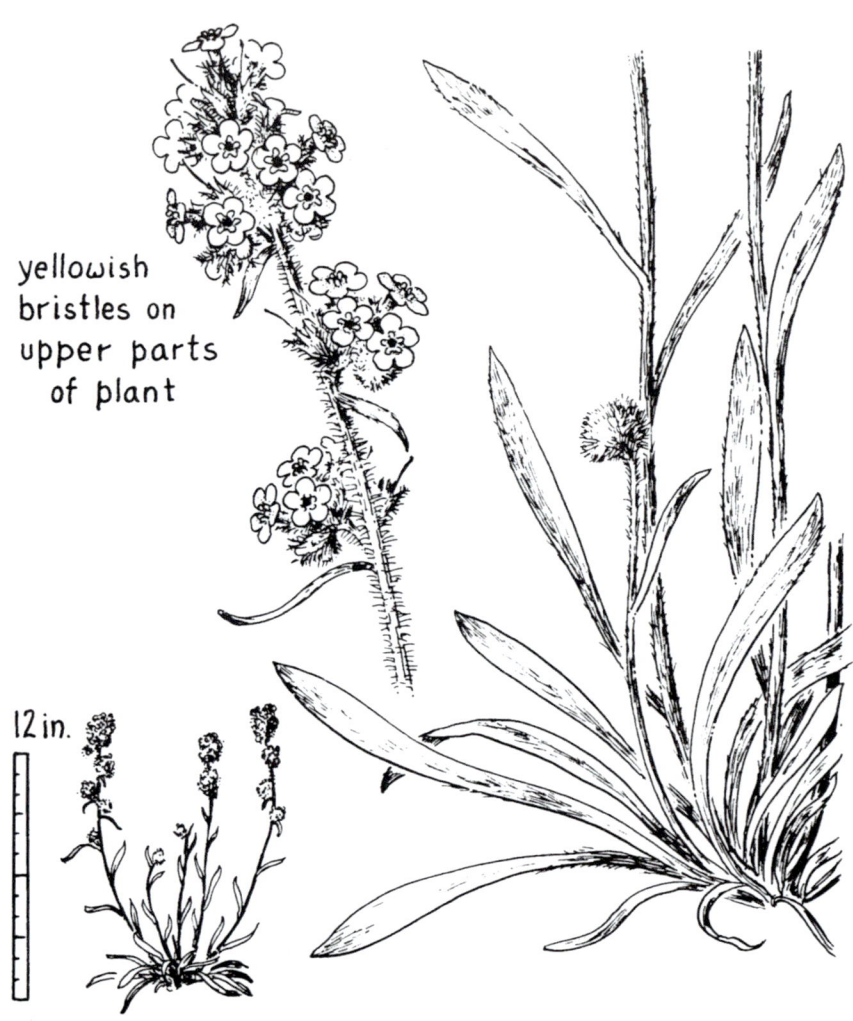

Golden cryptantha (Golden forget-me-not)
Cryptantha confertiflora   BORAGE FAMILY (Boraginaceae)
SYNONYM *Oreocarya confertiflora*
GROWTH FORM Perennial herb
DESCRIPTION **Golden cryptantha** has several stems a foot or more high rising from a woody base. Most of the leaves, which are silvery, are crowded at the bases of the plants, and the golden yellow flowers, which are nearly an inch across, are clustered toward the tops of the stems. These attractive plants may occasionally be seen as one drives through the pinyons. Like so many other plants of the Death Valley region, golden cryptantha can be found in southern Nevada and Utah as well as eastern California.
HABITAT Pinyon-juniper woodland.

Borage Family · YELLOW FLOWERS | 181

GOLDEN CRYPTANTHA

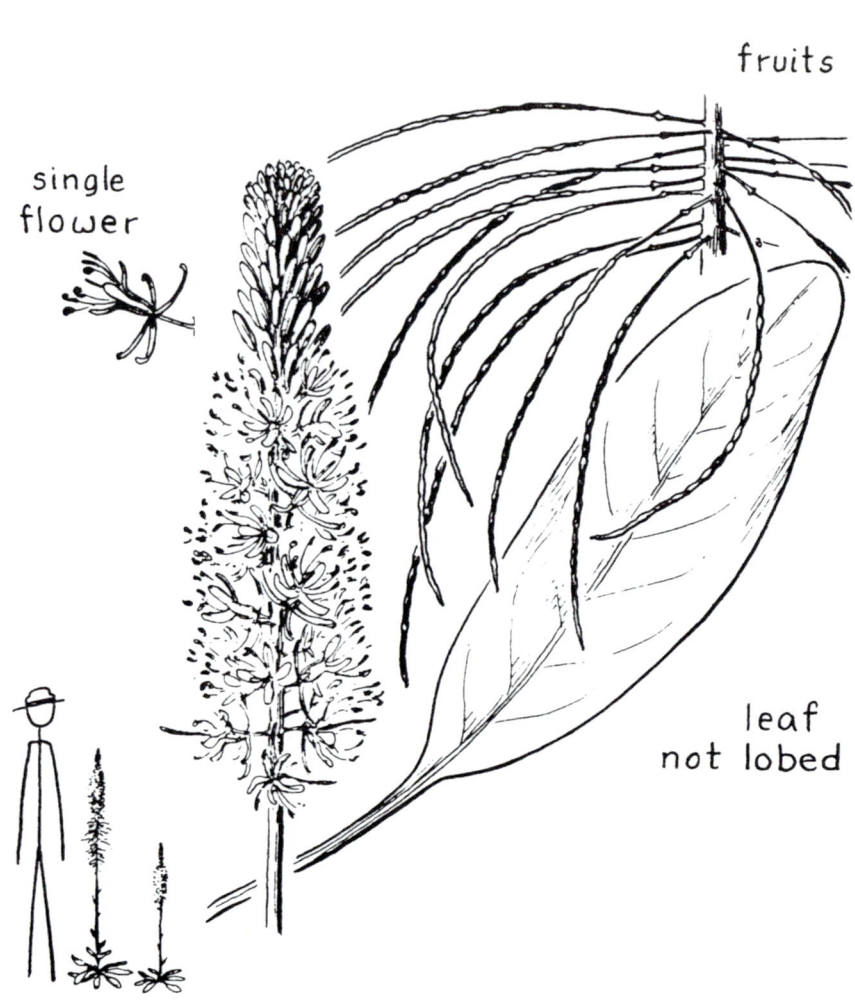

Panamint prince's-plume

Stanleya elata   MUSTARD FAMILY (Brassicaceae)

GROWTH FORM Perennial herb

DESCRIPTION This member of the mustard family grows on the slopes and mesas from about 3,000 to 3,500 feet. The tall unbranched plants (two to five feet high) are easily spotted by the long plume of yellow flowers which rise well above the rather large, entire leaves. This grows only in southern Nevada, northern Arizona, and the Death Valley region.

HABITAT Upper desert slopes.

Mustard Family | YELLOW FLOWERS | 183

PANAMINT PRINCE'S-PLUME

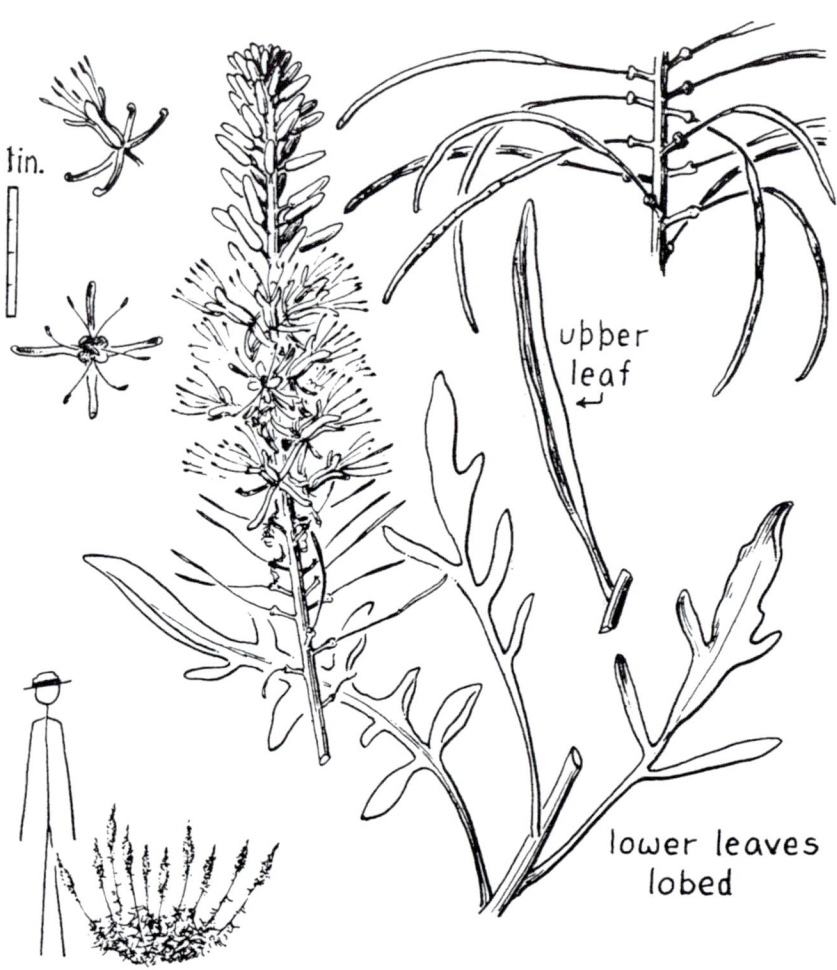

Desert prince's-plume

Stanleya pinnata MUSTARD FAMILY (Brassicaceae)

GROWTH FORM Perennial herb

DESCRIPTION The **desert prince's-plume** grows in this area and is often found at low elevations. The plants are about as high as the **Panamint prince's-plume** but are more often branched; the leaves are lobed and not entire, but the flowers are much the same as those of the other species. In years when all the flowers set seed the long slender curving pods on the tall flowering stalks (in both species) are as striking as the flowers. The desert prince's-plume is much more widespread than the Panamint prince's-plume and is found as far east as the plains of the Dakotas.

HABITAT Upper desert slopes and valley floor.

Mustard Family | YELLOW FLOWERS | 185

DESERT PRINCE'S-PLUME

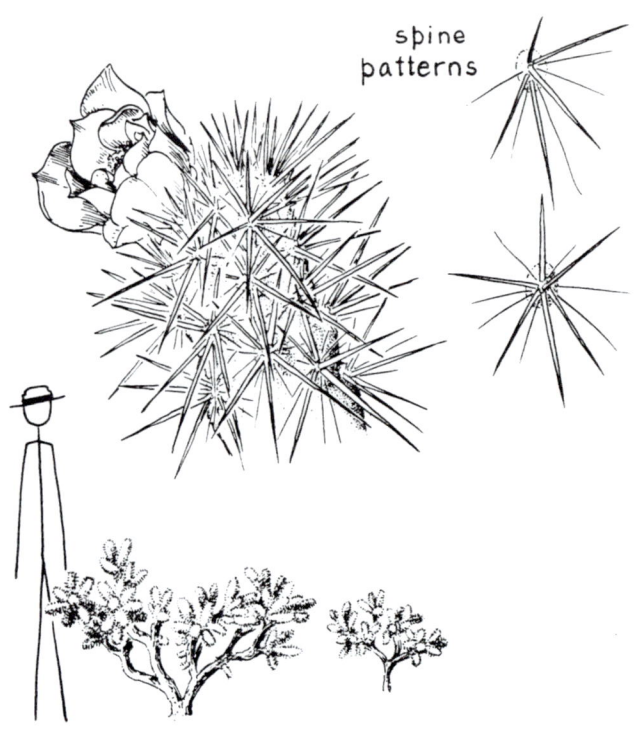

Strawtop cholla

Cylindropuntia echinocarpa CACTUS FAMILY (Cactaceae)

SYNONYM *Opuntia echinocarpa*
GROWTH FORM Cactus
DESCRIPTION This cholla usually has a distinct trunk and many short (four to six inches) branching joints. The whole plant is copiously covered with pale rigid spines. The flowers are greenish yellow, with sometimes a tinge of red on the outer petals, and blend rather than contrast with the appearance of the plant. The fruits are dry and spiny and harvesting them would be a real problem to the small hungry creatures of the desert.
NOTE There are two types of growth in the widespread genus *Opuntia:* those in which the joints are flattened and those in which the joints are rounded and the plants angularly branched (now separated as genus *Cylindropuntia*). The former are usually called pricklypears, the latter cholla. All the members of the cactus family that grow in the west have one thing in common—they have no leaves. The stems assume a fantastic variety of shapes. They may be flattened oval pads, branched canes, thick poles, huge "war clubs," large or small cylinders, heads or "barrels." They are always green and fleshy though the surface may be well-concealed by different kinds of spines. Several different kinds are found in Death Valley National Park.
HABITAT Upper desert slopes.

Cactus Family | **YELLOW FLOWERS** | **187**

STRAWTOP CHOLLA

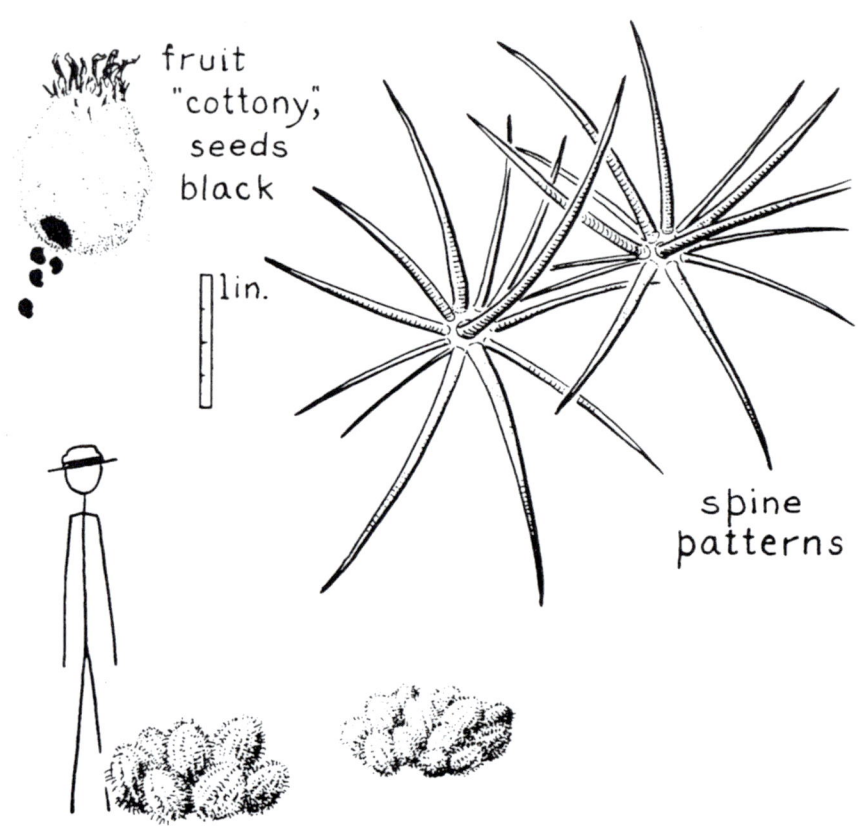

Cottontop echinocactus

Echinocactus polycephalus CACTUS FAMILY (Cactaceae)

GROWTH FORM Cactus

DESCRIPTION As you drive down the alluvial fans, through the desert shrubs you see clusters a foot or so high of ribbed spiny heads—sometimes as many as forty in a clump. They are beset with groups of strong flattish spines of unequal length. The yellow flowers, which grow only at the tops of the heads, are half-buried in white wool, and the dry fruit appears to be a woolly ball.

HABITAT Upper desert slopes.

Cactus Family | YELLOW FLOWERS | 189

COTTONTOP ECHINOCACTUS

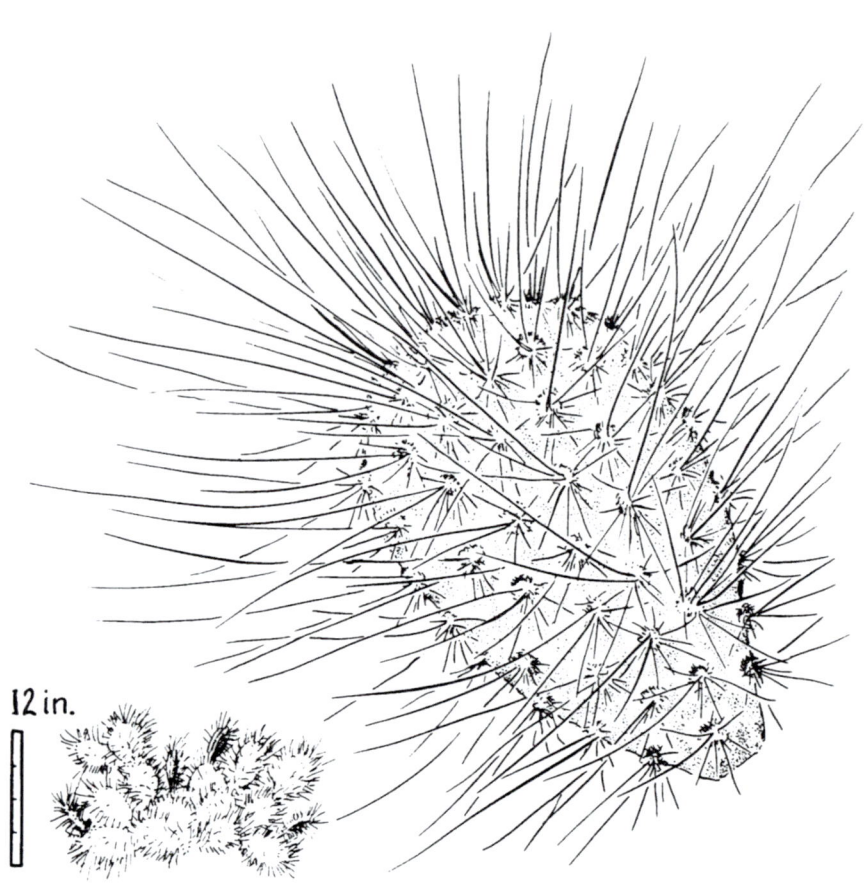

Grizzly bear pricklypear (Old man pricklypear)

Opuntia polyacantha var. *erinacea*   CACTUS FAMILY (Cactaceae)

GROWTH FORM Cactus

DESCRIPTION These are low-growing plants with flattened pad-like joints which form mats that may rise to a height of a foot or so. They almost conceal themselves in their slender spines, particularly the variety ursina. On this the spines are three to six inches long, or even eight inches, and very flexible. The common name implies a resemblance to the coarse fur of a bear. The flowers are yellow, though sometimes flushed with pink or red.

HABITAT Pinyon-juniper woodland.

Cactus Family — YELLOW FLOWERS | 191

GRIZZLY BEAR PRICKLYBEAR

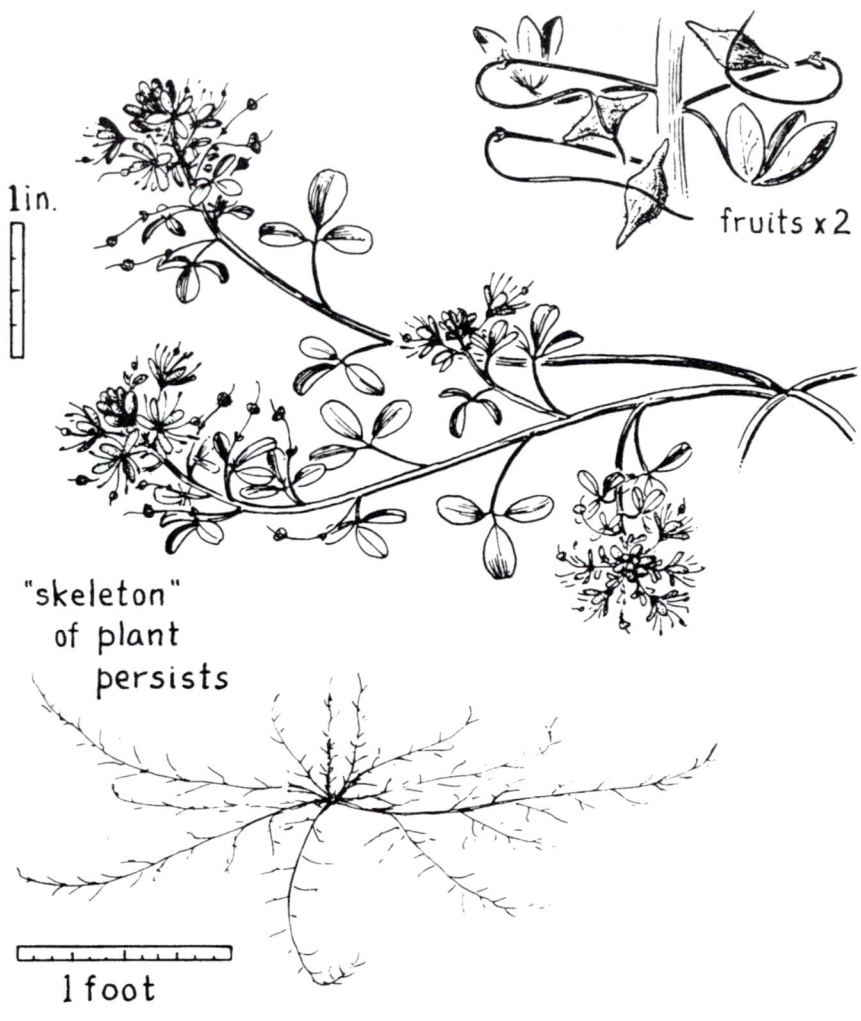

Bushy cleomella (Stinkweed)

Cleomella obtusifolia **SPIDER-FLOWER FAMILY** (Cleomaceae)

GROWTH FORM Annual herb

DESCRIPTION **Stinkweed** is not unattractive in spite of the unpleasant odor of the yellow-green foliage. The plants may be small (five to ten inches high) or the sprawling stems may spread about two feet. The flowers are yellow and the small leaves resemble clover leaves. The stalked capsule (dry fruit) has an angular shape, the angles often drawn out laterally into a pair of horns. The fruits are about the size of the pickled capers one finds on the grocery shelf, and the ripe seeds are reported to be relished by doves. It is common all over the Mohave Desert area and adjacent Nevada and Arizona, mostly growing in loose, alkaline loam.

HABITAT Valley floor and fans.

Spider-Flower Family | YELLOW FLOWERS | 193

BUSHY CLEOMELLA

BUSHY CLEOMELLA

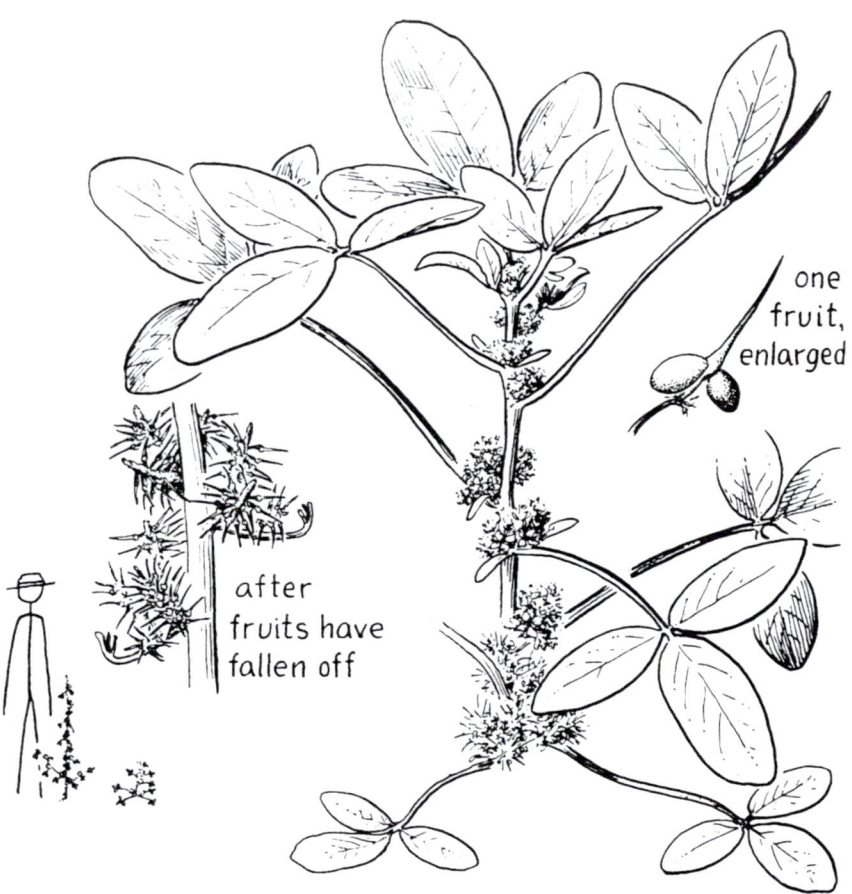

False-clover (Spiny caper)

Oxystylis lutea   SPIDER-FLOWER FAMILY (Cleomaceae)

GROWTH FORM Annual herb

DESCRIPTION The erect plants grow from a few inches to three feet in height; the leaves are in threes; the flowers are small and yellow and grow in clusters close to the stem; the fruits have a single sharp spine and the fruit clusters look like burrs along the stem and remain until the stout dead stalks blow away in the desert wind.

NOTE On April 28, 1844, John C. Fremont was returning along the Old Spanish Trail to the east from one of his expeditions. The party stopped at a stream called the Amargosa, "bitter water of the desert," where he saw a patch of yellow-green herbs which he thought belonged to the mustard family. The plants that he pressed and took home with him were described as a new genus and species, *Oxystylis lutea*. You will find the same kind of herb growing on the floor of the valley and in like areas to the eastward in saline places where the underground water is at a high enough level to supply its needs.

HABITAT Valley floor and fans, marshes.

Spider-Flower Family — YELLOW FLOWERS | 195

FALSE-CLOVER

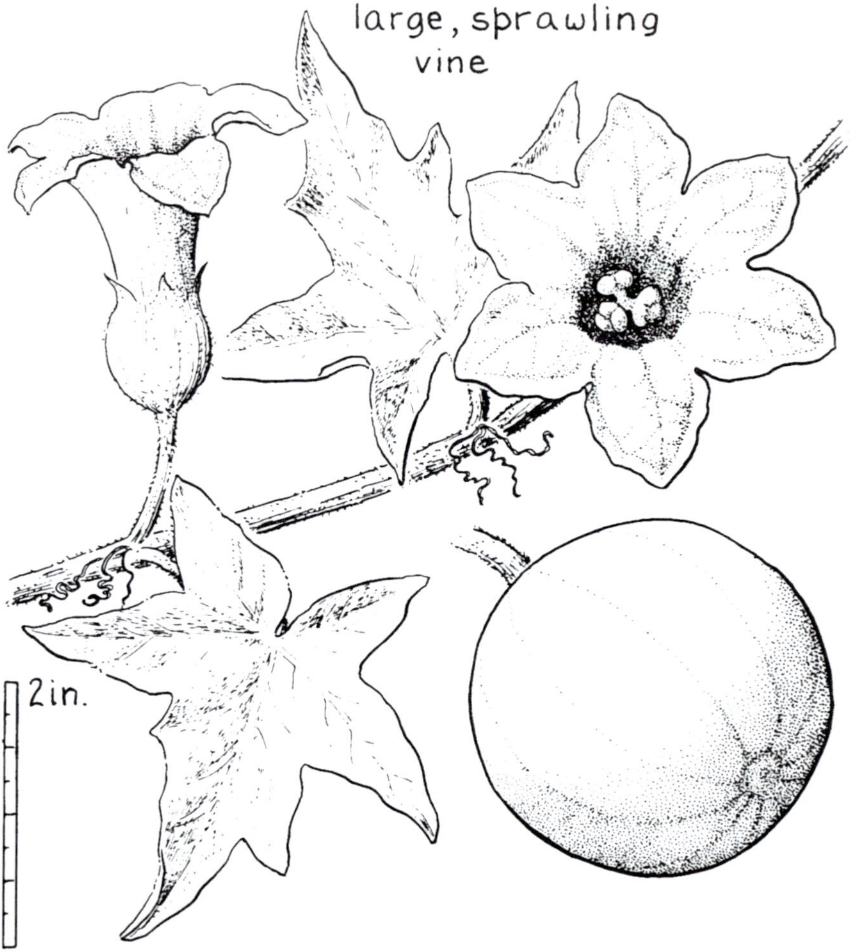

Palmleaf gourd (Coyote melon)
Cucurbita palmata   GOURD FAMILY (Cucurbitaceae)

GROWTH FORM Perennial herb

DESCRIPTION Occasionally in the washes you will see a familiar-looking vine with large yellow flowers and palmately lobed leaves trailing over the sand and gravel. Too many members of the gourd family—cucumbers, watermelons, squashes, for instance—are well known in the home vegetable garden for you not to recognize the familiar shape of the blossoms. Supposedly the gourds are edible; and possibly the Panamint Indians used the seeds at least, but better leave both for the desert rodents. The broken gourds give evidence that it has, for them, food value. This species grows in the California deserts and adjacent Arizona.

HABITAT Valley floor and fans, washes.

Gourd Family | YELLOW FLOWERS | 197

PALMLEAF GOURD

PALMLEAF GOURD

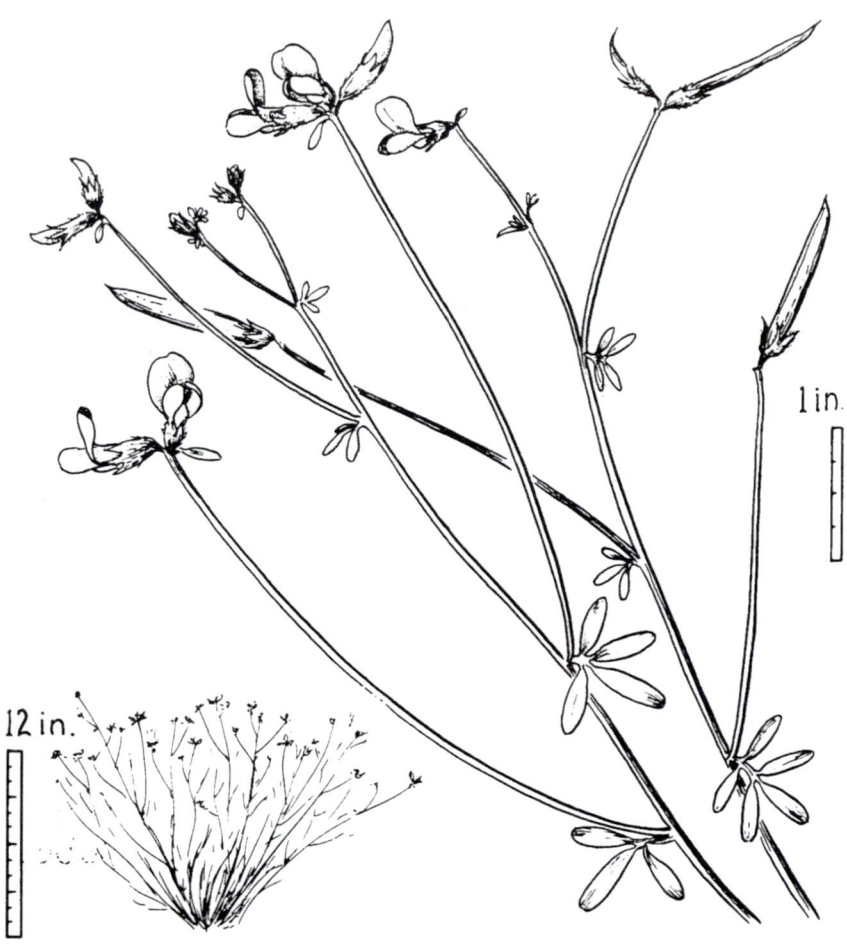

Shrubby deervetch

Acmispon rigidus   PEA FAMILY (Fabaceae)

SYNONYM *Lotus rigidus*

GROWTH FORM Perennial herb, sub-shrub

DESCRIPTION The **deervetch** is a half-shrubby perennial with several green stems rising from the woody base. The leaves, divided into three to five leaflets, are very apt to fall, leaving the stems and branches completely bare. The slender stalks that bear the clusters of two or three pea-shaped flowers are about an inch and one-half long, often longer. The yellow flowers are showy in spite of their small size (about one-half an inch) and the back of the upper petal (banner) is often tinged with red. The species is widespread throughout the western deserts but seldom abundant in one place.

HABITAT Upper desert slopes.

Pea Family   YELLOW FLOWERS | 199

SHRUBBY DEERVETCH

SHRUBBY DEERVETCH

YELLOW FLOWERS — Fabaceae

Honey mesquite
Prosopis glandulosa var. *torreyana* — PEA FAMILY (Fabaceae)

GROWTH FORM Tree

DESCRIPTION **Honey mesquite** is a friend of humans and wildlife. Perhaps it is not the friend to people that it was in the days when the Panamint Indians, and Indians elsewhere, harvested the nutritious pods and ground them into food. Now, at least the wood can be used for campfires, and its leafy canopy as protection from the sun, excepting those mesquites that have ceased to be trees because their trunks and branches are buried in the sand dunes. Throughout its wide range the pods and foliage are eaten by cattle; bees and other insects use the greenish yellow flower spikes. Mesquite is a deciduous tree about fifteen or twenty feet tall and much branched, and on the smaller branchlets there are cruelly strong spines. The **screwbean mesquite** (*Prosopis pubescens*), which has the woody pods tightly coiled, also grows in Death Valley.

HABITAT Valley floor and fans, salt flats and marshes.

Pea Family   YELLOW FLOWERS | 201

HONEY MESQUITE

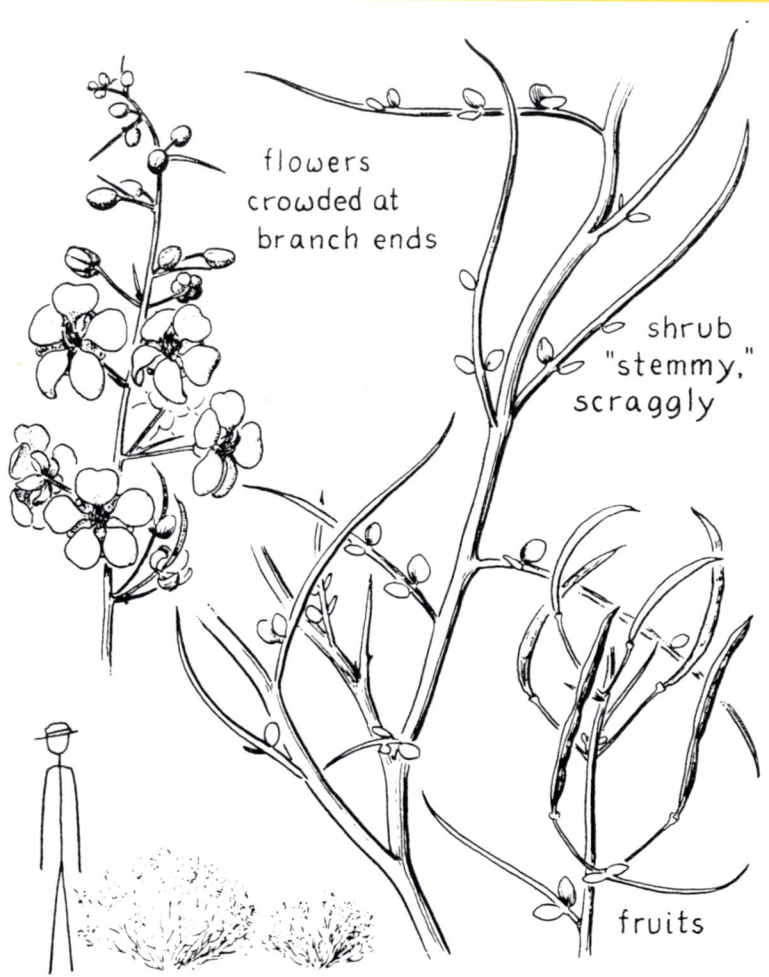

Desert senna

Senna armata

PEA FAMILY (Fabaceae)

SYNONYM *Cassia armata*
GROWTH FORM Shrub
DESCRIPTION Most of the year, **desert senna** is just another desert shrub that is hard to identify because it has no leaves, flowers or fruits; only smooth, grayish green stems almost a quarter of an inch in diameter that taper to a point. In the flowering season the shrub presents quite a different picture, as the tops of the now green stems are covered with yellow blossoms about an inch broad, and the leaves, though rather sparse, are interesting to examine. As in most members of the pea family a leaf is made up of small leaflets fastened to a central stemlike vein (midrib). In desert senna the midrib is flat and nearly as broad as each of the leaflets are wide. It is a native of both California and Arizona deserts and extends into northwestern Mexico.
HABITAT Upper desert slopes.

Pea Family | YELLOW FLOWERS | 203

DESERT SENNA

Desert mariposa

Calochortus kennedyi   LILY FAMILY (Liliaceae)

GROWTH FORM Perennial herb

DESCRIPTION The west is blessed with many species of this beautiful genus of the lily family. Various kinds of *Calochortus,* because of the shape of the petals or the hairs that sometimes cover them, have been called delightfully descriptive names: star tulip, pussy ears, fairy lantern, globe tulip. By far the most striking of them all is the group with large open flowers which are known as mariposas (butterflies in Spanish). The **desert mariposa**, which occurs in Death Valley as well as other parts of California, Arizona, and Nevada, grows in heavy soil. The stems, topped with one to six flowers, are three to ten or more inches high arid rise from deep-seated bulbs. The satiny petals (one to two inches long) are marked with purplish black at the base and may be vermillion, orange, or yellow—more often yellow in the Death Valley area. The lower leaves are often long and contorted.

HABITAT Upper desert slopes.

Lily Family | YELLOW FLOWERS | 205

DESERT MARIPOSA

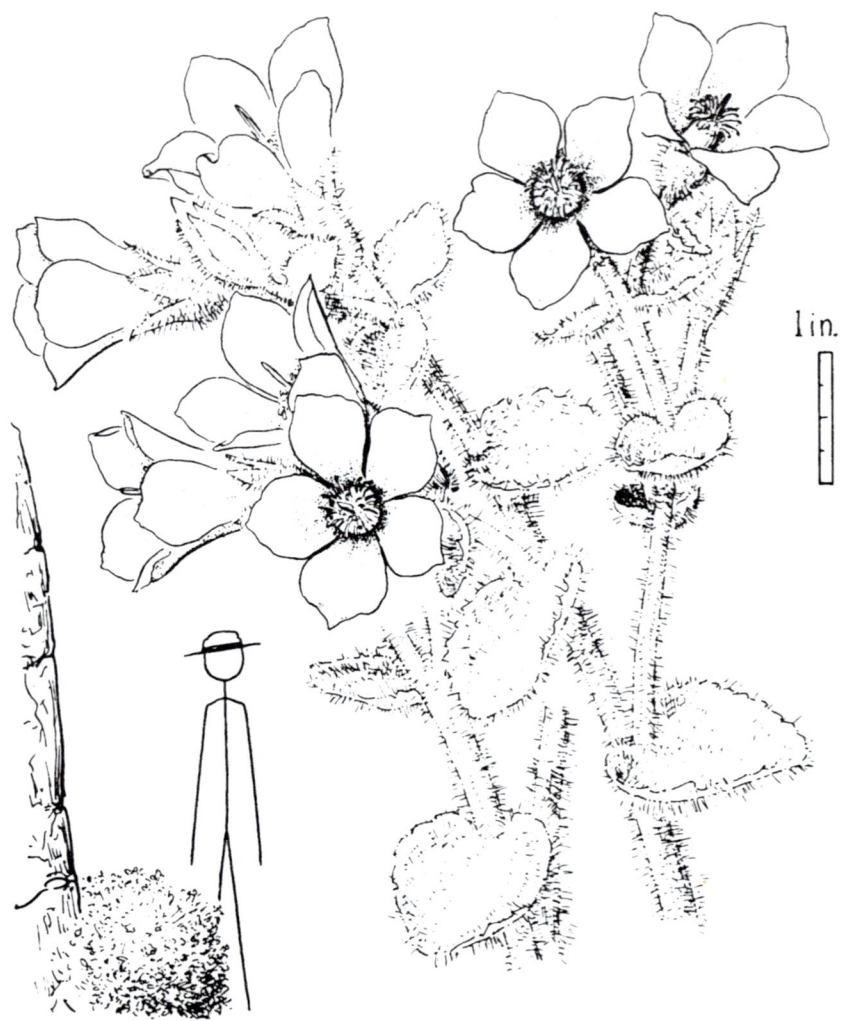

Stingbush (Desert rocknettle)
Eucnide urens BLAZINGSTAR FAMILY (Loasaceae)

GROWTH FORM Perennial herb

DESCRIPTION The **stingbush** is a handsome perennial to look at but definitely not a plant to touch because of the long sharp barbed bristles and the hairs which can be very irritating. In spite of this, the hardy desert bighorn enjoy browsing on it. This rather brittle shrub grows to a height of two feet and is even broader than it is high. It is found at the bases of canyon cliffs or the cut banks of the alluvial gravel at the mouths of the canyons and—but more rarely—on the fans. The leaves are broad, an inch or more long. The large flowers are pale yellow with a greenish tinge and appear in spring. It grows in similar places southward through the deserts.

HABITAT Valley floor and fans, canyons.

Blazingstar Family | YELLOW FLOWERS | 207

STINGBUSH

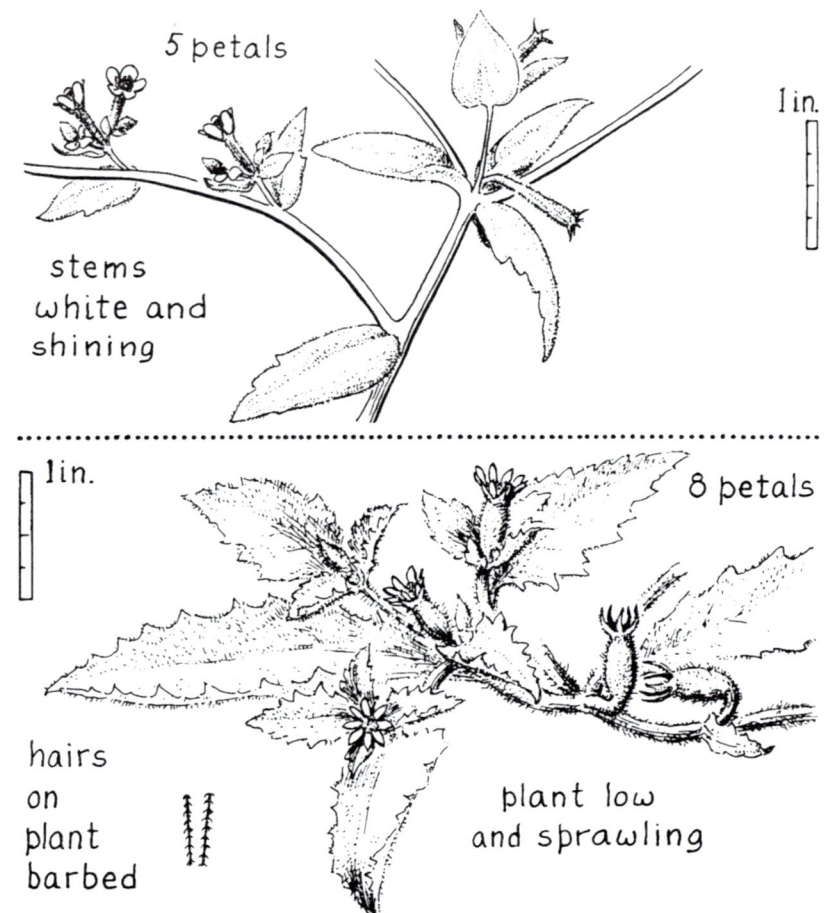

Death Valley mentzelia
Mentzelia reflexa   **BLAZINGSTAR FAMILY** (Loasaceae)

GROWTH FORM Annual herb

DESCRIPTION Though the **Death Valley mentzelia** is not as showy as one of the other mentzelias (*Mentzelia tricuspis*) which occur occasionally here, it is especially interesting, as it was long thought to grow only in the Death Valley region; it has more recently been found in central San Bernardino County. The plants are short and spreading and very leafy. The yellow petals and many stamens are conspicuous among the leaves, and when the seeds are ripe the stalk of the capsule is sharply turned downward. The leaves are covered with tiny barbed hairs that stick to anything they touch, hence the name "stick-leaf" has been sometimes used as a name for the whole group. The other kinds that grow in the region also have this clinging character. One of the small-flowered kinds, **whitestem mentzelia** (*Mentzelia albicaulis*) is illustrated at the top of the page.

HABITAT Valley floor and fans.

Blazingstar Family YELLOW FLOWERS | 209

DEATH VALLEY MENTZELIA

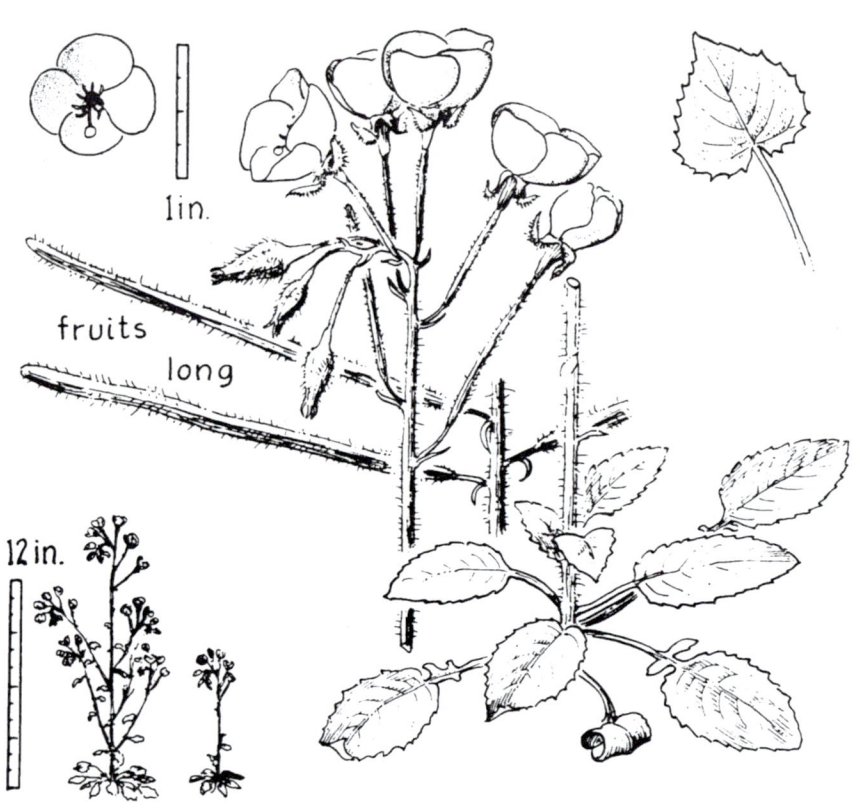

Golden evening-primrose

Chylismia brevipes **EVENING-PRIMROSE FAMILY** (Onagraceae)

SYNONYM *Oenothera brevipes*
GROWTH FORM Annual herb
DESCRIPTION From February through April from sea level to 4,000 feet this bright yellow evening-primrose may be seen someplace in travels around the Park. It may be found in the open desert among the black stones of the desert pavement or in sand in the washes, and it sometimes grows in stands thick enough to give color to the alluvial fans. The individual plants are often well over a foot high. The flowers, several on a stalk, are an inch or more across, and the ripening long narrow capsules spread almost at right angles. The leaves are mostly at the base and are attractive, too, with their toothed margins and reddish veins. The desert bighorn seem to relish it for early spring greens. It is common in the deserts of California and those of the states nearby. The flowers of a form of the **heartleaf evening-primrose** (*Chylismia cardiophylla*), a plant which grows in washes at the foot of canyon walls, much resemble this. The toothed heart-shaped leaves (upper right) help to distinguish it from golden evening-primrose.
HABITAT Valley floor and fans.

Evening-Primrose Family · YELLOW FLOWERS | 211

GOLDEN EVENING-PRIMROSE

GOLDEN EVENING-PRIMROSE

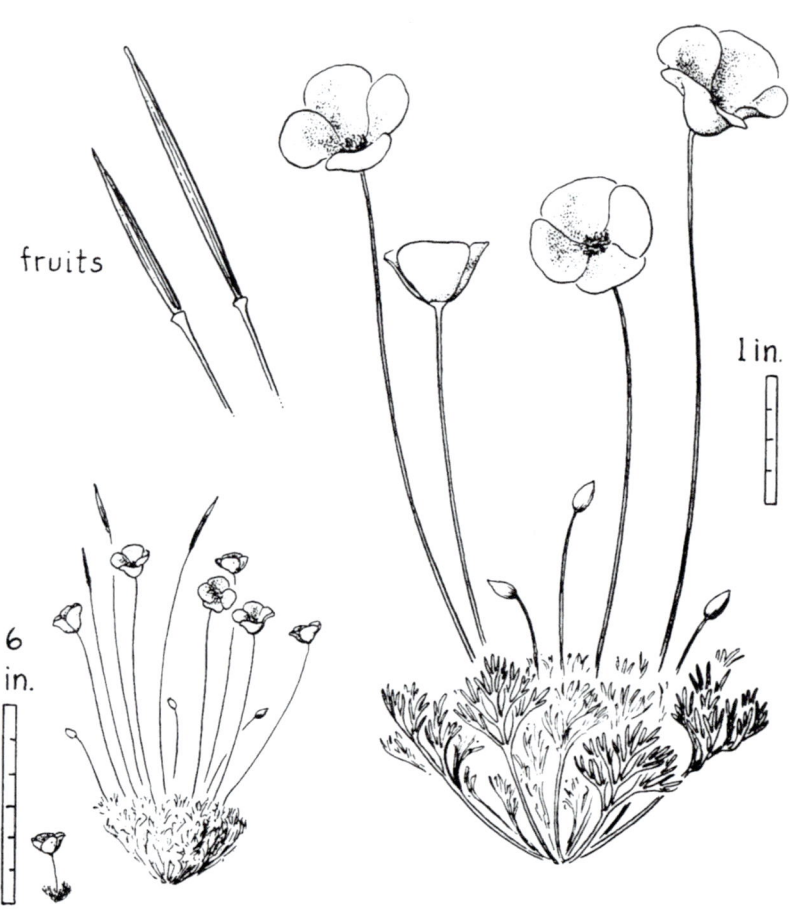

Desert goldpoppy

Eschscholzia glyptosperma POPPY FAMILY (Papaveraceae)

GROWTH FORM Annual herb

DESCRIPTION This small relative of the California state flower grows usually to a height of two to ten inches. The flowers are about an inch across, each one borne at the top of a leafless stalk which rises well above the clustered blue-green divided leaves at the base of the plant. Though small the plants are often very showy as they have many flower-bearing stems. This annual poppy grows in sand or on the desert pavement and is often seen while one is traveling on the roads in the Park.

HABITAT Valley floor and fans

Poppy Family — YELLOW FLOWERS | 213

DESERT GOLDPOPPY

DESERT GOLDPOPPY

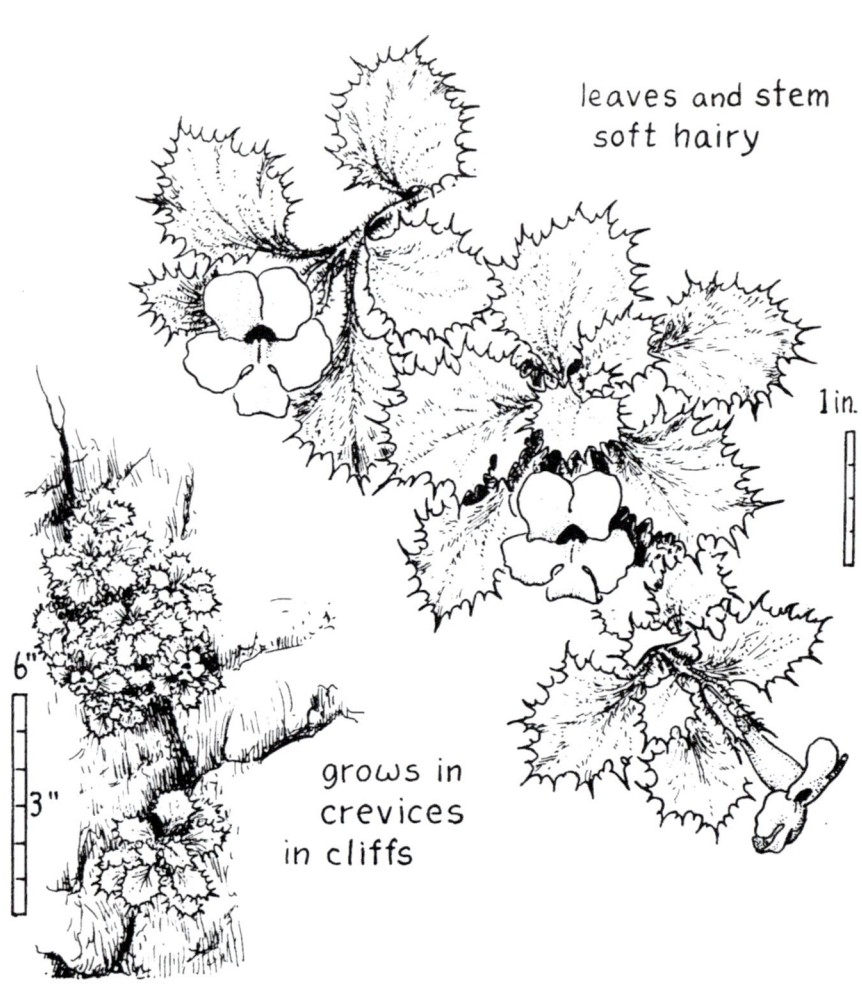

Rocklady

Holmgrenanthe petrophila   **PLANTAIN FAMILY** (Plantaginaceae)
SYNONYM *Maurandya petrophila*
GROWTH FORM Perennial herb
DESCRIPTION Rocklady is perhaps the rarest wildflower in the Park. So far this attractive little rock plant has been found in only one locality—hanging from the crevices of limestone cliffs. The flowers are pale yellow with a deeper yellow throat. The leaves are an inch or more long and wide and edged with bristly teeth.
HABITAT Upper desert slopes, canyon walls.

Plantain Family | YELLOW FLOWERS | 215

ROCKLADY

Death Valley mohavea

Mohavea breviflora   **PLANTAIN FAMILY** (Plantaginaceae)

GROWTH FORM Annual herb

DESCRIPTION This annual is quite commonly seen in the early spring growing in sand or gravel—later, sometimes, if rains are favorable. Though not as showy as its larger-flowered southern relative, *Mohavea confertiflora,* the short sticky-leaved plants are rather attractive with their yellow flowers which remind one of snapdragons. They are short-lived, however, and when the thin-walled capsules soon break and spill out the many black seeds, they look very different but still rouse your curiosity. This species grows in southern Nevada and northwestern Arizona as well as the Death Valley region.

HABITAT Valley floor and fans.

Plantain Family | YELLOW FLOWERS | 217

DEATH VALLEY MOHAVEA

DEATH VALLEY MOHAVEA

Yellow twining snapdragon

Neogaerrhinum filipes　　　　　　　　PLANTAIN FAMILY (Plantaginaceae)

SYNONYM *Antirrhinum filipes*
GROWTH FORM Annual herb
DESCRIPTION Like many of the desert annuals that are delicate and fragile, **twining snapdragon** gets its initial protection and additional moisture by starting its short life at the base of some desert shrub. The shrub then becomes the necessary support for this tangled green-stemmed plant with its scattered narrow leaves. The yellow flowers, which are about an inch long, are borne at the ends of the tendril-like branches. Yellow twining snapdragon grows in loose sandy soil in California deserts and in desert places as far east as Arizona and southern Utah.
HABITAT Valley floor and fans.

Plantain Family · YELLOW FLOWERS | 219

YELLOW TWINING SNAPDRAGON

YELLOW TWINING SNAPDRAGON

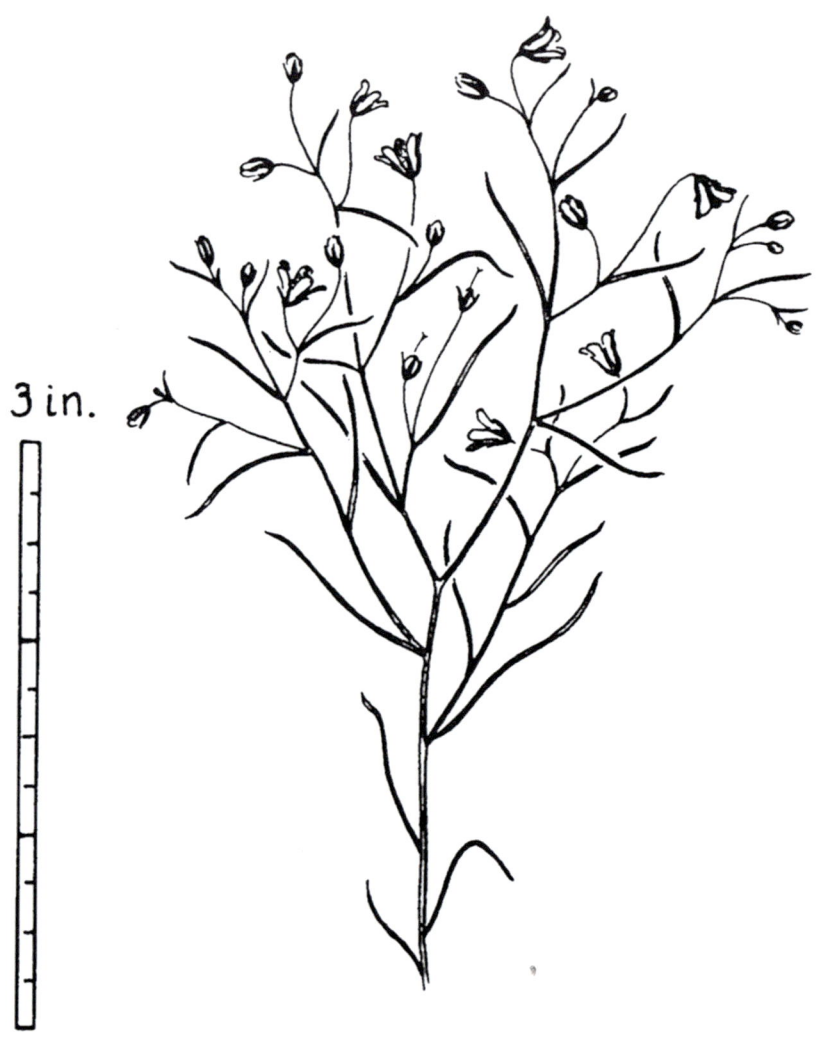

Threadstem gilia

Linanthus filiformis   PHLOX FAMILY (Polemoniaceae)

SYNONYM *Gilia filiformis*
GROWTH FORM Annual herb
DESCRIPTION The **threadstem gilia** has clear yellow flowers shaped like little bells; these are scattered among the thread-like leaves on the small plants. They will be found on gravelly mesas sometimes to elevations as high as 5,500 feet, though often much lower.
HABITAT Upper desert slopes.

Phlox Family · YELLOW FLOWERS | 221

THREADSTEM GILIA

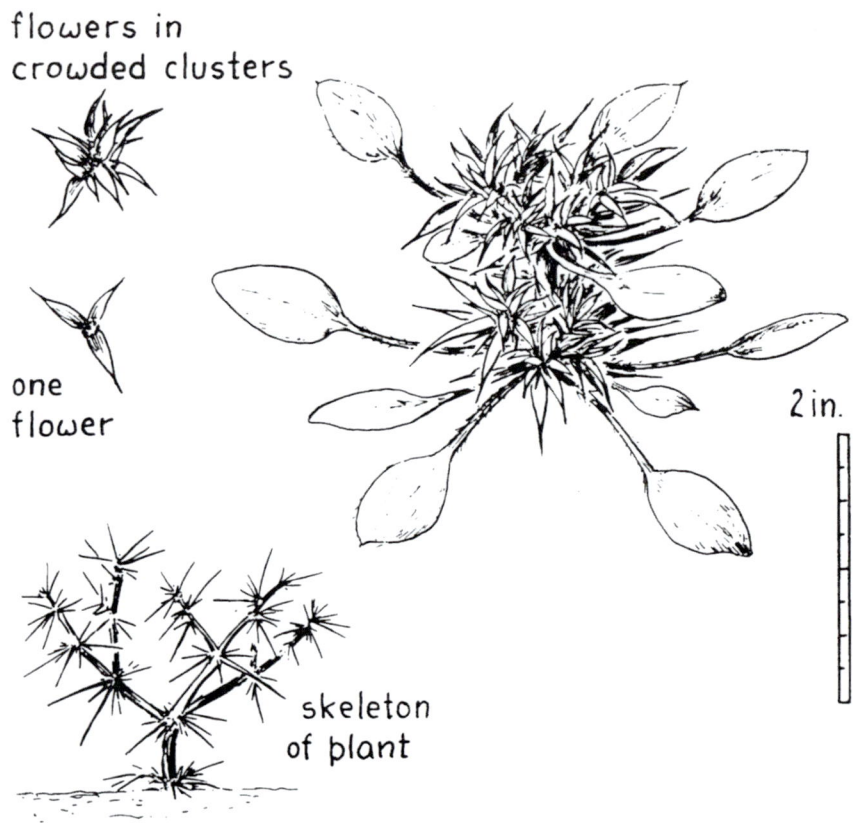

Spiny chorizanthe

Chorizanthe rigida   BUCKWHEAT FAMILY (Polygonaceae)

GROWTH FORM Annual herb

DESCRIPTION Here is a plant that can be identified by its "skeleton." This can be done with several other annuals you see in the fall and winter months when only the dead stalks remain of the spring and summer blooming. **Spiny chorizanthe**, as you see it on the gravelly or rocky flats, is more conspicuous dead than alive for the spiny bracts that surround the flowers become extremely rigid and darker, and the short stem (one to three inches long) takes on a woody texture. In life its most conspicuous feature is the woolly leaves, which have stalks much longer than the leaves themselves. The tiny greenish yellow flowers are so concealed by the spiny bracts that a hand lens is needed to examine them. The plants are rather common throughout the western deserts.

HABITAT Valley floor and fans.

Buckwheat Family | YELLOW FLOWERS | 223

SPINY CHORIZANTHE

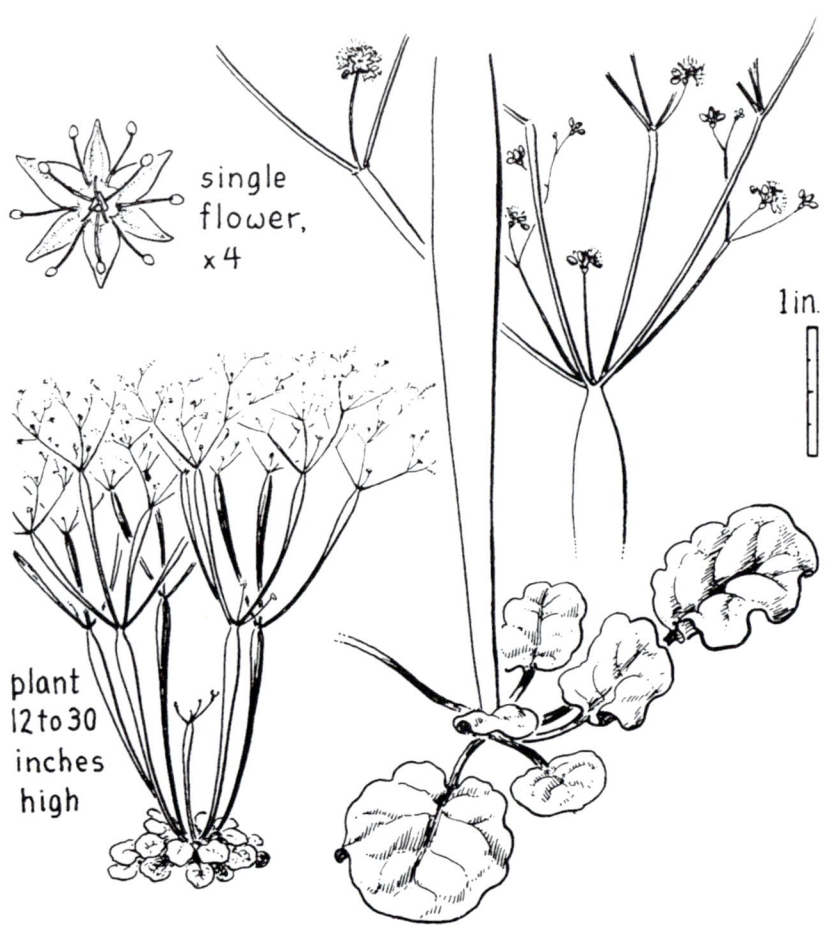

Desert-trumpet eriogonum

Eriogonum inflatum   BUCKWHEAT FAMILY (Polygonaceae)

GROWTH FORM Perennial herb

DESCRIPTION This eriogonum can be easily identified by its distinctive shape, a growth form which occurs to some degree in a few other species. The main blue-green hollow stem of **desert-trumpet** arises from the basal cluster of leaves, slender below and swelling above to a diameter of about one-half of an inch. From this summit, several branches spread out and they in turn become little "trumpets" and branch again into the slender branchlets that bear the small clusters of tiny yellow flowers. Even late in the season the dead trumpet-shaped stalks are easy to spot as one drives along the roads on the floor of the valley. It is a variable species in its wide range over the southwestern deserts, and the most marked variation was formerly known by the scientific name of *Eriogonum inflatum* var. *deflatum* (now considered synonymous with *E. inflatum*). You can doubtless figure out from the name what that looks like.

HABITAT Valley floor and fans.

Buckwheat Family — YELLOW FLOWERS | 225

DESERT-TRUMPET ERIOGONUM

DESERT-TRUMPET ERIOGONUM

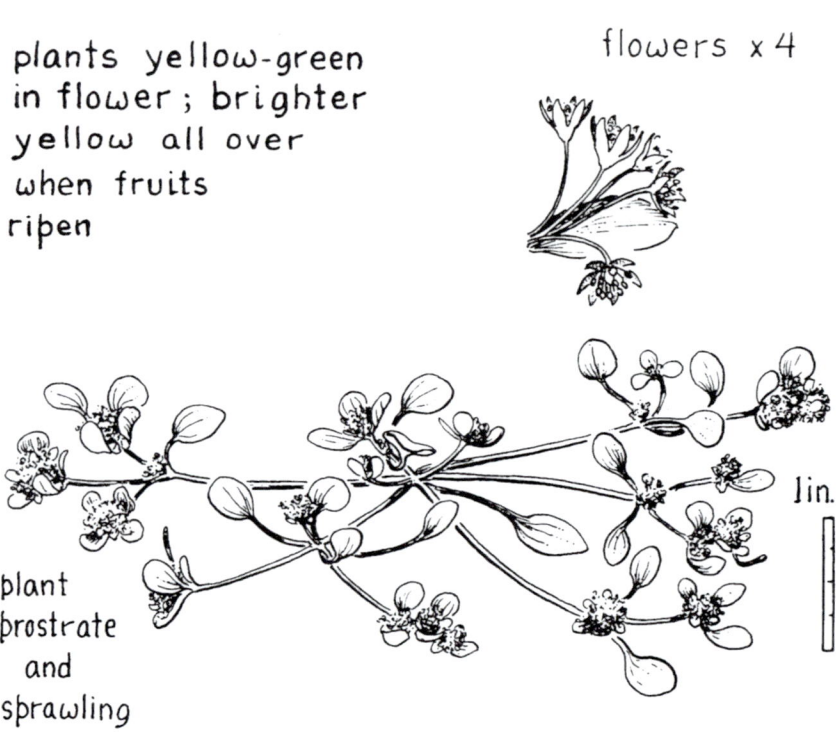

Death Valley gilmania (Goldcarpet)

Gilmania luteola   BUCKWHEAT FAMILY (Polygonaceae)

GROWTH FORM Annual herb

DESCRIPTION A botanist's delight is this small prostrate plant with small yellow-green leaves and yellow flowers. It is very rarely seen, except in the best years, and grows only on the lower parts of some of the washes in Death Valley and nowhere else.

NOTE Plants such as this that are restricted locally are known as "endemics." When this plant was first described as new by Frederick Coville, it had a different scientific name. Due to certain rules concerned with the naming of plants, another generic name must now be used. Fortunately, the new name honors another botanist who contributed much to the knowledge of the flora of Death Valley: M. French Gilman.

HABITAT Valley floor and fans.

Buckwheat Family   YELLOW FLOWERS | 227

DEATH VALLEY GILMANIA

DEATH VALLEY GILMANIA

YELLOW FLOWERS — Zygophyllaceae

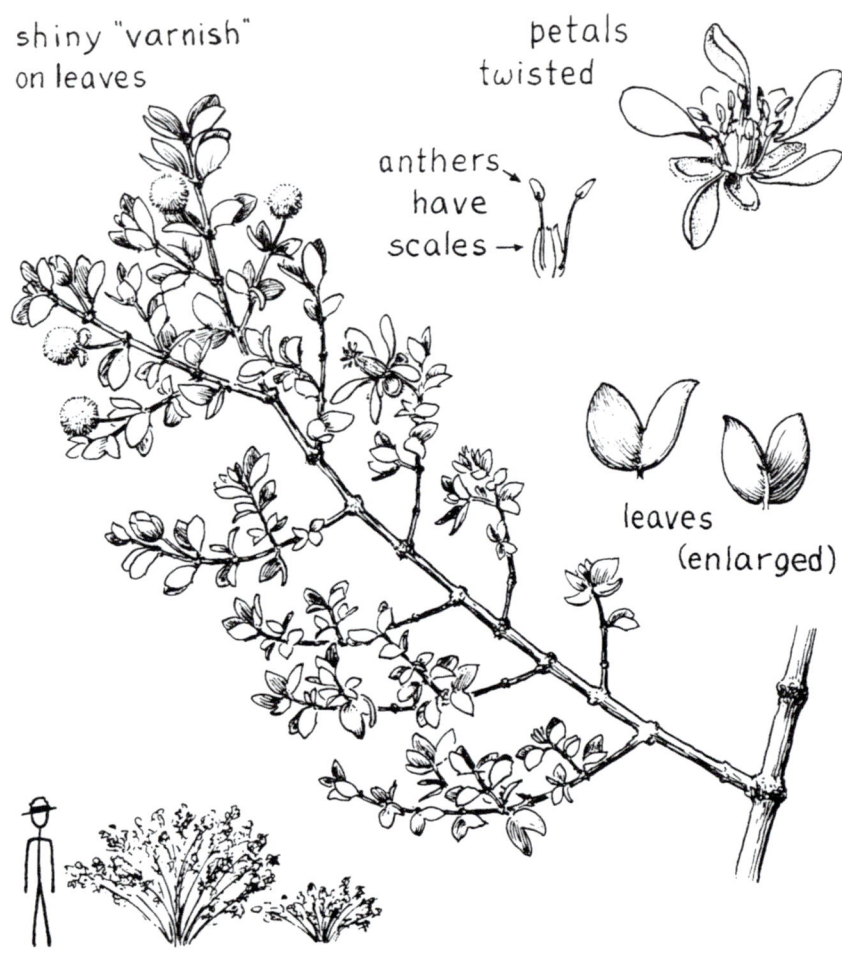

Creosotebush
Larrea tridentata   CREOSOTE-BUSH FAMILY (Zygophyllaceae)
GROWTH FORM Shrub
DESCRIPTION This is perhaps the most common shrub of the deserts of the west at elevations below the Joshua trees and the pinyon pines. It is not to be expected, however, on alkali sinks and salt pans. After the rains which may occur in its flowering periods, the **creosotebush** has the appearance of a well-kept garden shrub. The grayish stems with their blackish joints then have an abundance of dark green leaves, and the branchlets bear the conspicuous bright yellow flowers. The small fuzzy white fruits that develop later show up nicely against the evergreen foliage. The odor given off by the creosotebush is highly controversial; some find it extremely disagreeable, while others think it interesting and pleasant. After a rain the odor is intensified and one would know even in the dark that there were creosotebushes about.
HABITAT Valley floor and fans.

Creosote-Bush Family   YELLOW FLOWERS | 229

CREOSOTEBUSH

CREOSOTEBUSH

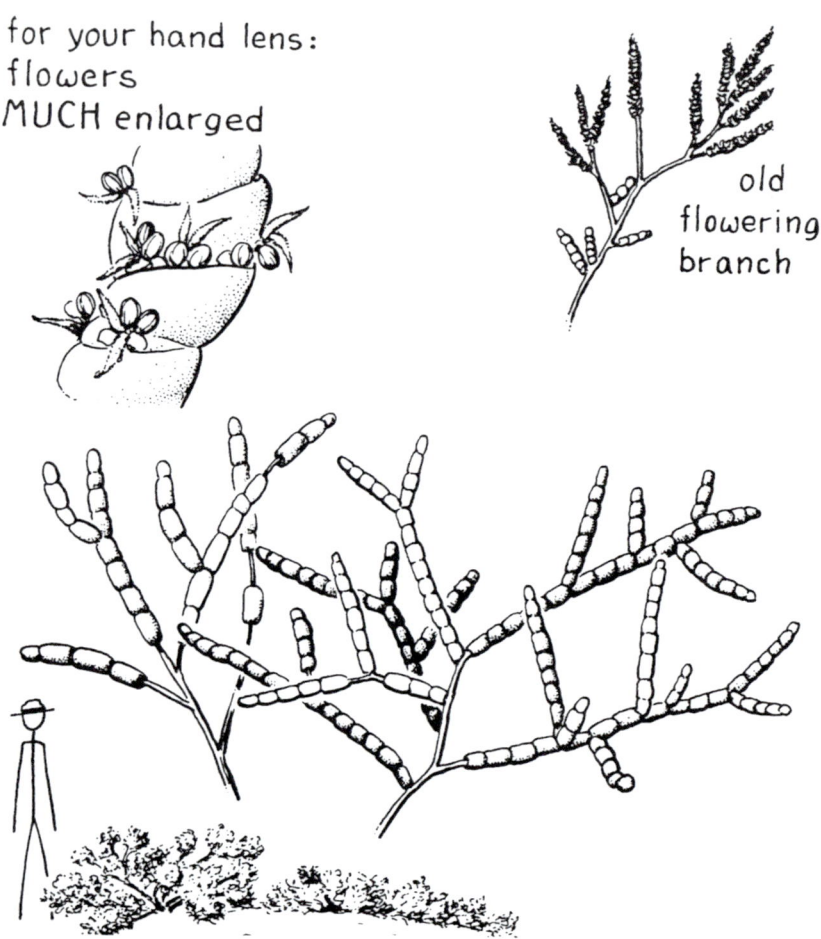

Pickleweed (Iodinebush)

Allenrolfea occidentalis   AMARANTH FAMILY (Amaranthaceae)

GROWTH FORM Shrub

DESCRIPTION **Pickleweed** is really a small shrub though often its woody stems are completely buried in drifting sand, much in the same manner in which the mesquite trees appear to be shrubs when buried in the sand dunes. It is most selective in the type of soil in which it will grow, and it will be found in strongly alkaline places in Death Valley, and in similar situations throughout its wide range in the west. As you leave the Devil's Golf Course or Salt Creek, the dark blue-green masses of vegetation catch the eye. If you stop and look at the pickleweed you will think that it has no flowers or leaves. It has, but they are so tiny and modified that you need a good hand lens to examine them. The stems are fleshy and green, and the joints are short. It makes one think of tiny green sausages strung along a slender twig.

HABITAT Valley floor, alkali flats.

Amaranth Family | **GREEN & BROWN FLOWERS** | 231

PICKLEWEED

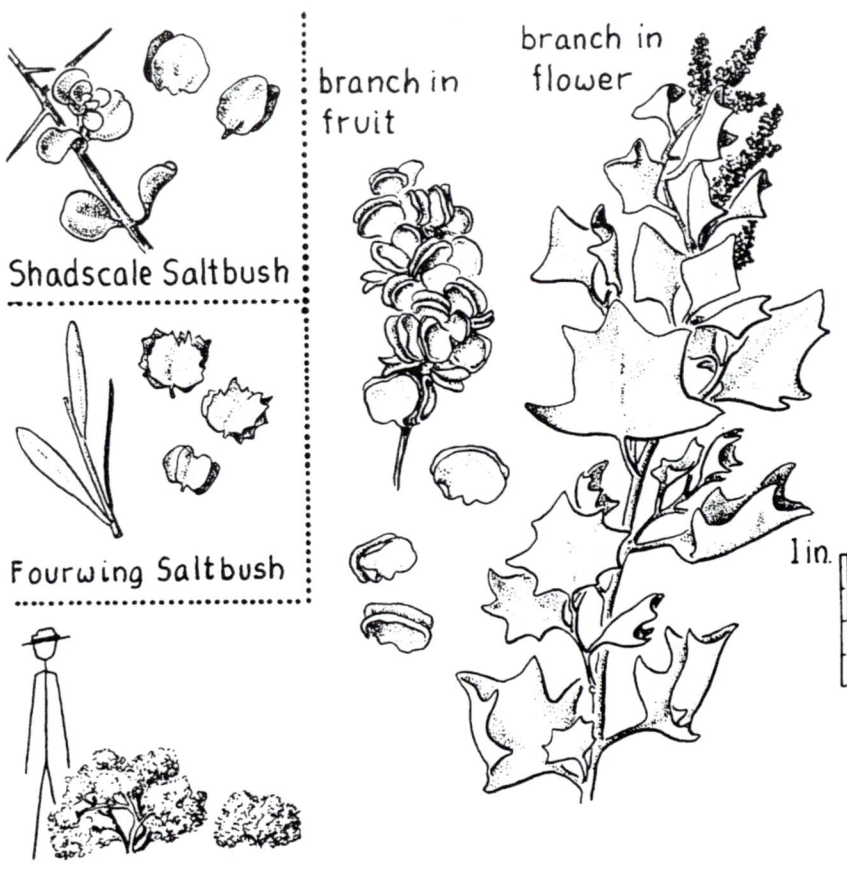

Desertholly

Atriplex hymenelytra   AMARANTH FAMILY (Amaranthaceae)

GROWTH FORM Shrub

DESCRIPTION Excepting creosotebush, **desertholly** is perhaps the best-known shrub in the Park, and it is not uncommon throughout the southwestern deserts. In the growing season, the toothed leaves (about one inch long and almost as wide) are white, and strongly flushed with green. In the hot season, the leaves are white, sometimes with a rosy tinge, as are also the round-winged fruits. The male and female flowers are on different plants. It is more tolerant of alkali than creosotebush and will even grow on the edges of the salt flats, but it is more commonly found growing in washes or alluvial fans to an elevation of 2,000 or 3,000 feet. Several other species of saltbush occur throughout the Park, and the fruits and leaves of two of them are illustrated above. **Shadscale** (*Atriplex confertifolia*), a grayish white shrub with spiny branches, is usually found on alluvial fans and lower slopes of mountains, while **fourwing saltbush** (*Atriplex canescens*) is commonly found in more well-watered areas on the valley floor.

HABITAT Valley floor and fans.

Amaranth Family **GREEN & BROWN FLOWERS** | 233

DESERTHOLLY

DESERTHOLLY

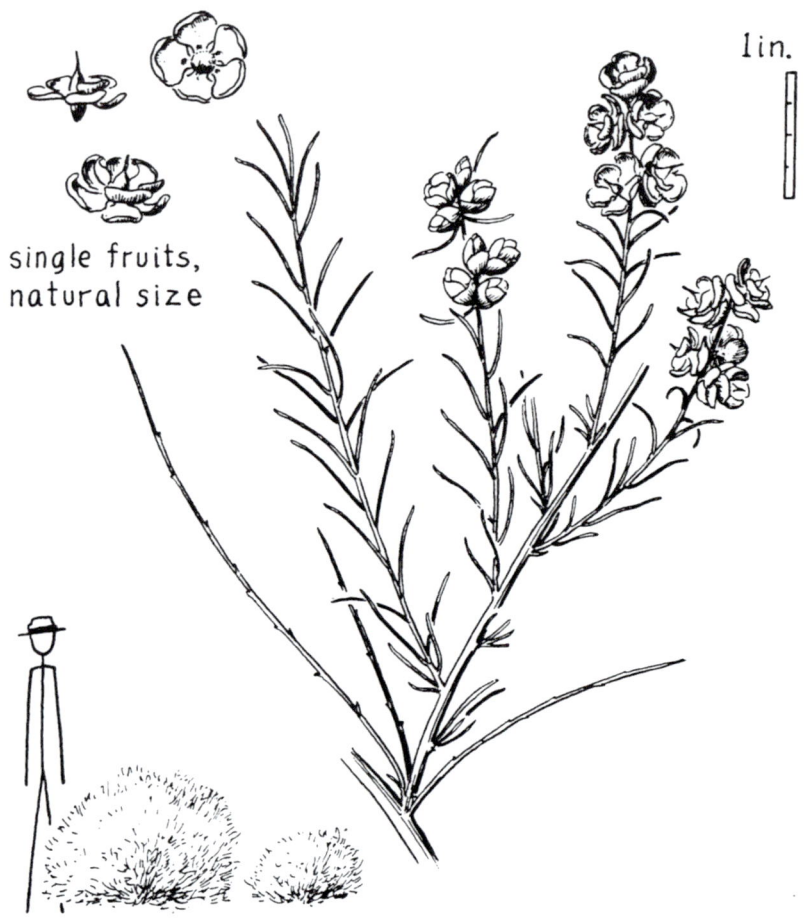

single fruits, natural size

White burrobrush

Ambrosia salsola   SUNFLOWER FAMILY (Asteraceae)

SYNONYM *Hymenoclea salsola*
GROWTH FORM Shrub
DESCRIPTION In almost any wash and along small drainage courses in the alluvial fans one can find the soft yellow-green mounds of the **white burrobrush**. Summer showers as well as winter rains bring out a new growth of young stems and thread-like leaves. The flowers (the male and female ones are separated) are not conspicuous, but the fruits are interesting and attractive. The shining, white or pink-tinged, dry scales are fastened spirally to a hard central core. When young the fruits are shaped like small dry rosebuds; when old the scales spread horizontally from the central core. This and related species are widely distributed in the west. It has been called cheesebush because of the odor of the crushed foliage, but it does not smell like the cheese most persons are fond of.
HABITAT Valley floor and fans, washes.

Sunflower Family | **GREEN & BROWN FLOWERS** | **235**

WHITE BURROBUSH

WHITE BURROBUSH

GREEN & BROWN FLOWERS — Asteraceae

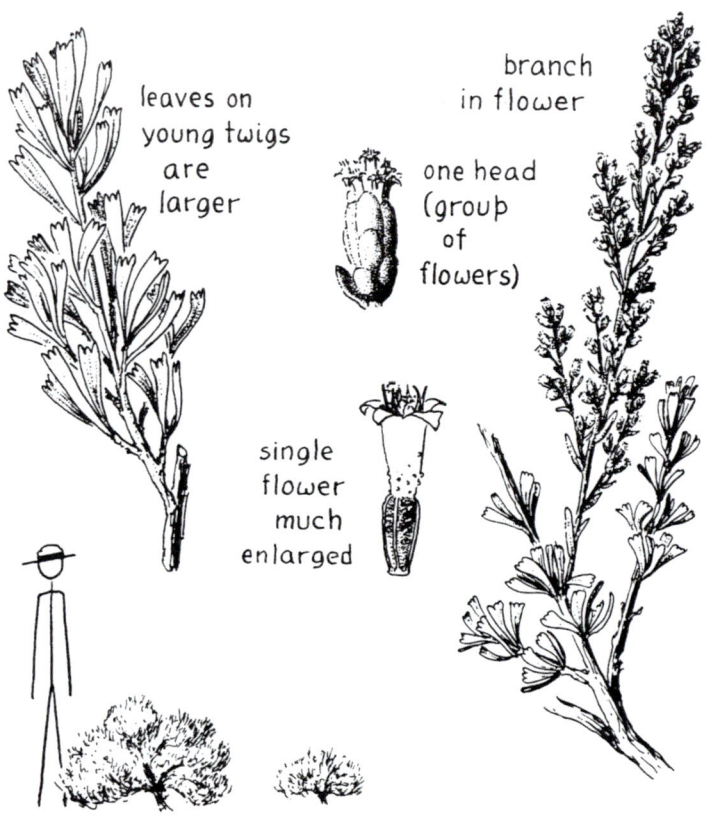

Big sagebrush
Artemisia tridentata SUNFLOWER FAMILY (Asteraceae)

GROWTH FORM Shrub

DESCRIPTION **Sagebrush**, tall or short, makes its presence known by its tangy aroma, which is especially noticeable after a shower. There is not the vast acreage of big sagebrush in Death Valley National Park that there is on the plains of the northwest, though it is abundant at higher elevations in the mountains of Death Valley; there it is usually much dwarfed. If one did not include the flowering stems with their multitude of tiny rayless flowers in measuring the height, the shrubs would be said to be only a few inches tall and look like gnarled miniature trees. The larger plants at a lower elevation have the same habit.

NOTE There are two species of the dwarfed sagebrushes, the low form of the big sagebrush and the **low sagebrush** (*Artemisia nova*). They resemble each other and are separated on quite technical details. The most obvious differences between the two are the shorter flower heads and the leaves which are one and one-half to three times as long as they are wide in the latter, while in the big sagebrush the leaves are three to six times as long as wide.

HABITAT Pinyon-juniper and limber pine-bristlecone pine woodland.

Sunflower Family | GREEN & BROWN FLOWERS | 237

BIG SAGEBRUSH

Bud sagebrush

Picrothamnus desertorum   SUNFLOWER FAMILY (Asteraceae)

SYNONYM *Artemisia spinescens*
GROWTH FORM Small shrub
DESCRIPTION **Bud sagebrush** is a small, compact shrub usually less than a foot high, much shorter than its associates, **horsebush** (*Tetradymia*), **white brittlebush** (*Encelia farinosa*), **spiny menodora** (*Menodora spinescens*), and others. It is leafless in winter—a rather spiny shrub, grayish with scales above and with shreddy bark on the older portion. The spines, which are an inch or more long, are really the flowering branches of preceding years. In spring the plant is covered with short divided cobwebby leaves and small yellowish green flower heads, and gives forth that pleasant sagebrush odor. Bud sagebrush grows commonly in the Great Basin and the adjacent Rocky Mountain region.
HABITAT Upper desert slopes.

Sunflower Family | **GREEN & BROWN FLOWERS** | 239

BUD SAGEBRUSH

BUD SAGEBRUSH

Olney bulrush
Schoenoplectus americanus SEDGE FAMILY (Cyperaceae)
SYNONYM *Scirpus olneyi*
GROWTH FORM Grass-like bulrush
DESCRIPTION **Olney bulrush**, in Death Valley at least, is one of that assemblage of plants associated with the alkaline marshes and meadows around wells and springs. However, it has to have its roots in surface water. Coville remarks upon it in the "Botany of the Death Valley Expedition." The plants growing so closely packed together always indicated the soft muck underneath. The Expedition found so frequently that their horses became mired in the clumps of it, that short-cuts through that type of marsh were never taken. Olney bulrush often grows to a height of more than four feet. The triangular stem is distinctive of this plant. The species grows from the coast to the desert.
HABITAT Valley floor and fans, marshes.

sedge Family | **GREEN & BROWN FLOWERS** | **241**

OLNEY BULRUSH

DEATH VALLEY EPHEDRA

EPHEDRA

This strange plant grows in desert regions in both the eastern and western hemispheres and many kinds have been described. For five thousand years, a tea made from one of the species was used in China to relieve congestion of the lungs, and now the extracted drug, ephedrine, is used all over the world for that purpose. Our American species contain little ephedrine but do contain other chemicals which give flavor to a palatable tea. The Indians, the early settlers, and people of the present day either like this brew or feel it is good for their health, but in any case, today's experts agree that small quantities are best.

Death Valley ephedra

Ephedra funerea   EPHEDRA FAMILY (Ephedraceae)

GROWTH FORM Shrub

DESCRIPTION Once you have learned the characteristic look of the genus *Ephedra* you can always recognize it, but the recognition of the kind of ephedra you are looking at is not always so easy. **Death Valley ephedra** fortunately has a typical growth habit. The short gray-green stems spread in a whorl from the main axis at an angle of about sixty degrees. The presence of three scale-like leaves is a very important character, but often these minute strawlike appendages have weathered off. Usually only one seed develops in each of the small "cones," while in the other two ephedras listed here the seeds are paired instead of single.

HABITAT Upper desert slopes, valley floor and fans.

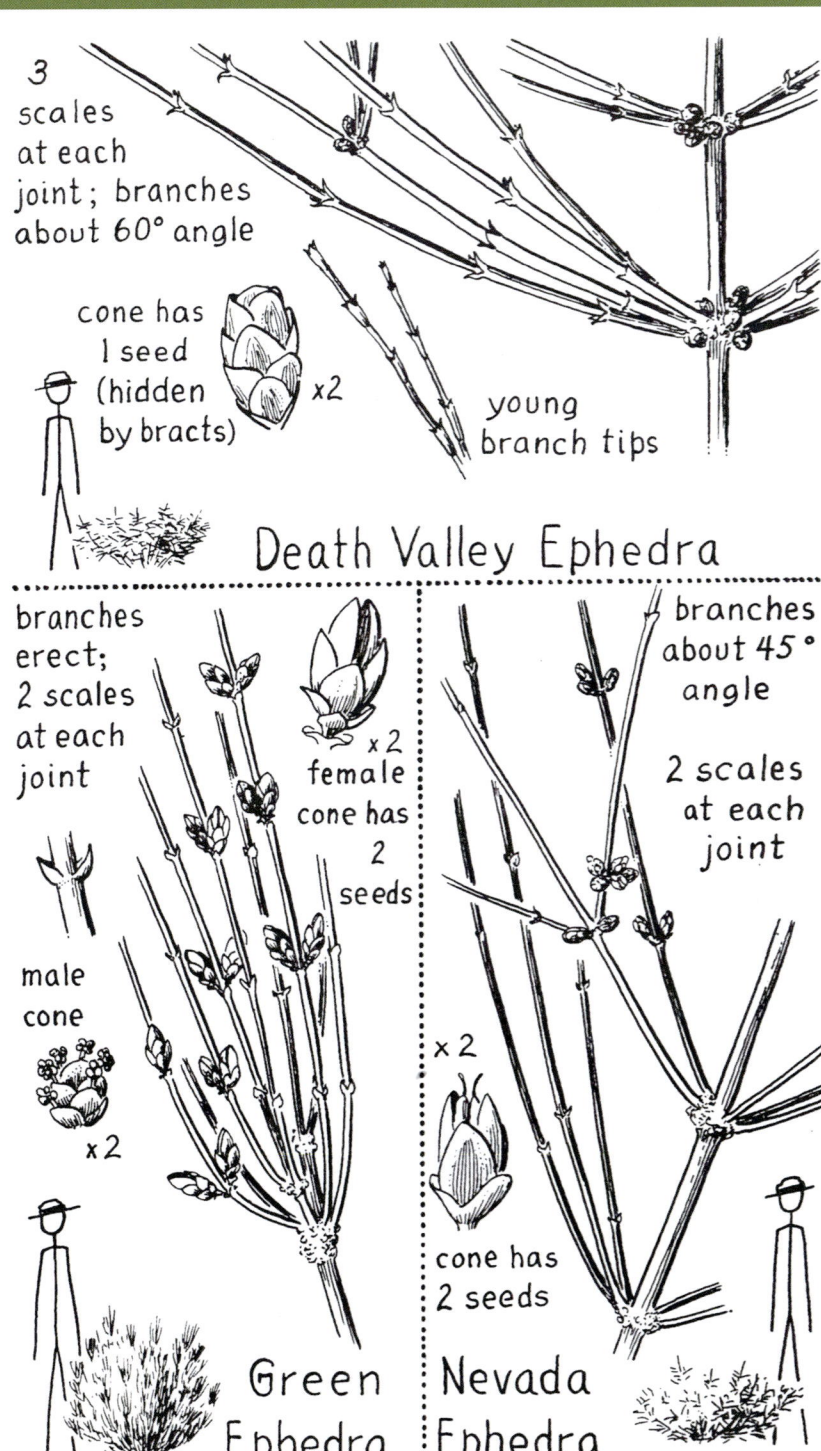

NEVADA EPHEDRA

Nevada ephedra

Ephedra nevadensis   EPHEDRA FAMILY (Ephedraceae)

GROWTH FORM Shrub

DESCRIPTION This is a low, gray-green shrub, with short, straggly branches sticking out in all directions from the nodes, at an angle of about forty-five degrees. **Nevada ephedra** is widespread and is found from eastern Oregon and from Utah south to eastern California and Arizona.

HABITAT Upper desert slopes.

Green ephedra (Mormon tea)

Ephedra viridis   EPHEDRA FAMILY (Ephedraceae)

GROWTH FORM Shrub

DESCRIPTION The **green ephedra** grows on rocky canyon slopes and on mesas in the pinyon-juniper area or even in the upper part of the creosote-bush belt. The bushes are three or four feet high and not quite as broad, and the stems are beset with many erect, bright green, broomlike branches. The slightly thickened "joints" are dark and the two tiny leaf scales break off in age. The male and female flowers of this strange gymnosperm are borne on different plants.

HABITAT Pinyon-juniper woodland.

Ephedra Family | **GREEN & BROWN FLOWERS** | 245

GREEN EPHEDRA

Cooper rush
Juncus cooperi   RUSH FAMILY (Juncaceae)

GROWTH FORM Grass-like rush

DESCRIPTION Many kinds of marsh plants grow around the springs, seeps, and wells of the valley floor and fans. The soil is pale gray or white with bleached-out minerals. Here and in no other habitat in the valley you find bulrushes and other members of the sedge family, and with them sacaton, saltgrass, yerba mansa, California satintail, screwbean mesquite, blue-eyed grass, thistle; also genera like goldenrod, loosestrife, epipactis, baccharis, arrowweed, and others which, though they need water, do not always demand so much alkalinity. **Cooper rush** is at home in these surroundings, here and in similar places in the southwestern deserts. It grows in large tufts one and one-half to nearly three feet high, and the round stems are stiff and pointed. The clusters of flowers are inserted below the sharp-pointed tip of the stem. The flower parts are dry and straw-colored and look the same when fresh as they do around the ripe capsule.

NOTE Rushes are one of the several plants Native Americans traditionally used in basket-making.

HABITAT Valley floor and fans, marshes.

Rush Family
GREEN & BROWN FLOWERS | 247

COOPER RUSH

COOPER RUSH

248 | GREEN & BROWN FLOWERS — Poaceae

old plant looks like bunch of white fluff

1 in.

Fluffgrass
Dasyochloa pulchella   GRASS FAMILY (Poaceae)

SYNONYM *Tridens pulchellus*
GROWTH FORM Perennial grass
DESCRIPTION This small bunchgrass will be noticed more in age than in youth. As it is commonly found growing among the blackened rocks of the desert pavement, the ripened fluffy grains and the thin straw-colored bracts that surround them make this tufted grass very conspicuous even though it is only a few inches high. In the Park there is another bunchgrass (*Blepharidachne kingii*) which might be confused with fluffgrass. It, too, is short and has hairy seeds, but the stems that bear the seeds are longer than the basal leaves. **Fluffgrass** can reproduce new plants from the old ones in an interesting fashion. The leaf-bearing branches arch over to the ground, root at the leaf cluster, and you have a new plant started. *Blepharidachne* reproduces new plants from seeds only.
HABITAT Valley floor and fans.

Grass Family | **GREEN & BROWN FLOWERS** | 249

FLUFFGRASS

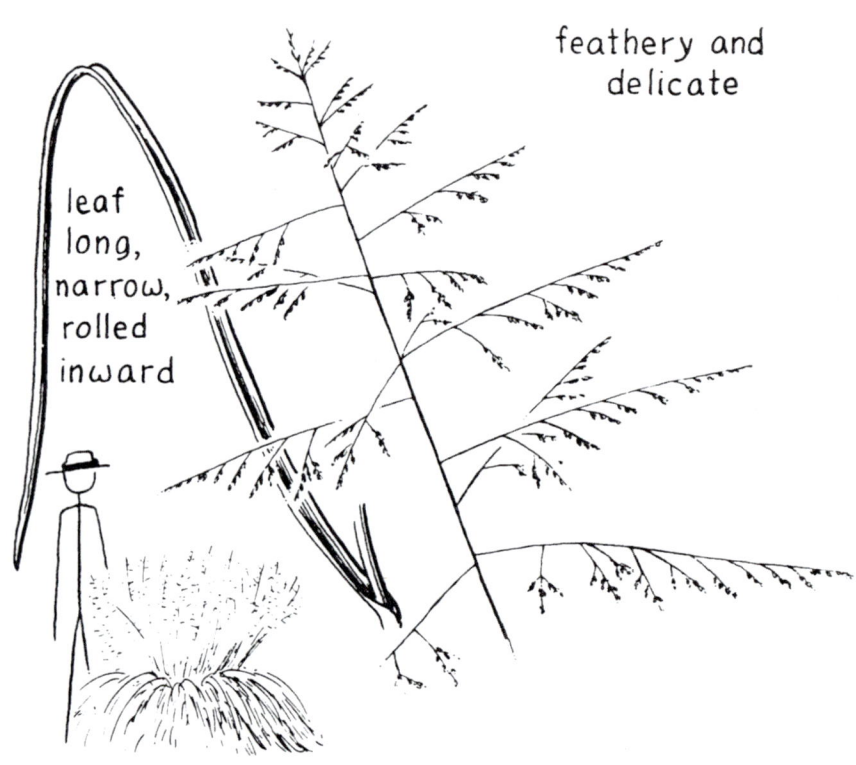

Alkali sacaton (Dropseed)
Sporobolus airoides   GRASS FAMILY (Poaceae)

GROWTH FORM Perennial grass

DESCRIPTION **Alkali sacaton**, which can be up to three feet in height, grows in large tough bunches. The stems that bear the flowers are slender and at least one-half the height of the whole plant. When the tiny seeds are ripe, the stems are much branched and very open and delicate-looking. The plants grow in more or less alkaline meadows with saltgrass and various sedges. It is a good forage plant; hence one may not be so fortunate as to see it in its feathery beauty because it has been grazed.

NOTE Ancient Indian storage barrows were often lined with this plant.

HABITAT Valley floor and fans, marshes.

Grass Family | **GREEN & BROWN FLOWERS** | 251

ALKALI SACATON

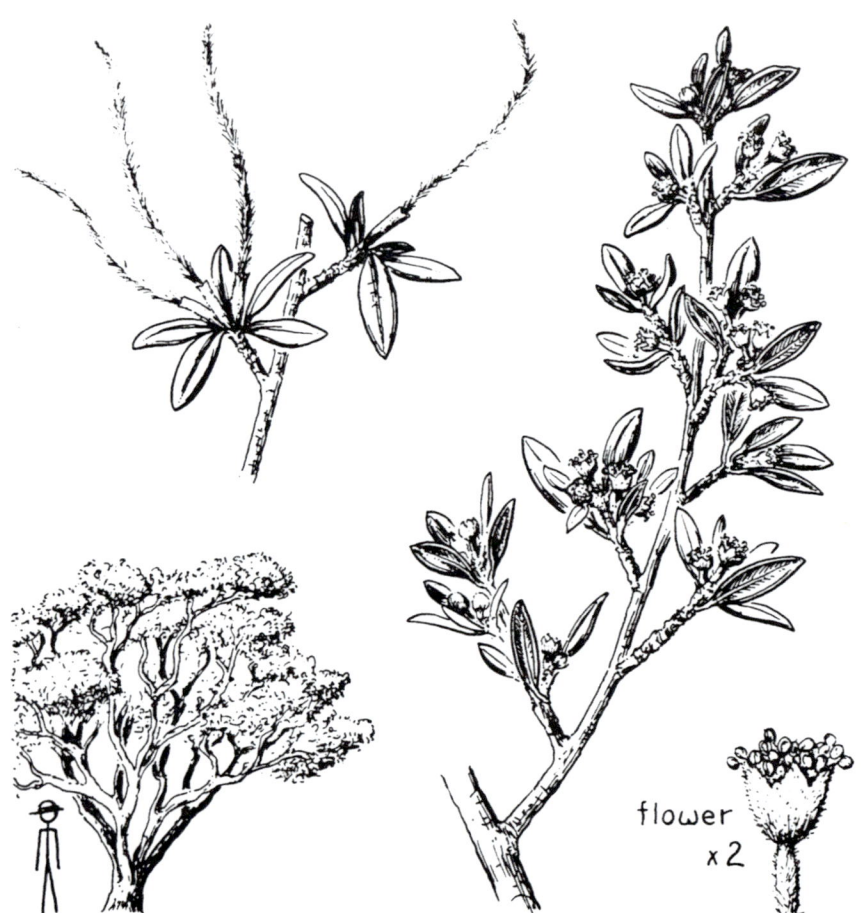

flower x2

Curlleaf mountain-mahogany
Cercocarpus ledifolius   ROSE FAMILY (Rosaceae)

GROWTH FORM Shrub, small tree
DESCRIPTION **Mountain-mahogany** is a conspicuous part of the pinyon pine woodland. In other places in its wide western distribution it is sometimes found at higher elevations. It is 15 to 25 feet tall and though it is bushy in habit, its sturdy furrowed trunk and stout rough branches give it the dignity of a tree. The wood is very hard. The lance-shaped leaves are thick in texture and are dark green above and pale below. Mountain-mahogany belongs to the rose family and is one of the members that have no petals on the flowers. The long white furry tails of the fruits give it eye appeal.
HABITAT Pinyon-juniper woodland.

Rose Family | GREEN & BROWN FLOWERS | 253

CURLLEAF MOUNTAIN-MAHOGANY

CURLLEAF MOUNTAIN-MAHOGANY

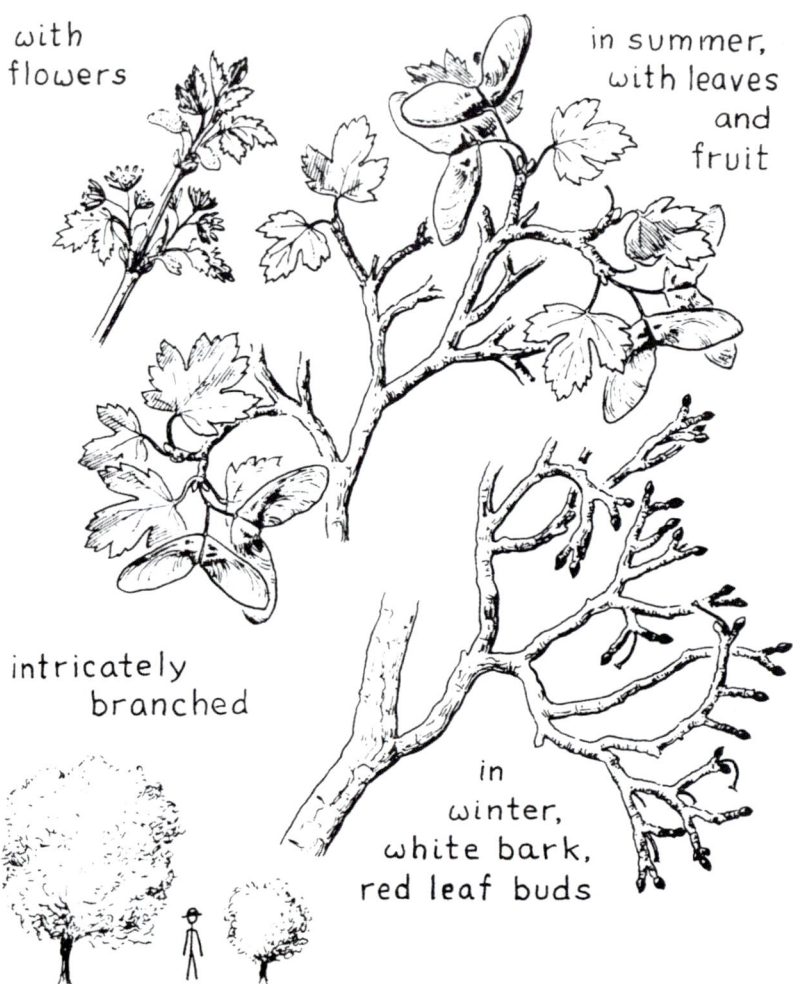

Rocky Mountain maple

Acer glabrum   SOAPBERRY FAMILY (Sapindaceae)

GROWTH FORM Shrub or small tree

DESCRIPTION In the high canyons of the Panamints, high enough to be in the area where the limber pines grow, a desert form of the maple tree is found. This desert form of the **mountain maple** (*Acer glabrum* var. *diffusum*) is not uncommon in desert ranges of southern California, Nevada and northern Arizona. The trees are 8 to 20 feet tall and have a rather bushy growth. In spring the small maple leaves, which are about one inch long and wide, unfold and the small greenish-yellow flowers bloom with them. By summer the winged paired seeds have developed. They fall in autumn with the yellowed leaves and the cycle is completed in winter with the startlingly white, leafless twigs and branches which bear the tiny red leafbuds of the next season.

HABITAT Limber-bristlecone pine woodland.

ROCKY MOUNTAIN MAPLE

ROCKY MOUNTAIN MAPLE

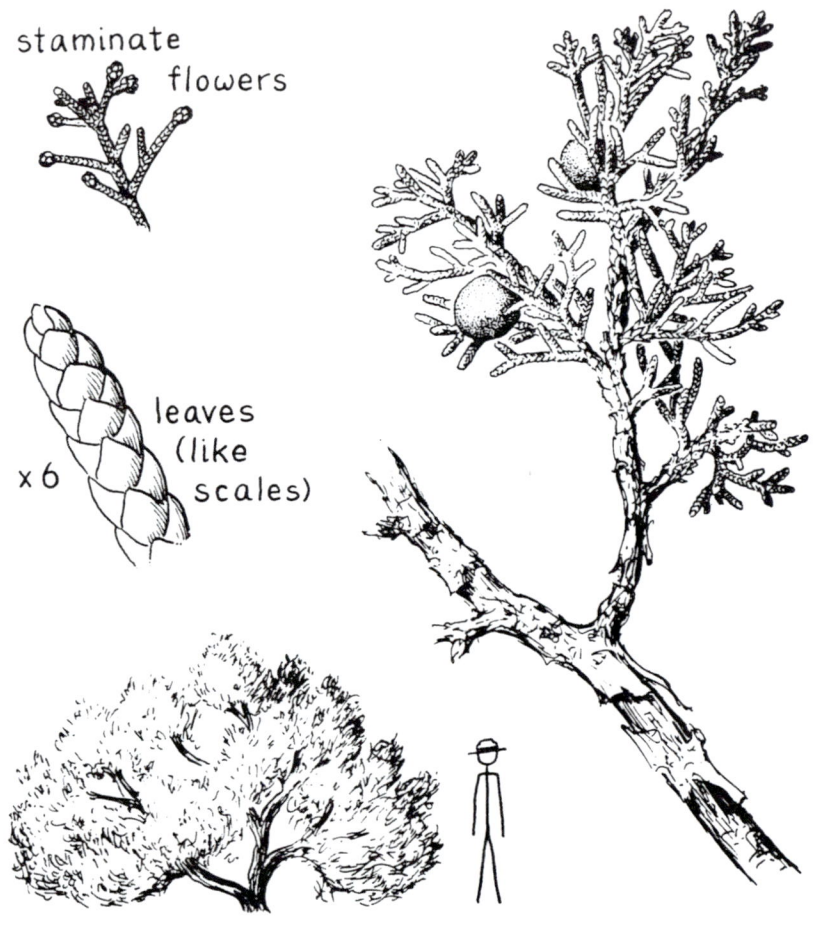

Utah juniper
Juniperus osteosperma   **CYPRESS FAMILY** (Cupressaceae)

GROWTH FORM Evergreen tree

DESCRIPTION The juniper and the pinyon pine form a belt on the higher mountains in Death Valley, roughly between the 5,000 and 7,500 foot levels, because it is around this elevation that the summer and winter temperatures, drainage, soil, and precipitation meet the growing needs of the trees. If Joshua trees were common in Death Valley, instead of occurring but rarely, they would begin below the lowest junipers and extend downward about 2,000 feet, as the growing conditions at that level would be right for them. Climate is a prime factor in the distribution of species but many other factors have to be studied, too. That is why the distribution of plants is so fascinating. Utah juniper is a native of the mountain ranges of the Great Basin.

NOTE It was useful to the Panamint Indians, so Coville reported; they used the wood to make their bows.

HABITAT Pinyon-juniper woodland.

UTAH JUNIPER

Great Basin bristlecone pine

Pinus longaeva   PINE FAMILY (Pinaceae)

SYNONYM *Pinus aristata* var. *longaeva*
GROWTH FORM Evergreen tree
DESCRIPTION The scales of the cones, which are from two and one-half to three and one-half inches long, bear an incurved prickle—hence the name "bristlecone." The short needles, which are in bundles of five, densely clothe the somewhat pendent branchlets.
NOTE Formerly treated as a variety of Rocky Mountain bristlecone pine (*Pinus aristata*), trees of the Park are now considered a separate species (*Pinus longaeva*), which ranges from eastern California to Nevada and Utah. A specimen in the White Mountains of California (north of Death Valley) has been dated at 5,069 years old, making it the oldest known (non-clonal) living organism in the world.
HABITAT Limber pine-bristlecone pine woodland.

GREAT BASIN BRISTLECONE PINE

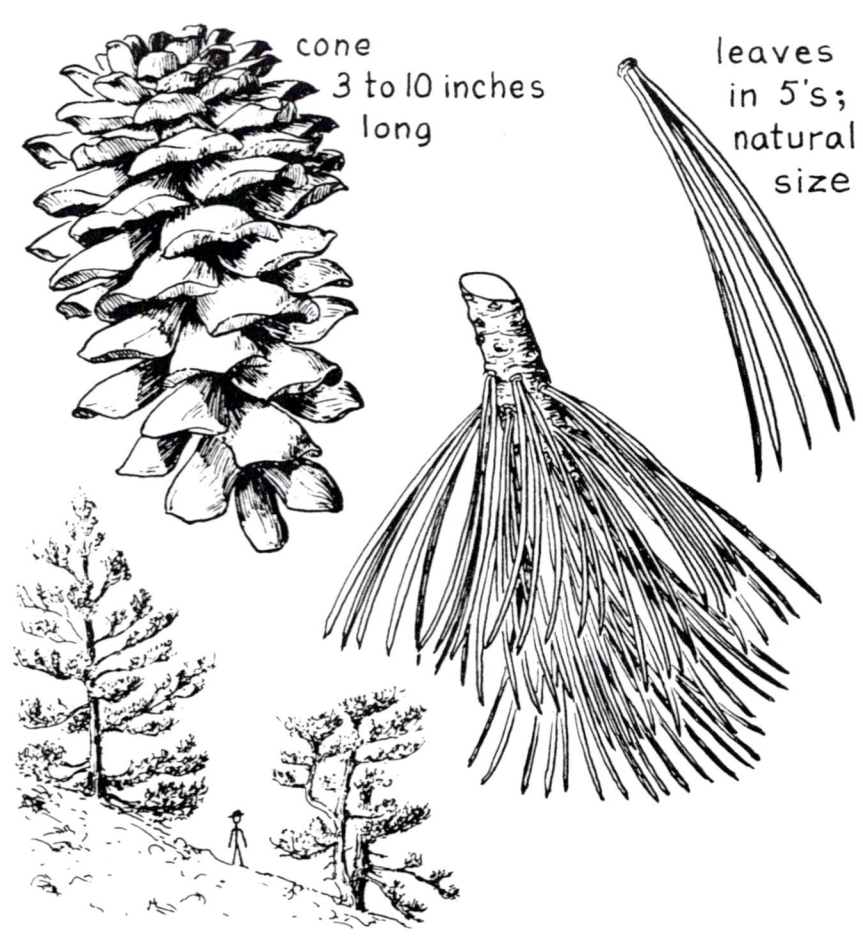

Limber pine

Pinus flexilis PINE FAMILY (Pinaceae)

GROWTH FORM Evergreen tree
DESCRIPTION The cones of the **limber pine** are larger than those of bristlecone pine, and the scales spread almost at right angles. The needles are also in bundles of five (as in bristlecone pine) but are longer than those of the bristlecone pine and not so densely set.
HABITAT Limber pine-bristlecone pine woodland.

LIMBER PINE

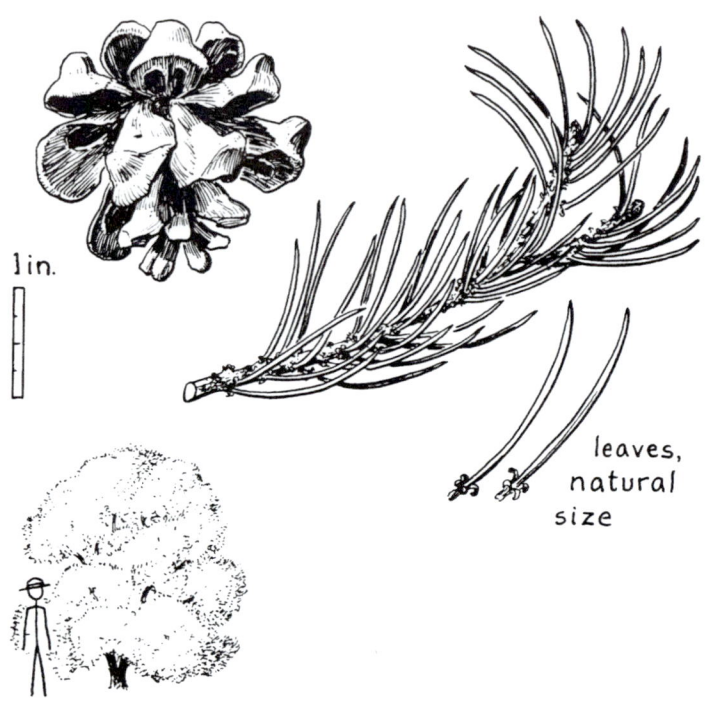

leaves, natural size

Singleleaf pinyon

Pinus monophylla   PINE FAMILY (Pinaceae)

GROWTH FORM Evergreen tree

DESCRIPTION In the days when the Indians were the only inhabitants in Death Valley, pine nuts and mesquite pods were their most dependable source of food, but now the gathering of pine nuts there is done by the jays. Even today Native Americans of the Great Basin area do a bit of harvesting of the nuts, though more as a source of income than of food. The trees are branching, usually with a divided trunk, and grow to a height of 15 to 45 feet. They usually grow at a higher elevation than the junipers with which they are associated. The wood of the pinyons furnished the source of the charcoal which formerly was made in the beehive-shaped kilns which are still standing in upper Wildrose Canyon. **Single-leaf pinyon** is the only one-needled pine. The **two-needle pinyon** (*Pinus edulis*) barely reaches the borders of California.

HABITAT Pinyon-juniper woodland

NOTE Very few kinds of the trees growing in Death Valley National Park are natives of the region. One might say that the tamarisks, the palms and such have been planted in self-defense against the sun. As is to be expected, the three pines that are natives grow at rather high elevations. The **singleleaf pinyon** will be met with more commonly, as it grows on mesas and slopes, mostly within the 5,000 to 7,000 foot levels, usually not too far from roads. But to see the **bristlecone** and the **limber pines** one must hike, as these grow high on the slopes of the Panamints. Specimens have been collected at 11,000 feet.

SINGLELEAF PINYON

Southern maidenhair fern
Adiantum capillus-veneris MAIDENHAIR FERN FAMILY (Pteridaceae)

GROWTH FORM Fern

DESCRIPTION **Southern maidenhair fern** is a delicate fern with many irregularly fan-shaped leaflets (pinnules) on the upper part of the slender, purplish black stalks and appears much like the one the florists use to set off their choice bouquets. This is not a plant that one thinks of meeting in so dry a place as Death Valley. It must have lots of moisture, however, and can be found growing in dripping seeps and springs or on the canyon walls in the ranges about the valley. Southern maidenhair fern is not restricted to this area and can be found in subtropical regions in both the Old and the New World.

HABITAT Upper desert slopes, springs.

Maidenhair Fern Family | **NON-FLOWERING PLANTS** | 265

SOUTHERN MAIDENHAIR FERN

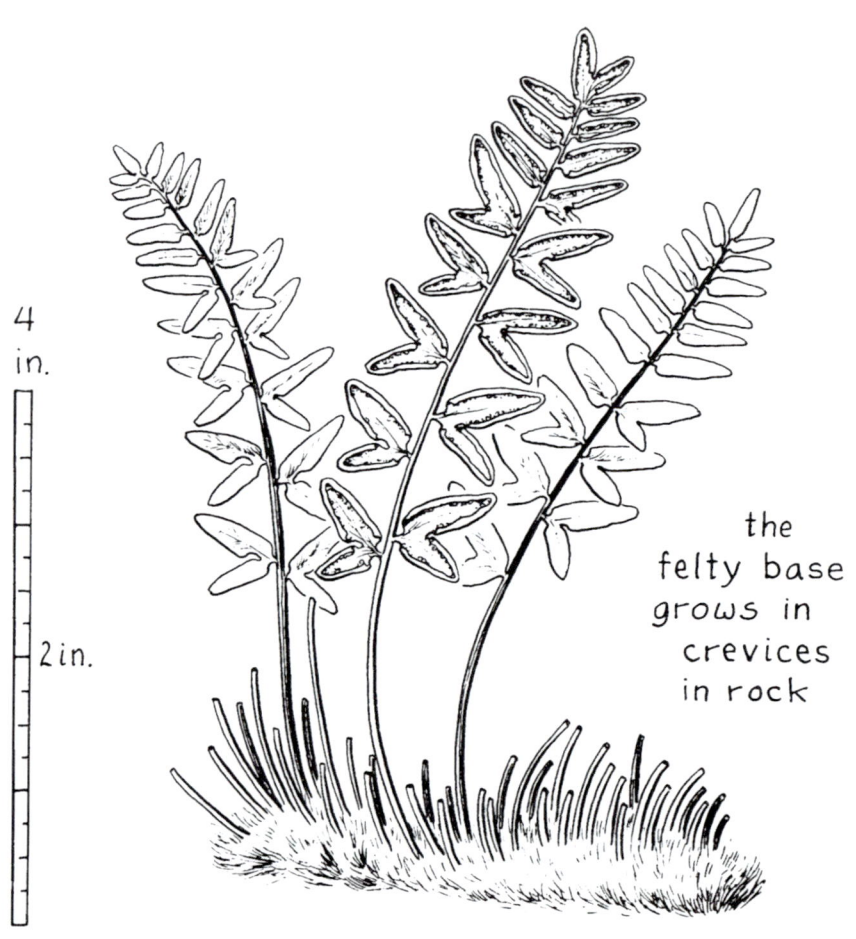

the felty base grows in crevices in rock

Brewer's cliffbrake
Pellaea breweri   MAIDENHAIR FERN FAMILY (Pteridaceae)

GROWTH FORM Fern

DESCRIPTION High up in the Panamints where the limber and bristlecone pines grow, one finds the short, densely tufted, bright green fronds of **Brewer's cliffbrake** among the rocks. Though short in stature, the fronds, with their closely set, two-parted pinnae, are conspicuous early in the season. Later they cannot be found, as the stems (stipes) snap off above the brown, felty base buried among the rocks. The cliffbrake is a fern of the western mountains from Montana south.

HABITAT Limber pine-bristlecone pine woodland.

Maidenhair Fern Family | **NON-FLOWERING PLANTS** | 267

BREWER'S CLIFFBRAKE

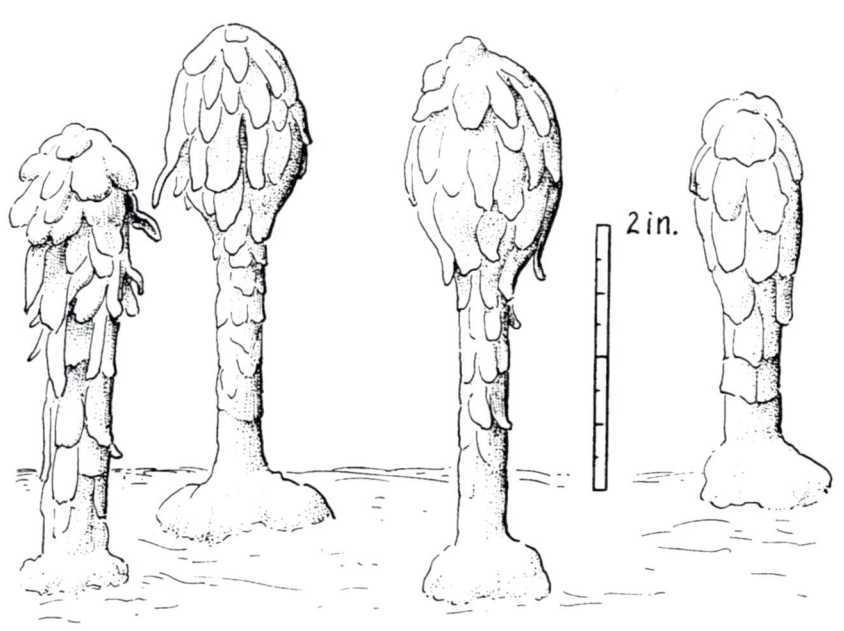

Desert puffball

Podaxis farlowii   PUFFBALL FAMILY (Agaricaceae)

GROWTH FORM Fungus

DESCRIPTION Driving along the roads, you may catch sight of a few gleaming white objects in the compacted silty soil on alluvial fans and valley floor, or even pushing through the blacktop of the roads. You will doubtless stop, expecting to pick up something that has been tossed out of a passing car, and find, instead of a bit of refuse, a mushroom. **Desert puffball** is bright white, grows sometimes to a height of six inches, and has an egg-shaped scaly top to the stalk. Do not feel inspired to use this in cooking, for it is very dry. It is not at all the kind of mushroom that you are accustomed to see in the woods but is a kind of puffball instead, one which someone has been aptly described as a "puffball on a stick."

HABITAT Valley floor and fans.

Acknowledgments

Much of the text of this book and the line drawings originally appeared in *Death Valley Wildflowers,* published by the Death Valley Natural History Association in 1962. The plant family assignments and scientific names have been updated in nearly all cases to those used and accepted in **ITIS**, the *Integrated Taxonomic Information System* (www.itis.gov).

Photographs were obtained, where possible, from public domain sources, from the author's own collection, and from a number of photographers on Flickr who have made their work available under Creative Commons commercial use licences (see www.flickr.com). Special thanks go to photographers Joe Decruyenaere and Andrey Zharkikh.

AUTHOR AND ILLUSTRATOR

After Roxana Judkins Stinchfield Ferris (1895–1978) received an A.M. in botany from Stanford University (1916), she joined the research and curatorial staff of the university's Dudley Herbarium. Throughout her career, and even after her official retirement in 1963, she collected over 14,000 botanical specimens, served as co-editor of the classic reference work Illustrated *Flora of the Pacific States,* and wrote such books as *Death Valley Wildflowers* and *Flowers of Point Reyes National Seashore.*

Jeanne R. Janish's (1902–1998) first introduction to botany was her meeting scientists Dr. Frederick and Edith Clements who were working in the "Alpine Laboratory" in Colorado, a part of of the University of Minnesota's Botany Department.

She would go on to attend Vassar College as a Latin major and graduated in 1924. She took a masters degree in Geology at Stanford where she was asked by her Paleontology professor, Dr. James Perrin Smith, to illustrate a monograph, which was the beginning of her career as a botanical illustrator.

In 1929 she travelled to China with her cousin, to become a rug designer with a rug company in Peking. There she met her husband Carl, who after serving in the marines, stayed on in Peking to work at the *New York Times.* They married and stayed there until 1934. Upon their return to the States, they moved to Nevada, where Carl, an expert engineer, found building opportunities, and Jeanne could continue her drawing.

From 1927-1974, Janish prepared illustrations for thirty-two major books, plus for many short papers, articles and booklets. Her artwork, with its clear and accurate depictions of plants, remains a standard of excellence in the field of botanical illustration.

Steve Chadde (1955–) received degrees in Range Management and Plant Ecology from the University of Wyoming and Montana State University. He has worked in many regions of the USA as a botanist and ecologist for the USDA Forest Service, the Nature Conservancy, and as an environmental consultant. He is the author of numerous field guides on plant identification.

Resources

The following websites offer a wealth of information on the plant life of Death Valley:
- Death Valley National Park (www.nps.gov/deva/index.htm)
- Death Valley area plants (www.dvplants.com/PLANTS/)
- SEINet (swbiodiversity.org/seinet)
- Southwest Desert Flora (southwestdesertflora.com)
- The Jepson eFlora (ucjeps.berkeley.edu/eflora/)

A number of books are available that provide addional information and illustrations of the flora of Death Valley and the Mojave Desert, including:
- *Mojave Desert Wildflowers: A Field Guide To Wildflowers, Trees, And Shrubs Of The Mojave Desert, Including The Mojave National Preserve, Death Valley National Park, and Joshua Tree National Park.* Pam Mackay. Published by Falcon Guides, (2nd edtion, 2013)
- *Mojave Desert Wildflowers.* Jon Stewart. Published by Jon Stewart Photography, 1998.
- *The Jepson Desert Manual: Vascular Plants of Southeastern California.* Bruce Baldwin et al. Published by University of California Press, 2002.
- *Flowers and Shrubs of the Mojave Desert.* Janice Bowers. Published by Western National Parks Association, 1998.

DEATH VALLEY

ABOVE General location of the Mojave Desert and Death Valley.

Index

NOTE Synonyms are listed in *italics*.

Abronia villosa, 74
Acamptopappus shockleyi, 152
Acer glabrum, 254
Acmispon rigidus, 198
Acton encelia, 162
Adiantum capillus-veneris, 264
alkali sacaton, 250
Allenrolfea occidentalis, 230
Ambrosia
    dumosa, 52
    salsola, 234
amphipappus, 94
Amphipappus fremontii, 154
Anemopsis californica, 142
anisocoma, 156
Anisocoma acaulis, 156
Antirrhinum filipes, 218
Anulocaulis annulatus, 48
Aquilegia shockleyi, 96
Arabis glaucovalvula, 24
Arctomecon merriamii, 126
Argemone munita, 128
Arizona lupine, 32
arrowweed pluchea, 64
Artemisia
    nova, 236
    spinescens, 238
    tridentata, 236
Asclepias erosa, 98
Aster abatus, 16
Astragalus
    coccineus, 86
    funereus, 28
    layneae, 30
Atrichoseris platyphylla, 100
Atriplex
    canescens, 232
    confertifolia, 232
    hymenelytra, 232

Bahiopsis reticulata, 158
beaked penstemon, 92
beardtongue
    Death Valley, 58
    Panamint, 76
bearpoppy, desert, 126
beautiful rockcress, 24
beavertail pricklypear, 68
Bebbia juncea, 160
bebbia, sweetbush, 160
big sagebrush, 236
birdnest eriogonum, 94
bladdersage, Mexican, 44
blue-podded rockcress, 24
Boechera
    glaucovalvula, 24
    pulchra, 24
Boerhavia annulata, 48
Brewer's cliffbrake, 266
brickellia
    pungent, 102
    spearleaved, 102
Brickellia atractyloides, 102
bristlecone pine, Great Basin, 258
brittlebush, 158, 162
brittlebush, white, 162
broad-flowered gilia, 78
broom snakeweed, 172
broomrape, desert, 52
browneyes, 120
bud sagebrush, 238
bulrush, Olney, 240
bur-sage, white, 52
burrobrush, white, 234
bushy cleomella, 192

Calochortus
    flexuosus, 116
    kennedyi, 204
calthaleaf phacelia, 20

Calycoseris
    parryi, 104
    wrightii, 104
Camissonia boothii, 122
caper, spiny, 194
Cassia armata, 202
Castilleja
    chromosa, 90
    linariifolia, 90
Caulanthus
    crassicaulis, 26
    inflatus, 26
cedar, pygmy, 176
Cercocarpus ledifolius, 252
Chaenactis carphoclinia, 106
chaenactis, pebble, 106
Chamaebatiaria millefolium, 138
cholla, strawtop, 186
Chorizanthe rigida, 222
chorizanthe, spiny, 222
Chrysothamnus
    nauseosus, 166
    paniculatus, 168
Chylismia
    brevipes, 210
    cardiophylla, 210
    claviformis, 120
Cirsium mohavense, 14
Cleomella obtusifolia, 192
cleomella, bushy, 192
cliffbrake, Brewer's, 266
cliffrose, Stansbury, 140
columbine, desert, 96
Cooper rush, 246
cottontop echinocactus, 188
Cowania stansburiana, 140
coyote melon, 196
crenate phacelia, 20
creosotebush, 228
Cryptantha
    confertiflora, 180
    utahensis, 110
cryptantha
    golden, 180
    scented, 110

Cucurbita palmata, 196
curlleaf mountain-mahogany, 252
Cylindropuntia echinocarpa, 186
Cymopterus gilmanii, 12

daisy, Panamint, 164
Dalea fremontii, 36
dalea, Fremont, 36
dandelion, desert, 104, 174
Dasyochloa pulchella, 248
Datura inoxia, 144
Datura wrightii, 144
datura, sacred, 144
Death Valley
    beardtongue, 58
    ephedra, 242
    gilmania, 226
    goldeneye, 158
    locoweed, 28
    mentzelia, 208
    mohavea, 216
    monkey-flower, 56
    phacelia, 22
    sage, 40
deervetch, shrubby, 198
Delphinium parishii, 60
desert bearpoppy, 126
desert broomrape, 52
desert columbine, 96
desert dandelion, 104
desert dandelion, 174
desert fivespot, 72
desert globemallow, 88
desert gold, 170
desert goldpoppy, 212
desert Indian-paintbrush, 90
desert mariposa, 204
desert milkweed, 98
desert pricklepoppy, 128
desert prince's-plume, 184
desert puffball, 268
desert rabbitbrush, 168
desert rocknettle, 206
desert sage, 38
desert sand-verbena, 74

desert senna, 202
desert snowberry, 70
desert sunflower, 170
desert tobacco, 146
desert wire-lettuce, 104
desert wire-lettuce, 66
desert-candle, 26
desert-rue, Mohave, 62
desert-star, Mohave, 108
desert-trumpet eriogonum, 224
desertholly, 232
desertsweet, 138
Diplacus rupicola, 56
dropseed, 250

Echinocactus polycephalus, 188
Encelia
    actonii, 162
    farinosa, 158
Enceliopsis
    argophylla, 164
    covillei, 164
ephedra, 242
Ephedra
    funerea, 242
    nevadensis, 244
    viridis, 244
ephedra
    Death Valley, 242
    green, 244
    Nevada, 244
Epipactis gigantea, 50
Eremalche rotundifolia, 72
Eremothera boothii, 122
Ericameria
    nauseosa, 166
    paniculata, 168
Eriogonum
    brachypodum, 134
    fasciculatum, 136
    inflatum, 224
    nidularium, 94
    panamintense, 82
    rixfordii, 134

eriogonum, 134
    birdnest, 94
    Panamint Mountain, 82
    Rixford, 134
    rosemary, 136
Eschscholzia glyptosperma, 212
Eucnide urens, 206
Euphorbia
    albomarginata, 114
    parishii, 114
euphorbia
    Parish, 114
    white-margin, 114
evening-primrose
    golden, 210
    heartleaf, 210
    shredding, 122
    tufted, 124

false-clover, 194
fern, southern maidenhair, 264
fivespot, desert, 72
flat-crown eriogonum, 134
flax, prairie, 46
fluffgrass, 248
forget-me-not, golden, 180
fourwing, 232
Fremont dalea, 36
Fremont phacelia, 22

Geraea canescens, 170
giant helleborine, 50
Gilia
    filiformis, 220
    latiflora, 78
gilia
    broad-flowered, 78
    granite, 132
    threadstem, 220
Gilman cymopterus, 12
Gilmania luteola, 226
gilmania, Death Valley, 226
globemallow
    Rusby, 88
    desert, 88

gold desert, 170
goldcarpet, 226
golden cryptantha, 180
golden evening-primrose, 210
golden forget-me-not, 180
goldeneye, Death Valley, 158
goldenhead, Shockley, 152
goldpoppy, desert, 212
gourd, palmleaf, 196
granite gilia, 132
gravelghost, 100
Great Basin bristlecone pine, 258
green ephedra, 244
grizzly bear pricklypear, 190
Gutierrezia
    microcephala, 172
    sarothrae, 172

heartleaf evening-primrose, 210
Heliomeris multiflora, 158
helleborine, giant, 50
Holmgrenanthe petrophila, 214
Holodiscus discolor, 138
honey mesquite, 200
honeysweet tidestromia, 148
Hymenoclea salsola, 234

incienso, 162
Indian-paintbrush
    desert, 90
    Wyoming, 90
iodinebush, 230

Juncus cooperi, 246
juniper, Utah, 256
Juniperus osteosperma, 256

Langloisia setosissima, 130
langloisia, spotted, 130
larkspur, Parish, 60
Larrea tridentata, 228
Layne locoweed, 30
Leptodactylon pungens, 132
lilac sunbonnet, 130
limber pine, 260

Linanthus
    filiformis, 220
    pungens, 132
Linum lewisii, 46
locoweed
    Death Valley, 28
    Layne, 30
    scarlet, 86
Lomatium parryi, 150
lomatium, Parry, 150
Lotus rigidus, 198
low sagebrush, 236
lupine
    Arizona, 32
    yelloweye, 34
Lupinus arizonicus, 32
Lupinus flavoculatus, 34

maidenhair fern, southern, 264
Malacothrix glabrata, 104, 174
Malvastrum rotundifolium, 72
maple, Rocky Mountain, 254
mariposa
    desert, 204
    weakstem, 116
Maurandya petrophila, 214
melon, coyote, 196
Menodora spinescens, 118
menodora, spiny, 118
Mentzelia
    albicaulis, 208
    reflexa, 208
    tricuspis, 208
mentzelia
    Death Valley, 208
    whitestem, 208
mesquite
    honey, 200
    screwbean, 200
Mexican bladdersage, 44
milkweed, desert, 98
Mimulus
    bigelovii, 54
    rupicola, 56
Mohave aster, 16

Mohave desert-rue, 62
Mohave desert-star, 108
Mohave thistle, 14
Mohavea
    breviflora, 216
    confertiflora, 216
mohavea, Death Valley, 216
monkey-flower
    Death Valley, 56
    yellow-throat, 54
Monoptilon bellioides, 108
Mormon tea, 244
mountain-mahogany, curlleaf, 252

Nama demissa, 18
Neogaerrhinum filipes, 218
Nevada ephedra, 244
Nevada showy goldeneye, 158
New Mexican rafinesquia, 104
Nicotiana obtusifolia, 146

Oenothera
    brevipes, 210
    cespitosa, 124
    claviformis, 120
    decorticans, 122
old man pricklypear, 190
Olney bulrush, 240
Opuntia
    basilaris, 68
    echinocarpa, 186
    polyacantha, 190
Oreocarya confertiflora, 180
Orobanche cooperi, 52
Oxystylis lutea, 194

palmleaf gourd, 196
Panamint
    beardtongue, 76
    daisy, 164
    phacelia, 112
    prince's-plume, 182
Panamint Mountain eriogonum, 82
Parish euphorbia, 114

Parish larkspur, 60
Parry lomatium, 150
pebble chaenactis, 106
Pellaea breweri, 266
Penstemon
    floridus, 76
    fruticiformis, 58
    rostriflorus, 92
penstemon, beaked, 92
Peucephyllum schottii, 168, 176
Phacelia
    calthifolia, 20
    crenulata, 20
    fremontii, 22
    perityloides, 112
    vallis-mortae, 22
phacelia
    calthaleaf, 20
    crenate, 20
    Death Valley, 22
    Fremont, 22
    Panamint, 112
Phlox stansburyi, 80
phlox, Stansbury, 80
pickleweed, 230
Picrothamnus desertorum, 238
pine, limber, 260
Pinus
    aristata, 258
    edulis, 262
    flexilis, 260
    longaeva, 258
    monophylla, 262
pinyon
    singleleaf, 262
    two-needle, 262
Pluchea sericea, 64
Podaxis farlowii, 268
prairie flax, 46
pricklepoppy, desert, 128
pricklypear
    beavertail, 68
    grizzly bear, 190
    old man, 190

prince's-plume
    desert, 184
    Panamint, 182
Prosopis
    glandulosa, 200
    pubescens, 200
Psathyrotes ramosissima, 178
Psorothamnus fremontii, 36
puffball, desert, 268
pungent brickellia, 102
purple sage, 38
purplemat, 18
Purshia mexicana, 140
pygmy cedar, 176

rabbitbrush
    desert, 168
    rubber, 166
Rafinesquia neomexicana, 104
rafinesquia, New Mexican, 104
Rixford eriogonum, 134
rock spiraea, 138
rockcress
    beautiful, 24
    blue-podded, 24
rocklady, 214
rocknettle, desert, 206
Rocky Mountain maple, 254
Rosa woodsii, 84
rose sage, 42
rose, Woods', 84
rosemary eriogonum, 136
rubber rabbitbrush, 166
Rusby globe-mallow, 88
rush, Cooper, 246

sacred datura, 144
sage
    Death Valley, 40
    desert, 38
    purple, 38
    rose, 42
sagebrush
    big, 236
    bud, 238

low, 236
Salazaria mexicana, 44
saltbush, 232
Salvia
    dorrii, 38
    funerea, 40
    pachyphylla, 42
sand-verbena, desert, 74
scarlet locoweed, 86
scented cryptantha, 110
Schoenoplectus americanus, 240
Scirpus olneyi, 240
screwbean mesquite, 200
Scutellaria mexicana, 44
Senna armata, 202
senna, desert, 202
shadscale, 232
Shockley goldenhead, 152
showy goldeneye, Nevada, 158
shredding evening-primrose, 122
shrubby deervetch, 198
singleleaf pinyon, 262
snakeweed
    broom, 172
    threadleaf, 172
snapdragon, yellow twining, 218
snowberry, desert, 70
southern maidenhair fern, 264
spearleaved brickellia, 102
Sphaeralcea
    ambigua, 88
    rusbyi, 88
spiderling, wetleaf, 48
spiny caper, 194
spiny chorizanthe, 222
spiny menodora, 118
spiraea, rock, 138
Sporobolus airoides, 250
spotted langloisia, 130
sprucebush, 168, 176
Stanleya
    elata, 182
    pinnata, 184
Stansbury cliffrose, 140
Stansbury phlox, 80

Stephanomeria
    parryii, 66
    pauciflora, 66, 104
stingbush, 206
stinkweed, 192
strawtop cholla, 186
sunbonnet, lilac, 130
sunflower, desert, 170
sweetbush, 160
sweetbush bebbia, 160
Symphoricarpos longiflorus, 70

tackstem, white, 104
tansybush, 138
Thamnosma montana, 62
thick-stem wild-cabbage, 26
thistle, Mohave, 14
threadleaf snakeweed, 172
threadstem gilia, 220
Tidestromia oblongifolia, 148
tidestromia, honeysweet, 148
tobacco, desert, 146
tobaccoweed, 100
Tridens pulchellus, 248
tufted evening-primrose, 124
turtleback, 178
two-needle pinyon, 262

Utah juniper, 256

Viguiera reticulata, 158

weakstem mariposa, 116
wetleaf spiderling, 48
whiskbroom, 94
white brittlebush, 162
white bur-sage, 52
white burrobrush, 234
white tackstem, 104
white-margin euphorbia, 114
whitestem mentzelia, 208
wild-cabbage, thick-stem, 26
wire-lettuce, 66, 104
Woods' rose, 84
Wyoming Indian-paintbrish, 90
Xylorhiza tortifolia, 16

yellow twining snapdragon, 218
yellow-throat monkey-flower, 54
yelloweye lupine, 34
yerba-mansa, 142

www.ingramcontent.com/pod-product-compliance
Lightning Source LLC
Chambersburg PA
CBRC100215040426
42333CB00035B/69